AMERICA'S
TEST KITCHEN

ALSO BY THE EDITORS AT AMERICA'S TEST KITCHEN

100 Recipes: The Absolute Best Ways to Make the True Essentials
Cook's Country Eats Local
The Cook's Illustrated Meat Book
The America's Test Kitchen New Family Cookbook
The Complete Cooking for Two Cookbook
The Cook's Illustrated Baking Book
The Cook's Illustrated Cookbook
The Science of Good Cooking
The America's Test Kitchen Cooking School Cookbook
The America's Test Kitchen Menu Cookbook
The America's Test Kitchen Quick Family Cookbook
The America's Test Kitchen Healthy Family Cookbook
The America's Test Kitchen Family Baking Book

The America's Test Kitchen Library Series
The Best Mexican Recipes
The Complete Vegetarian Cookbook
The Make-Ahead Cook
The How Can It Be Gluten Free Cookbook Volume 2
The How Can It Be Gluten Free Cookbook
Healthy Slow Cooker Revolution
Slow Cooker Revolution Volume 2: The Easy-Prep Edition
Slow Cooker Revolution
The Six-Ingredient Solution
Pressure Cooker Perfection
Comfort Food Makeovers
The America's Test Kitchen D.I.Y. Cookbook
Pasta Revolution
Simple Weeknight Favorites
The Best Simple Recipes

The TV Companion Series
The Complete Cook's Country TV Show Cookbook
The Complete America's Test Kitchen TV Show Cookbook 2001–2016
America's Test Kitchen: The TV Companion Cookbook (2002–2009
and 2011–2015 Editions)

America's Test Kitchen Annuals
The Best of America's Test Kitchen
(2007–2016 Editions)
Cooking for Two (2010–2013 Editions)
Light & Healthy (2010–2012 Editions)

For A Full Listing Of All Our Books Or To Order Titles
CooksIllustrated.com
AmericasTestKitchen.com

PRAISE FOR OTHER AMERICA'S TEST KITCHEN TITLES

"Ideal as a reference for the bookshelf . . . will be turned to time and again for definitive instruction on just about any food-related matter."
Publishers Weekly on *The Science of Good Cooking*

"A one-volume kitchen seminar, addressing in one smart chapter after another the sometimes surprising whys behind a cook's best practices. . . . You get the myth, the theory, the science and the proof, all rigorously interrogated as only America's Test Kitchen can do."
NPR on *The Science of Good Cooking*

"Carnivores with an obsession for perfection will likely have found their new bible in this comprehensive collection."
Publishers Weekly (starred review) on *The Cook's Illustrated Meat Book*

"This encyclopedia of meat cookery would feel completely overwhelming if it weren't so meticulously organized and artfully designed. This is *Cook's Illustrated* at its finest."
The Kitchn on *The Cook's Illustrated Meat Book*

"The perfect kitchen home companion . . . The practical side of things is very much on display . . . cook-friendly and kitchen-oriented, illuminating the process of preparing food instead of mystifying it."
The Wall Street Journal on *The Cook's Illustrated Cookbook*

"The 21st-century *Fannie Farmer Cookbook* or *The Joy of Cooking*. If you had to have one cookbook and that's all you could have, this one would do it."
CBS San Francisco on *The New Family Cookbook*

"This book upgrades slow cooking for discriminating, 21st-century palates—that is indeed revolutionary."
The Dallas Morning News on *Slow Cooker Revolution*

"Buy this gem for the foodie in your family, and spend the extra money to get yourself a copy too."
The Missourian on *The Best of America's Test Kitchen 2015*

"The sum total of exhaustive experimentation . . . anyone interested in gluten-free cookery simply shouldn't be without it."
Nigella Lawson on *The How Can It Be Gluten Free Cookbook*

"Even ultra-experienced gluten-free cooks and bakers will learn something from this thoroughly researched, thoughtfully presented volume."
Publishers Weekly on *The How Can It Be Gluten Free Cookbook*

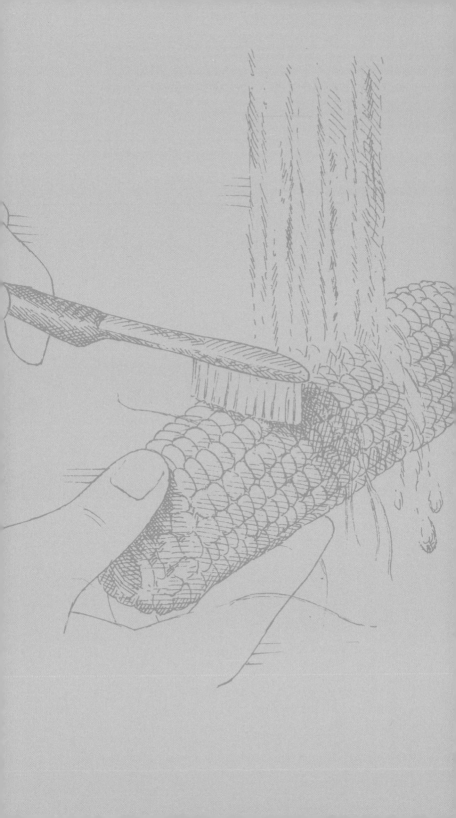

Kitchen Hacks

How Clever Cooks Get Things Done

THE EDITORS AT
AMERICA'S TEST KITCHEN

ILLUSTRATIONS BY
JOHN BURGOYNE

Copyright © 2015 by the Editors at America's Test Kitchen

All rights reserved. No part of this book may be reproduced or transmitted in any manner whatsoever without written permission from the publisher, except in the case of brief quotations embodied in critical articles or reviews.

America's Test Kitchen
17 Station Street, Brookline, MA 02445

Library of Congress Cataloging-in-Publication Data

Cook's illustrated kitchen hacks : how clever cooks get things done / the editors of America's Test Kitchen.
    pages cm
Includes index.
ISBN 978-1-940352-00-8
1. Cooking--Handbooks, manuals, etc. I. America's Test Kitchen (Firm)
 TX652.C7367 2015
 641.5--dc23
                                                2015006557
Paperback: US $19.95 / $19.95 CAN

Manufactured in the United States of America
10 9 8 7 6 5 4 3 2 1

Distributed by Penguin Random House Publisher Services
Tel: 800.733.3000

Editorial Director
Jack Bishop
Editorial Director, Books
Elizabeth Carduff
Executive Editor
Lori Galvin
Assistant Editor
Rachel Greenhaus
Editorial Assistant
Samantha Ronan
Design Director
Amy Klee
Art Director
Greg Galvan
Deputy Art Director
Taylor Argenzio
Designer
Jen Kanavos Hoffman
Illustration
John Burgoyne
Photography Director
Julie Cote
Photography
Carl Tremblay

Staff Photographer
Daniel J. van Ackere
Food Styling
Catrine Kelty, Sally Staub
Production Director
Guy Rochford
Senior Production Manager
Jessica Lindheimer Quirk
Project Manager
Britt Dresser
Digital Asset Management Specialist
Ian Matzen
Production and Imaging Specialists
Heather Dube, Sean MacDonald, Dennis Noble, Lauren Robbins, Jessica Voas
Copy Editor
Cheryl Redmond
Proofreader
Elizabeth Emery
Indexer
Elizabeth Parson

This book has been tested, written, and edited by the folks at America's Test Kitchen, a very real 2,500-square-foot kitchen located just outside of Boston. It is the home of *Cook's Illustrated* magazine and *Cook's Country* magazine and is the Monday-through-Friday destination for more than four dozen test cooks, editors, food scientists, tasters, and cookware specialists. Our mission is to test recipes over and over again until we understand how and why they work and until we arrive at the "best" version. As we like to say in the test kitchen, "We make the mistakes, so you don't have to."

All of this would not be possible without a belief that good cooking, much like good music, is indeed based on a foundation of objective technique. There is a right way to sauté, there is a best way to cook a pot roast, and there are measurable scientific principles involved in producing perfectly beaten, stable egg whites. This is our ultimate goal: to investigate the fundamental principles of cooking so that you become a better cook. It is as simple as that.

If you're curious to see what goes on behind the scenes at America's Test Kitchen, check out our daily blog, The Feed, at AmericasTestKitchenFeed.com, which features kitchen snapshots, exclusive recipes, video tips, and much more. You can watch us work (in our actual test kitchen) by tuning in to *America's Test Kitchen* (AmericasTestKitchen.com) or *Cook's Country from America's Test Kitchen* (CooksCountryTV.com) on public television. Listen to *America's Test Kitchen Radio* (ATKradio.com) on public radio for insights, tips, and techniques that illuminate the truth about real home cooking. Enroll in a cooking class at our online cooking school at OnlineCookingSchool.com. And find information about subscribing to *Cook's Illustrated* magazine at CooksIllustrated.com or *Cook's Country* magazine at CooksCountry.com. Both magazines are published every other month. However you choose to visit us, we welcome you into our kitchen, where you can stand by our side as we test our way to the best recipes in America.

facebook.com/AmericasTestKitchen

pinterest.com/TestKitchen

twitter.com/TestKitchen

americastestkitchen.tumblr.com

youtube.com/AmericasTestKitchen

google.com/+AmericasTestKitchen

instagram.com/TestKitchen

Vermonters are legendary hackers— they can find 100 uses for baling twine, towropes, and come-alongs. They can change a clutch with a crescent-head wrench, a hammer, and pair of pliers. And don't even ask what they can do with a feed bucket, a length of wire, and a metal post. I'm sure they could have built the pyramids with less.

We also have hacks in the kitchen. They are called quick tips, shortcuts, or time-savers. They help you organize; clean up; repair mistakes; transport, revive, and store food; and impress your friends. There are fun hacks, serious hacks, silly hacks, and money-saving hacks. There are boozy, green, gadget, introverted, shortcut, lunchtime, memory, and coffee hacks. In fact, there is a hack for just about everything and anything one does in and around the kitchen.

Having trouble removing coconut meat from the shell? Freeze the coconut overnight, whack the equator with the dull side of a cleaver, and the shell will detach easily from the meat. And, the coconut water is frozen into a ball, making it easy to remove without spillage or waste.

Want steamed milk for a cappuccino? Fill a Mason jar halfway with milk, put on the lid, and shake vigorously for 30 seconds. Remove the lid and microwave for 30 seconds on high to warm and stabilize the foam.

Techies love this tip: Take a snapshot on your phone of kitchen supplies that are empty and save them to a album entitled "Groceries." Now you have an image-based grocery list.

Or, to rescue oversoftened butter, throw in a few ice cubes and stir for 1 minute. The rapid cooling will reestablish the tiny crystals that stabilize the air bubbles in the butter.

Some of my favorite hacks use hair dryers, miniature marshmallows, toothpicks, beach towels, paper towel and toilet paper tubes, rubber shelf liners, rubber bands, and binder clips. Others use the plastic lid from a yogurt container, an adhesive coat hook, or a shower cap.

Yet others just use smarts—no special tools or leftovers—just a good imagination and quick thinking.

Of course, you will never have a problem like I once had. My International 404 tractor jumped out of gear on a hill, ran off an embankment, and ended up in the crotch of a tree. So how do you hack a tractor in a tree? Well, with a chainsaw of course!

Enjoy the book. Enjoy the hacks. Have more fun in the kitchen!

Christopher Kimball
Founder and Editor,
Cook's Illustrated and *Cook's Country*
Host, *America's Test Kitchen* and
Cook's Country from America's Test Kitchen

HACK
THIS BOOK!

What Kind of Kitchen Hacker Are You?

Use these alternative tables of contents to help you navigate this book. Whether you're a loner, a party animal, an environmentalist, or just a clueless cook, there's a hack for you!

HACKS FOR CAFFEINE FIENDS

HACKS FOR HAPPY HOUR

HACKS FOR THE FORGETFUL

HACKS FOR YOUR RECYCLING

HACKS FOR THE LAZY

HACKS FOR ONE

HACKS IN PLAIN SIGHT

HACK YOUR APPLIANCES

HACKS FOR MINIMALISTS

HACKS TO EAT AND DRINK

CHAPTER 1

CLEAN KITCHEN HACKS

Because No One Likes to Get Sick (or Dirty)

1.1 PUTTING YOUR BEST HAND FORWARD

SING WHILE YOU SCRUB

Washing your hands is one of the best ways to stop the spread of food-borne pathogens. Wash before and during cooking, especially after touching raw meat and poultry. The U.S. Food and Drug Administration recommends at least 20 seconds in hot, soapy water. How long is that? Try singing "Happy Birthday."

BEATING BEET STAINS

No matter how hard you scrub your hands, simple soap and water do little to remove lingering red beet stains. However, rubbing a dab of whitening toothpaste with peroxide over the area can help erase the stains. Or you can try avoiding the stains altogether by rubbing the hand that will be holding the beets with about ½ teaspoon vegetable oil, taking care to keep the knife-holding hand dry, and then cutting the beets as desired. Afterward, wash your hands with hot, soapy water.

(LESS) TIME TO COME CLEAN

Here's a trick for shortening your scrubbing time after kneading sticky dough.

1. Standing over the sink, "wash" your hands with a handful of flour or cornmeal instead of soap and water.

2. Rinse your hands with cold water. (Hot water causes the starches in the dough to gelatinize, thus requiring more scrubbing.)

MINTY FRESH HANDS

After working with pungent ingredients such as garlic, onions, or fish, many cooks use a little lemon juice to wash away any lingering odors from their hands. But sometimes the smell is stronger than the citrus. For those tough cases, try washing your hands with a couple of tablespoons of mouthwash. Any inexpensive brand is fine.

FRUIT FLY CATCHERS

Since so-called fruit flies are actually vinegar flies attracted to the odor of fermenting fruits and vegetables, there's a simple solution to rid your kitchen of these annoying pests. Place a few drops of dish soap in a small bowl of vinegar on the counter and stir to combine. The vinegar lures the flies into the liquid, and the soap breaks the surface tension, preventing them from escaping. For an alternate solution, pour ¼ cup of orange juice in a small drinking glass and then top it with a funnel. Placed next to a fruit bowl, the juice lures the tiny flies into the funnel, where they are unable to escape, and keeps them away from your ripening produce.

STOP KITCHEN STENCH

Some foods leave an unpleasant smell in the kitchen after cooking. Here's a simple tip to freshen the air: Simmer 2 tablespoons of ground cinnamon in 2 cups of water until the offending odor is replaced with the scent of the simmering spice.

REMOVING FUNKY FRIDGE ODORS

Here's a technique that works better than baking soda to deodorize a refrigerator: Place a handful of charcoal briquettes in a disposable plastic container (with no lid) in the refrigerator or freezer. Once the offending smell has dissipated, simply discard the charcoal.

DISPOSAL FRESHENER

Rather than throwing out the remnants of zested citrus peels, try grinding leftover pieces of lemon, lime, orange, and grapefruit rind in your kitchen sink disposal. The strong, fresh scent of the fruit helps to mask unpleasant odors that sometimes collect in the disposal. Another option to freshen things up is to freeze cubes of distilled white vinegar and then grind a few in the disposal with cold water running.

1.3 EVERYTHING *AND* THE KITCHEN SINK

SANITIZE YOUR SINK

Studies have found that the kitchen sink is crawling with even more bacteria than the garbage bin (the drain alone typically harbors 18,000 bacteria per square inch). The faucet handle, which can reintroduce bacteria to your hands after you've washed them, is a close second. Though hot, soapy water is amazingly effective at eliminating bacteria, for added insurance, clean these areas frequently with a solution of 1 tablespoon bleach per quart of water (the bleach will also kill off some of those microbes in the drain).

SPONGE ON A ROPE

For a handy way to keep track of sponges dedicated to surface cleaning, poke a small hole in the sponge and thread a string through the hole. Loop the sponge over the neck of a spray bottle filled with vinegar and water or any cleaning solution.

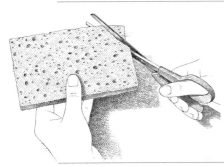

KEEPING SPONGES STRAIGHT

To avoid using the same sponge for washing dishes as for cleaning grimy countertops and kitchen surfaces, snip off a corner from sponges that you intend to use for cleaning counters and stovetops, reserving uncut sponges for washing dishes.

HOMEMADE SPONGE HOLDER

Letting air circulate around wet kitchen sponges— instead of laying them flat on the counter—helps them dry faster and stay mildew-free. Rather than purchasing a caddy or a tray, you can fashion a stand with a large binder clip. Attach the clip to the short end of a sponge and then press the "arms" of the clip flat against the sponge.

CLEAN YOUR SPONGE—REALLY CLEAN IT

Whenever possible, use a paper towel or a clean dishcloth instead of a sponge to wipe up. If you do use a sponge, disinfect it. We tried microwaving, freezing, bleaching, and boiling sponges that had seen a hard month of use in the test kitchen, as well as running them through the dishwasher and simply washing them in soap and water. Lab results showed that microwaving and boiling were most effective, but since sponges can burn in a high-powered microwave, we recommend boiling them for 5 minutes.

A LITTLE DAB WILL DO YA

Here's a tip to bring the neatness and ease of dispensing hand soap from a small pump to another cleaning product: dishwashing liquid. This is especially helpful if you buy supersize bottles, which are usually a bargain but are also ungainly.

1. Recycle a hand-soap dispenser bottle by refilling it with dishwashing liquid.

2. When it comes time to wash the dishes, simply pump the desired amount of soap onto the sponge.

HANG UP YOUR GLOVES

If you prefer to hang your dishwashing gloves so that they're always at hand, but your pair lacks tabs to do so, you can create your own by folding a piece of duct tape over the top edge of each one and then piercing the tape with a hole puncher.

FOILING HARD-TO-CLEAN POTS AND PANS

If you run out of steel wool but need to get tough, baked-on food off glass baking dishes or an oven rack, try dishwashing liquid and a crumpled-up ball of aluminum foil. The craggy foil is more abrasive than a sponge. This is a great way to recycle used—but still clean—sheets of foil.

CLEANING BOTTLENECK CONTAINERS

Narrow-mouthed bottleneck containers require a long, slim brush to reach the bottom and clean the interior. In lieu of purchasing a specialized tool, try adding a handful of uncooked rice, water, and dish soap to the bottle, covering the top, and shaking vigorously. The grains' friction against the sides loosens any grime and offers a nearly scrub-free solution.

DOUBLE-DUTY ONION BAG

Try using an onion bag as a replacement scrub pad for cleaning dirty pots and pans or vegetables.

1. Wrap an empty perforated plastic onion bag around a sponge, or simply fold it around itself to form a compact shape. Secure with a rubber band.

2. Use the wrapped scrubber to scour cookware in hot, soapy water or to clean vegetables under cool running water. In both cases, discard the bag when finished.

CLEAN UTENSILS AT THE READY

Every cook knows the frustration of having to stop in the middle of dinner preparation to wash a utensil, such as a paring knife, which you've dirtied but need to use again. To eliminate this frustration, start your cooking preparations by filling a glass or jar with hot, sudsy water. Slip dirty utensils into the water (sharp ends down) to soak as soon as you're done with them, and, if you need them again, just a quick rinse under the faucet makes them ready to go.

WINE-GLASS BUFFER ZONE

Washing fragile glassware by hand is the best way to stave off breakage—unless it slips out of your grasp and crashes down into the sink. As a precautionary measure, place rubber shelf liners in the sink for a breakage-free cleaning session.

SPOT-FREE GLASSWARE

For sparkling stemware free of water spots, wash glasses by hand and rinse them with distilled water, which has none of the spot-producing impurities of regular tap water.

1. Fill a squirt bottle with distilled water. Rinse the glasses inside and out with the water.

2. Air-dry the glasses, first upside down, then right side up.

CHEMICAL-FREE CLEANING

To avoid cleaning kitchen countertops with chemicals that might contaminate food, use a spray bottle filled with equal parts white vinegar and water.

QUICK DRY FOR BAKING UTENSILS

Most home bakers have just one piece of any given type of equipment, such as a strainer or sifter. Of course, these tools must be completely dry before you use them, but waiting for a just-washed strainer or sifter to dry fully can be frustrating, and it is easy to miss spots if you hand-dry with a dish towel. If you're in the midst of a holiday baking bonanza and in a rush to use your sifter, try this way to dry it off quickly and completely: Because the oven is on anyway, put the utensil in it to dry out. Set a timer for about 2 minutes to remind yourself that the utensil is in the oven. Just be sure that the utensil does not have any plastic parts that can melt. After 2 minutes, the utensil will be quite hot, so use a mitt to protect your hand when you remove it from the oven.

AIR-DRYING LARGE VASES

Drying a wine carafe or glass vase upright can leave behind unwanted residue, but balancing these fragile items upside down to dry can be tricky. For a sturdier solution, try placing the vase or carafe upside down on an empty vertical paper towel stand, allowing it to properly drain and dry. Alternatively, try anchoring a wooden spoon in the dish rack, handle-end up. Vases and bottles fit easily over the handle so they can drain properly.

JUMP-STARTED DISH DRYING

Many cooks who wash dishes by hand would prefer to wash, dry, and put away the dishes in one fell swoop. Rather than waiting for them to air-dry and putting them away later, try propping up a small table fan level with the dishes in the rack and directing the air flow onto the dishes, which will dry in record time.

1.3 EVERYTHING *AND* THE KITCHEN SINK

MAKESHIFT DISH-DRYING RACKS

Everyone dreads the huge pile of dishes that builds up after a dinner party or holiday gathering. In these situations, when the dishwasher and dish rack are already full, drying space can be hard to come by. To create extra drying space for glasses and dishes, try one of the following tricks.

A. | **B.**
C. | **D.**

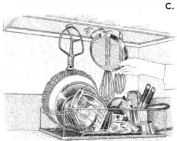
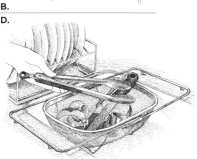

A. Wire cooling racks used for baking are an ideal source of drying space, especially for delicate wine glasses. Place a towel underneath the rack to absorb the water that drips off the glasses.

B. Set an oven rack or wire rack over the sink. The air circulating on all sides of the rack will help dry dishes, glasses, and any other items placed on it.

C. If you keep your dish-drying rack underneath a cabinet, try attaching hooks to the under-side of the cabinet for those times when the rack is overflow-ing with dishes and utensils. Extra items can be suspended from the hooks to drip dry.

D. Try repurposing a colander with extending arms as an extra, over-the-sink drainer for small dishes, utensils, or cutlery when the countertop rack is full.

TAKING YOUR DISHES TO THE MAT

If you hand-wash your pots and pans, you may find that a dish towel is never absorbent enough to soak up all of the water that trickles from the cookware. Instead of a towel, try placing a clean terrycloth bath mat beneath your dish rack to catch all of the drips. The bath mat can be laundered and used repeatedly.

VINEGAR IN THE DISHWASHER IS A NATURAL

Here's a cheaper, environmentally friendly alternative to dishwasher rinse agent: Fill the compartment with plain white vinegar, which works just as well to keep spots from forming and costs mere pennies per load.

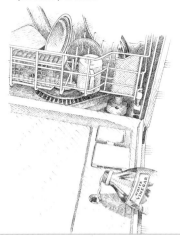

KEEPING CHOPSTICKS SAFE IN THE DISHWASHER

Chopsticks are useful utensils, but they can be frustrating to wash in the dishwasher because they slide right through the holes in the silverware bin. Here's one way to keep the chopsticks from straying: With a paring knife, cut a small "x" for each chopstick in the plastic lid from a yogurt or sour cream container. Slide each chopstick into an "x" and place the lid in the top rack of the dishwasher. The plastic will keep the chopsticks secure during the wash cycle.

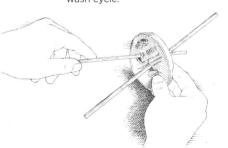

SECURING SMALL ITEMS IN THE DISHWASHER

It's easy for small kitchen utensils such as cake testers or trussing needles to fall through the slots in the dishwasher silverware bin. To keep utensils where they belong, follow this tip.

1. Stuff a small nylon pot scrubber into the bottom of the cutlery container.

2. Secure small items by sticking them into the pot scrubber. The scrubber will prevent anything from falling through.

PREVENTING CONTAINER FLIP-OUT

To keep plastic storage containers from turning over and filling with water during the wash cycle, place them on the upper rack of the dishwasher and set a wire rack on top. The rack keeps the containers in place while soapy water flows through.

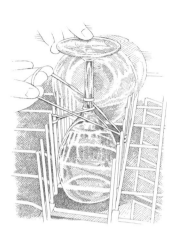

ANCHORING TIPSY WINEGLASSES

While most dishwashers do a fine job of cleaning wineglasses, few have rack space engineered to prevent jostling (and breaking) during the cycle. Here's how to lock wineglasses into place.

1. Place the wineglass, bowl side down, on the upper rack. Loop a rubber band around one spoke and pull the opposite end over the stem of the glass.

2. Loop the rubber band around a spoke on the other side of the rack and bring it up around the stem again. Repeat, if necessary, until the wineglass is secure.

KEEPING TABS ON DISH DUTY

Tired of guessing whether or not the dishwasher has been run? Erase all doubt by writing an X on a light-colored clothespin or bag clip with a nontoxic dry-erase marker and attaching it to one of the dishwasher racks prior to running the appliance. The cycle washes away the mark—a quick visual indicator of a clean load.

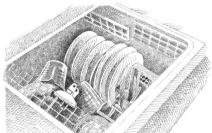

UNLOADING, SIMPLIFIED

Unloading the dishwasher is a dreaded chore. However, a little extra care while loading the silverware makes unloading go faster. Separate the silverware as you go; all forks together, knives together, and so on. At unloading time, simply grab each bunch of silverware and transfer to the appropriate drawer.

TRASH BAG TIPS

A. Here's a clever way to save both time and space while changing trash bags: Store the container of trash bags in the bottom of the trash can; when a full bag is removed, all you have to do is reach down and grab a fresh bag to replace it.

B. Recycle plastic shopping bags by using them to line small trash cans. Keep them from sliding to the bottom of the can by attaching small adhesive coat hooks (with the hooks facing downwards) on either side of the can, about 4 inches from the top. To secure the bag, simply slip the bag handles around the hooks.

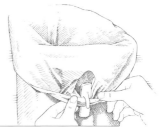

BAND YOUR BAGS

Most kitchen garbage bags tend to slip down inside the trash can, inviting an unpleasant mess to clean up later. Try securing the bag to the receptacle with a lightweight bungee cord. Just make sure you don't throw out the cord along with the trash when you change the bag!

CLIP FOR A TIGHTER FIT

To fix garbage and compost bags that are too wide for a narrow pail, gather and twist the excess to one side and fasten it in place with a bread bag clip to keep the top secure and open.

SWIFT SCRAP CLEANUP

Save plastic produce bags from the supermarket and use them to clean up kitchen scraps. Spread a bag on the counter next to your cutting board or in one half of the sink and sweep scraps such as vegetable peelings and onion skins onto it as you prep. When you're done, just gather up the bag and toss it away.

FRYING OIL DISPOSAL

Instead of pouring a small amount of used frying oil into an empty bottle or can, try sopping up the mess with the leftover flour, egg, and bread crumbs that were used to coat pan-fried foods.

1. Off the heat, add leftover flour, egg, and bread crumbs to the hot oil; stir.

2. Once the oil has been absorbed by the flour mixture, let cool and discard.

CLEANING UP SPILLS

Minor spills are a frequent occurrence in most kitchens. Here's a trick for keeping counters tidy: Use the small rimmed baking sheet from a toaster oven as a miniature dust pan, holding the pan under the edge of the counter and sweeping spilled food onto it for disposal.

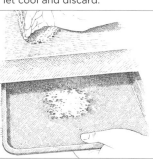

BREAKING NEWS: NEW AND IMPROVED CLEANUP

Whether they have built-in disposals or not, many cooks peel and pare fruits and vegetables directly into the sink. Those without disposals are then left with the task of fishing all of the scraps out of the sink and rinsing it out.

1. Make this chore much simpler by lining the empty sink with newspaper before you begin any prep work.

2. That way, when you're done prepping all you have to do is gather up the newspaper and its contents and put them in the trash (or the compost heap) in one fell swoop.

CORRALLING GERMS

When handling raw meat, such as chicken, avoid cross-contamination from bacteria by placing the plastic-wrapped chicken on a rimmed baking sheet. Cut open the package with kitchen shears, leaving the empty package, shears, and any other dirty utensils on the sheet, and pat the chicken dry. Then discard the packaging and transfer the baking sheet and tools to the sink to clean.

KEEPING A DIGITAL SCALE CLEAN

Weighing raw meat directly on the platform of a digital scale is not a great idea in terms of kitchen hygiene. Instead, cover the platform with a sheet of plastic wrap or slide the entire scale into a large zipper-lock bag. The buttons are usable and the readout visible through the plastic, which can be washed and reused for the same purpose.

STOP! DON'T RINSE THAT CHICKEN

Avoid rinsing raw meat and poultry. Contrary to what some cookbooks (or your grandmother) advise, rinsing is more likely to spread contaminants around the sink (and perhaps onto nearby foods like lettuce sitting on the counter) than to send them down the drain. Our kitchen tests also failed to demonstrate any flavor benefit to rinsing meat or poultry before cooking.

DOUBLE-DUTY DISHES

Keep your food safe and clean while still saving yourself from having to wash any extra dishes by reusing the same platter to hold meat before and after cooking. Simply cover the dish with plastic wrap or foil before putting the meat on it. Remove the protective layer after all the meat is in the pan or on the grill and *voilà*—you have a clean platter ready for the cooked food.

1.6 AVOIDING CROSS-CONTAMINATION

NEATLY UNWRAPPING VACUUM-SEALED PACKAGES

When opening poultry or meat wrapped in vacuum-sealed plastic, it's hard to prevent leakage onto your countertop. Try this simple mess-minimizing technique.

1. With a sharp knife, cut a large X in the plastic on the top of the package, being careful not to cut into the poultry or meat.

2. Gently pull the corners of the plastic away from the center of the X and remove the poultry or meat, leaving all of the juices in the bottom of the package.

WHEN RECYCLING IS NOT OK

Used marinade is contaminated with raw meat juice and is therefore unsafe to consume. If you want a sauce to serve with cooked meat, make a little extra marinade and set it aside before adding the rest to the raw meat.

SEASON SAFELY

Though bacteria can't live for more than a few minutes in direct contact with salt (which quickly dehydrates bacteria, leading to cell death), it can live on the edges of a box or shaker. To avoid contamination, transfer a little salt and ground pepper to small bowls. This way, you can reach into the bowls for seasoning without having to wash your hands every time you touch raw meat or fish. Afterward, the bowls go right in the sink or the dishwasher.

PREVENTING SPICE RUB CONTAMINATION

We developed many of our spice rub recipes to yield about a cup, so some will be left for the next session at the grill. To avoid contaminating the entire batch with raw food, portion out only as much spice rub as you'll need in a separate bowl, then seal and store the remaining spice rub.

MESS-FREE PERCOLATOR

If you hate the messy chore of cleaning damp coffee grounds out of the plastic basket of your coffee percolator, here's a way to make cleanup easier.

1. Snip a small hole in the center of a small (4- to 6-cup) basket-style coffee filter.

2. Fit the filter over the percolator tube and into the basket. Fill the filter-lined basket with ground coffee and brew as directed.

3. When it's time to clean up, just dump out the filter with the grounds.

PUDDLE-FREE COFFEE MAKING

The poorly designed spouts of most modern coffee carafes make it difficult to pour water into the coffee-maker reservoir without splashing the countertop. To prevent puddles, try filling the reservoir directly from the sink using the spray hose, avoiding the wet mess while also saving a step.

TAKE THE STRESS OUT OF CLEANING A FRENCH PRESS

French presses are hard to clean; the spent grounds cling to the bottom of the carafe and collect between the plates and screen of the plunger. Here are two tricks to make cleanup easier.

A. To easily get rid of the grounds without any going down the disposal (usually considered inadvisable), fill the carafe with water, pour its contents into a fine-mesh strainer over the sink, and dump the grounds into the trash.

B. To clean the whole press if you find anything left behind, fill the empty carafe halfway with soapy water. Then insert the plunger and rapidly move it up and down a few times. The force of the water dislodges any stuck grounds—and scrubs the sides of the carafe.

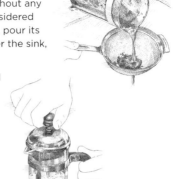

1.7 A NEAT START TO THE DAY

STABILIZING COFFEE FILTERS

When using a manual drip coffee maker, the grounds can spill down into the pot because the paper filter folds over on itself when the water is poured into it. To avoid this problem, dampen the paper filter just a little bit and press it against the sides of the plastic cone. When you add the coffee and pour the water through, the filter adheres to the cone.

REMOVING COFFEE STAINS

If you're unable to adequately scrub the inside of your thermal coffee carafe, try this clever trick.

1. Fill a carafe with a handful of rice and a cup of hot water.

2. Cover, then swirl and shake the carafe vigorously. Once the inside is clean, discard the rice and water. Rinse several times with hot water to remove any remaining residue.

CLEANING TOUGH TEA STAINS

If you brew a fresh pot of tea every morning, you know that tannin stains build up quickly on ceramics. Here's an easy way to remove them: Fill the stained teapot, teacup, or any tainted piece of ceramic with water and drop in a denture cleansing tablet. Let soak for 2 or 3 hours, then wash with dishwashing liquid and hot water. Light stains will disappear, leaving the cup or pot looking as good as new. Heavier stains may need several treatments followed by a scrubbing with hot, soapy water. Another option for cleaning tea- and coffee-stained ceramics is to try cutting a fresh lemon in quarters and using the fruit as a scrubber, gently squeezing its juice into a stained coffee mug or teapot. For extra cleaning power, first dip the lemon in kosher salt, which acts as an abrasive. Follow with a wash in hot, soapy water.

NEATER FRENCH TOAST

No one likes to waste French toast batter by dripping it all over the stovetop while transferring soaked slices of bread from bowl to skillet. Here's a clever way to soak up each and every drop: Simply place one piece of plain bread between the bowl and the skillet. Once you've used up all of the other slices, use the catchall slice for the last piece of French toast.

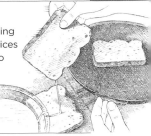

MUFFIN-TIN SHIELDS

Tired of scrubbing off the burnt batter from your muffin tins? Try this tip to avoid spills and simplify cleanup.

1. Cover the muffin tin tightly with aluminum foil. Cut slits in each hole and press the foil into each indentation.

2. Drop paper or foil liners into each hole and fill with your favorite muffin batter. After removing the muffins, simply peel off the dirty foil.

(SPLATTER) SCREEN TEST

Splatter screens prevent hot grease from making a mess of the stovetop while you're frying bacon, and the perforated flat surfaces can double as platters to hold cooked slices. After removing the screen to retrieve cooked bacon from the pan, replace it and lay the strips on top while other slices finish cooking. The cooked bacon not only sheds excess fat (blot it further before serving, if desired) but also stays warm.

DOWN THE TUBE

Hot bacon grease can be poured into a container and thrown away, but bacon grease that has cooled in the pan and adhered to the sides is harder to remove. Try using the end of an empty paper towel roll to scoop out the leftover grease. The hollow tube offers a channel for the grease to collect in and allows you to remove every last bit without dirtying your hands.

1.8 BEST PRACTICES FOR THE TIDY BAKER

MINIMIZING FLOUR SPRAY

No matter how gingerly you try to open a new bag of flour, the results are the same: A cloud of fine white dust rains down on the counter. For a no-mess fix, try slapping the top of the bag a few times before opening it to settle the flour so that it stays inside.

STAND MIXER SPLASH-GUARD

Dry ingredients can puff out in a cloud of fine particles when mixed, while wet ingredients, such as cream or liquid batters, can splatter. Here's a good way to keep your counter clean when using a stand mixer: Once the ingredients are in the bowl, drape a clean, very damp dish towel over the front of the mixer and bowl. Draw the towel snug with one hand and then turn on the mixer. When done, simply wash the towel.

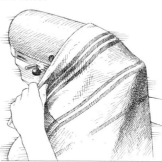

MITIGATING MIXER MESS

Bakers who use a stand mixer know well the mess that dry ingredients make if you add them to the mixer bowl too quickly. If you own the type that lifts the bowl up off the base, the mess is easy to control: Spread a kitchen towel between the base and the bowl. If you have a model where the bowl affixes to the base, try placing a piece of plastic wrap between the base of the mixer and the bowl. This provides a layer of protection without inter-fering with the way the bowl attaches to the base.

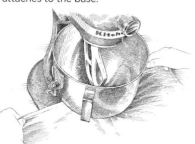

A TRAY'S THE WAY

To avoid a mess and fussy clean-up when using a stand mixer, put a plastic serving tray (like the kind found in cafeterias) under the mixer. Not only is it easier to slide the mixer on the counter-top, but any mess can be easily cleaned up with a quick rinse of the tray.

SHOWER CAPS AS DUSTBUSTERS

It makes sense to store the attachments for an electric mixer inside the bowl. But doing so can also expose them to dust. To avoid this, use a clean shower cap as a portable cover for the bowl and the attachments stored inside. You can use the same trick to keep dust from collecting on utensils stored upright in a crock. Whenever you're cooking or have company, all you have to do is slip off the cap and stick it in a kitchen drawer.

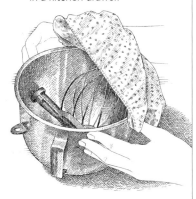

A FLEXIBLE SOLUTION FOR MIXER MESSES

Adding dry ingredients to a stand mixer from a wide mixing bowl can often lead to spills on the countertop. To make adding ingredients like flour and sugar easier, use a flexible plastic container, like a large yogurt or cottage cheese tub. Once the ingredients are placed in the container, pinch the edges to control the flow of spill-prone ingredients.

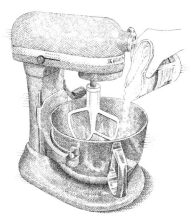

SPLASH-PROOF MIXER

To avoid ingredients splattering out of the bowl when using a handheld mixer, take a plastic gallon-size ice cream lid, cut it to fit around the beater, and place it on top of the bowl. No more dirty countertops.

SIFTER COASTER

Keep your counters clean with this simple trick: When you have to put down your sifter in the midst of a baking project, try placing it on the lid from your flour canister to catch any flour that falls through.

DISPOSING OF OIL NEATLY

Deep-fried foods are a real treat, but cleaning up after frying is not. Disposing of the spent oil neatly and safely is a particular challenge. Try making a quadruple- or quintuple-layered bag using four or five leftover plastic grocery bags. With someone holding the bag open over a sink or in an outdoor area, carefully pour the cooled frying oil from the pot into the innermost bag. Tie the bag handles shut before disposing of the oil.

THE PAN FLIP THAT STOPS DRIPS

Pouring melted butter, warm oil, sauce, or almost any liquid from a pan often creates a drip down the outside of the pan. This not only makes a mess on the pan's exterior but the drips can burn onto the pan bottom if you place it back on a hot burner. But you can prevent the drip with a simple flick of the wrist. Instead of immediately turning the pan right side up after pouring out the contents, continue to turn the pan in the direction of the pour, through one full rotation, until it eventually ends right side up. This forces the liquid to run back into the pan instead of down its side.

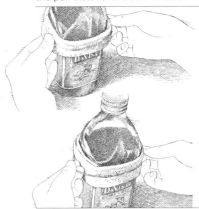

DON'T SWEAT OIL DRIPS

A. To prevent unsightly oil stains on pantry shelves, try wrapping a clean sweatband around the middle of the bottle of oil to catch drips. When the band becomes too dirty, clean it in the washing machine.

B. Alternatively, a band of folded paper towels can be fastened around the bottle with a rubber band and simply thrown away when dirty.

GETTING A GRIP ON SLICK BOTTLES

Because grabbing an olive oil bottle or can of vegetable oil spray with floured or greasy hands can be a slippery task, you might want to add some traction. Place a rubber band around the container. Now you have a no-slip grip on the spray.

SPLASH-FREE POURING

Tired of the splashes that occur when transferring tomato sauce, soup, or stew from a pot to a storage container? With the help of a spoon, the mess can be averted. Place the backside of a large wooden or metal spoon under the pouring stream to deflect the liquid into the container.

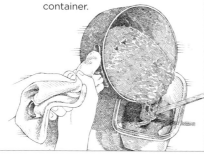

STOPPING HOT SPLASHES

An immersion blender creates a one-pot solution for pureeing ingredients into smooth soups. However, unlike a traditional blender with an airtight top, the handy tool is little more than a stick with a blade and the hot contents can splatter out when it's in use. For an easy solution, cut a hole in a disposable aluminum pie plate, invert it on top of the pot, and insert the immersion blender in the hole to prevent any mess.

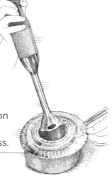

SAUCEPAN SPLASH GUARD

To keep simmering sauces from splattering onto the stovetop, fashion a splash guard from a disposable aluminum pie plate.

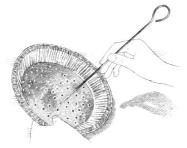

1. Using a metal skewer, poke at least a dozen holes in the pie plate.

2. Using tongs, invert the pie plate onto the pan. The holes allow the steam—not the splatters—to escape.

MINIMIZING SAUTÉ SPLATTER

When you are browning meat for a soup or stew, grease splatters on the stovetop and burners make for a nasty mess and an unpleasant cleanup job. The stovetop is easy enough to wipe off, but cleaning the burners and burner plates is more involved. To keep unused burners from getting dirty in the first place, position inverted disposable aluminum pie plates over them. The pie plates can be wiped clean and used again. You can also use a large cookie sheet to cover more than one burner at a time.

PREVENTING BOILOVERS

Most cooks with electric stoves who need to quickly cool down a hot pot move it to another burner. Instead of risking a burn while trying to move a large pot of angrily bubbling water, toss in one or two ice cubes. This brings down the temperature quickly and takes up the slack while the stove slowly cools down.

A STOVETOP KETTLE GRILL

A grill pan is a good alternative when outdoor grilling is not an option, but it tends to create messy grease splatters and imparts minimal smoke flavor to food. Try inverting a disposable aluminum roasting pan over the top of your grill pan to catch splatters. This also concentrates smoky flavor in whatever food you are grilling, much like the closed lid of a kettle grill.

MESS-FREE BROILING

When you're broiling greasy meats such as ground beef, the fat often produces smoke and is hard to clean up. Lining the broiler pan with aluminum foil helps, but you can take this method one step further.

1. Line the bottom of the broiler pan with foil and cover it with a few slices of bread to soak up the grease. Cover with the perforated broiler pan top and proceed to broil the meat.

2. When it comes time to clean up, simply gather the foil and grease-soaked bread together and discard.

TONGS CADDY

Tongs are the tool of choice for a wide range of cooking projects. When cooking with tongs, try keeping them at the ready by resting them in a heavy beer or coffee mug. This way, any juices on the tongs drip into the mug, keeping your counters mess-free and simplifying cleanup.

BETTER BLENDING

Oil or melted butter added to dressings or sauces in a whirring blender can splatter back up through the opening in the lid and make a mess. Eliminate this problem by placing a small funnel in the opening and pouring the liquid through it slowly and steadily.

THE GREAT GRATER-CLEANING PROBLEM

Graters coated with the sticky residue from soft cheeses can be a chore to clean. Here's an easy way to handle this task.

1. Rub a hard, stale crust of bread (such as the end of a baguette) over the dirty grater to remove most of the mess.

2. Scrub the grater in hot soapy water to finish the job.

CLEANING RASP-STYLE GRATERS

A rasp-style grater is an invaluable tool, but food can get trapped in its holes, making it a challenge to clean. Try using a clean toothbrush to scrub its hard-to-reach nooks and crannies.

SMARTER KNIFE CLEANING

Scrub pads do a fine job of removing gunk from knife blades but eventually damage the finish. To keep knives shiny, use a wine cork instead. Angling the blade toward the cutting board, simply rub the cork over the knife to remove food residue, then wash the knife in hot, soapy water with a soft sponge.

SALTING BASTING BRUSHES

Cleaning a basting brush can be a tricky business, with lots of goo and grease clinging stubbornly to its bristles—and the brush just gets worse with every use. Try this clever technique to ensure a thorough cleaning job. After washing the dirty brushes with liquid dish soap and very hot water, rinsing them well, and shaking them dry, place the brushes, bristles pointing down, into a cup and fill the cup with coarse salt until the bristles are covered. The salt draws moisture out of the bristles and keeps them dry and fresh between uses.

NO MORE STINKY WOODEN SPOONS

We love wooden spoons, but because they retain odors and transfer flavors, a hint of yesterday's French onion soup can end up in today's beurre blanc. Since it isn't advisable to put wood in the dishwasher, we had to find another way to clean these utensils. We rinsed dirty spoons with water, then cleaned them with the following substances: dish detergent and water, vinegar and water, bleach and water, a lemon dipped in salt, a tablespoon of baking soda mixed with a teaspoon of water, and more plain water as a control. The only spoon that came out odor-free was the one scrubbed with baking soda. Here's why: Odors left behind in the porous surface of a wooden spoon are often caused by weak organic acids. Baking soda neutralizes such acids, eliminating odor. Furthermore, since baking soda is water soluble, it works its magic as far as the water penetrates.

TLC FOR WOODEN UTENSILS AND CUTTING BOARDS

While most cooks know that butcher-block countertops or cutting boards should be treated with mineral oil to boost longevity, some forget that wooden utensils also benefit from an occasional dip.

1. Pour food-grade mineral oil into a baking dish to a ⅛-inch depth. (If your utensils are too long for the pan, use a rimmed baking sheet.) Lay clean utensils in the oil for 15 minutes; flip and let sit for 15 minutes longer.

2. Remove the utensils from the oil and wipe away the excess. Let them dry for 24 hours. Funnel any leftover oil into a container to reserve for future use.

PREVENTIVE CARE FOR CUTTING BOARDS

Some cooks have multiple cutting boards for different purposes, but cooks with more limited storage space often make do with one. Here are two tips that keep them from picking up stains and odors.

A. Put garlic cloves in a plastic sandwich bag, mash them with a pan or rolling pin right in the bag, and dump them directly from the bag into the pot. This way, no odor pervades the board because no garlic ever touches it.

B. If you like roasted beets but hate the way they stain cutting boards when you peel and slice them, try lining the roasting pan with a square of aluminum foil that is large enough to act as a board liner when it comes time to prep the roasted beets.

1.11 CONQUERING TRICKY CLEANING CHALLENGES

OUT, DAMNED SPOT

Slicing pomegranates, beets, or cherries can leave bright pink or red stains on your cutting board that even endless scrubbing can't get out. But you can make the marks disappear with distilled white vinegar by blotting it on with a sponge. After a quick scrub and rinse, the surface is as good as new.

DON'T CRY OVER SPILLED WINE

Try this homemade solution for removing red wine stains. Combine equal parts hydrogen peroxide and dish detergent. Pour on the stain to saturate. The stain should disappear within an hour. (Be sure to test the solution on an inconspicuous spot first.)

ALL THE NEWS THAT'S FIT TO DE-STINK

Raw garlic and onions can leave behind unpleasant odors in plastic containers, which can subsequently permeate any food stored in them. You can use newspaper to solve the problem.

1. Fill the odoriferous container with crumpled pieces of newspaper and seal the lid. The newspaper will absorb the odor.

2. After a day or two, remove the newspaper and wash the now odor-free container in hot, soapy water.

CLEANING CAST IRON

To clean a cast-iron pan without ruining the finish, it is important to avoid using too much soap. One way to accomplish this it to let the pan cool, then take a plastic mesh produce bag (the kind that holds lemons or onions) and swipe the pan clean. The mesh bag doesn't damage seasoning the way steel wool will, and you don't have to ruin a scrubber pad with grease. A wad of heavy-duty aluminum foil will also work. In either case, you can reseason the pan after cleaning by using paper towels to wipe it with about 1 tablespoon of oil.

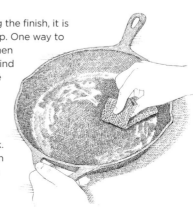

STICKING IT TO STUCK-ON FOOD

Try this effective solution for removing burnt-on food from your pots and pans.

1. Fill the pan 2 inches high with water. Add ¼ cup baking soda and ¼ cup distilled white vinegar. Bring to a boil and cook for 15 minutes. Turn off heat and let sit until cooled.

2. Drain the water and clean the pot as usual. If any burnt patches remain, repeat.

REMOVING BAKED-ON GOO

The baked-on coating of burnt cheese and sauce left at the bottom of a fondue dish or macaroni-and-cheese pan may be tasty, but hardened food residue presents a formidable cleaning task. Here are two ways to handle the challenge.

A. Cover the burnt-on mess with dishwashing soap and a small amount of boiling water and allow it to rest overnight. The next morning, the mess will wash away with ease.

B. To deal with large pans even in a small sink, soak a dish towel thoroughly in warm water and place it directly on the surface of the dirty pan. In as little as a few minutes, the mess washes right off, just as if the pan had been soaked in a sink.

SMOOTHING A STICKY SALAD BOWL

Years of exposure to oily salad dressings can leave wooden salad bowls with a gummy, rancid residue that all the soap and hot water in the world can't wash off. The best way to restore your bowl is to completely remove the accumulated layers of oil with sandpaper and start fresh. Using medium-grit sandpaper (80 to 120 grit), gently rub the bowl's surface until it turns matte and pale; thoroughly wash and dry the bowl; and give it a new coat of food-grade mineral oil (don't use vegetable oil or lard, both of which turn rancid and sticky). With a paper towel, liberally apply the oil to all the surfaces of the bowl, let it sink in for 15 minutes, and then wipe it with a fresh paper towel. Reapply oil whenever the bowl becomes dry or dull. It's fine to use a mild dish soap and warm water to clean wooden bowls; doing this will help maintain the seasoning and prevent oil buildup. Dry the bowl thoroughly after cleaning and never put it in the dishwasher or let it soak; otherwise, it can warp and crack.

DIY CHARCOAL MITT

Filling a chimney starter with a precise amount of charcoal can be a messy enterprise. Try repurposing the long plastic bags in which newspapers are delivered as mitts. The bags keep hands clean as you reach into the sack to grab handfuls of coal.

CLEANING GRILL TOOLS ON THE GO

Here's a new way to tote soiled grilling tools home from picnics and campsites: Put them in a large plastic sealable container filled with water and a few drops of dishwashing soap. The grungy tools get a presoak on the road, which makes for easy cleaning at home.

PROTECTING GAS-GRILL CONTROLS

The ignition and burner control knobs on some gas grills can be persnickety if they get wet or dirty from exposure to the elements, especially if the grill is kept outdoors in the snow during the winter. If you're unable to find a cover for the entire grill, try this impromptu solution: Invert a disposable aluminum roasting pan over the control panel and tape it in place on either end with duct or electrical tape.

OILED GRATE SCRAPER

One of the test kitchen's favorite ways to clean a grill without a grill brush is to use balled-up aluminum foil.

1. Lay an 18 by 12-inch piece of foil on a counter, then center two paper towels on the foil. Drizzle the paper towels with 2 tablespoons vegetable oil.

2. Crumple the foil around the paper towels and poke several holes in it with a wooden skewer.

3. Using long-handled tongs, brush the hot grill surface with the foil ball, letting some of the oil leak out and season the grill.

EASY ASH DISPOSAL

No matter how you do it, emptying a kettle grill of cool ashes is a messy procedure. You can neaten things up by fashioning a grill scoop out of a plastic one-quart or half-gallon milk jug with a handle.

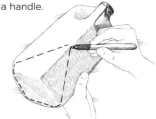

1. Cut off a bottom corner of the jug to form a scoop.

2. The plastic conforms to the curve of the grill bottom, which makes it easier to collect more ashes with a single sweep.

CLEANING AN IMMERSION BLENDER

Scrubbing the blade of an immersion blender with a thick sponge can be a frustrating, dangerous task. For a better, and safer, approach, fill a bowl with hot, soapy water and place it in the sink. Place the dirty blender blade in the water. Turn the blender on to whirl away the stuck-on food, then rinse the tool clean with hot water.

EASIER FOOD PROCESSOR CLEANUP

Some food processor lids have non-removable sliding feed tubes that don't get completely clean in the dishwasher because the pieces stick together. To solve the problem, pull up the top portion of the lid and insert a chopstick between the tube and the lid to separate the pieces. Soapy water can now flow through, and the entire lid emerges from the dishwasher perfectly clean.

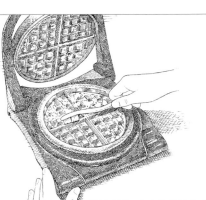

BRUSH AWAY THE MESS

While most waffle irons and panini presses feature an easy-to-clean nonstick cooking surface, you may find that food still gets stuck in the deep ridges. A firm-bristle toothbrush is perfect for this cleaning task. The bristles are stiff enough to remove stubborn stuck-on food yet soft enough for a nonstick surface. If you still find any residue left in the ridges, try a cotton swab.

NO-CLEAN PANINI PRESS

Panini presses simplify the process of whipping up Italian-style grilled sandwiches, but scrubbing away grease and melted-on cheese after each use can be a chore. Try wrapping your sandwiches in parchment paper before placing them in the press. The parchment can take the heat and catches spills, eliminating the need for cleanup.

CUSTOM SPONGE FOR PANINI GRILLS

Because of their many grooves, panini grills, grill pans, and sandwich presses can be difficult to clean. However, you can create a customized cleaning tool with a sponge and a chef's knife.

1. Using a sharp chef's knife, cut several ½-inch-deep slits lengthwise into the sponge, spacing the slits so that they accommodate the grooves of the grill.

2. When the grill is cool and ready to be cleaned, dip the sponge into hot, soapy water and fit it into the grooves for scrubbing.

PREVENTING MICROWAVE SPLATTERS

Food often splatters when it is being heated in the microwave. A basket-style coffee filter is ideal for covering food and keeping the walls of the microwave clean.

EASY MICROWAVE CLEANING

In busy households where the microwave sees a lot of use, people sometimes forget to cover a dish when reheating food. This results in splatters inside the oven. Since scrubbing is tedious and has the potential to damage the interior surfaces, you need a simple cleaning method. Place a microwave-safe bowl full of water in the oven and heat it on high for 10 minutes; the steam loosens dried food particles so they can be wiped off with ease.

CLEANING MICROWAVES AND BLENDERS

Nooks, crannies, and crevices on kitchen appliances can be a particular cleaning challenge. Here are two good suggestions for these tricky spots.

A. The corners of a microwave oven pose a cleaning problem. A small foam paintbrush with a beveled edge can be used to brush away crumbs and other residue with ease.

B. The buttons on a blender are situated very close together, so it's a chore to clean between them when something spills. Use a nail brush to get into the tight spaces.

FUME-FREE OVEN CLEANING

Spraying oven cleaner in the oven to remove grime from the racks can fill the kitchen with harsh fumes. To clear the air, try taking the process outdoors.

1. Place the dirty oven rack in a large garbage bag. Take the bag outside and, keeping the rack in the bag, spray it with oven cleaner. Close the bag and let it sit outside overnight.

2. Wearing rubber gloves, remove the rack from the bag and place it on several sheets of newspaper. Wipe the rack clean with a damp dish towel before returning it to the oven.

Microwave Caramel Sauce

⚲ **WHY THIS RECIPE WORKS:** Many cooks shy away from making caramel. The process involves nothing more than melting sugar on the stovetop, but it can be tricky—and messy—nonetheless. The sugar must be heated slowly and carefully to avoid over-cooking, which is an all-too-easy occurrence even when you're using a thermometer. And there's always the risk of getting splattered by the molten syrup as you stir. But there's an easier, virtually hands-off approach with very little cleanup: Use the microwave. This appliance makes clean, safe caramel a breeze; then simply add cream and butter for a perfect sauce for ice cream, bread pudding, or anything else. Homemade caramel doesn't get any easier than this. This recipe makes about 1 cup.

1   **cup sugar**
2   **tablespoons corn syrup**
2   **tablespoons water**
⅛   **teaspoon lemon juice**
½   **cup hot heavy cream**
1   **tablespoon unsalted butter**

1. Stir sugar, corn syrup, water, and lemon juice together in 2-cup microwave-safe measuring cup or glass bowl.

2. Microwave on full power until mixture is just beginning to brown, 5 to 8 minutes (depending on strength of your microwave).

3. Remove caramel from microwave and let it sit on dry surface for 5 minutes or until it darkens to rich honey brown.

4. Add hot cream a few tablespoons at a time (so caramel won't seize up), followed by butter.

CHAPTER 2

KITCHEN ORGANIZATION HACKS

DIY Without a Trip to Ikea

2.1 A PLACE FOR EVERYTHING

STACKED SUPPLIES

Utilize deep kitchen drawers by stacking cutlery trays on top of each other. For easy access, use the top tray for the items that you use most often (everyday utensils, such as can openers, spatulas, and large spoons) and the bottom tray for less frequently needed items (such as spreaders, skewers, straws, and chopsticks). It's a simple matter to grasp the top tray and lift it aside when you need access to the bottom layer.

TWO CORKING IDEAS

A. Very few tools bring order to the kitchen like a utensil holder. To keep your holder from knocking against the sides of the drawer every time you open and close it, make a better fit with a wine cork. Cut the cork to fill the space between the holder and the drawer, creating a wedge that locks the holder in place.

B. If you have kitchen cabinets that always slam shut after you reach in for dishes, spices, or other culinary sundries, try slicing a wine cork into thin disks and gluing them onto the inside corners of the cabinets.

ROLLING PIN PERCH

Storing large, awkward rolling pins with handles and ball bearings is often difficult, especially with limited drawer and cupboard space. Here's a clever solution: Hang it on the wall. First, measure the distance between the handles of the rolling pin. Next, measure that same distance at a convenient spot on your kitchen wall and mount two inexpensive curtain rod holders or hooks, one at each end. Then simply suspend your rolling pin by its handles.

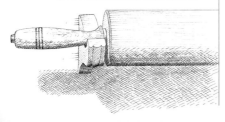

DUTCH OVEN HANGUPS

If you're short on cabinet space, consider this trick for alternative storage of your large Dutch oven: Affix two sturdy coat hooks, spaced about 8 inches apart, to the side of your cabinet. Hang the pot by its handle on the lower rungs and prop the lid on top of the hooks.

SAFER STORAGE FOR BAKING STONES

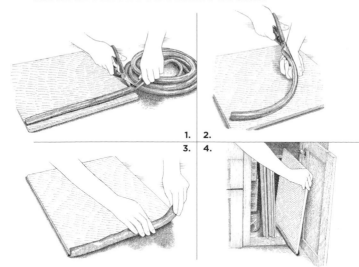

1. | 2.
3. | 4.

A baking stone helps create crisp, evenly browned pizza and bread, but its rough edges can scrape cabinet linings. To keep your cabinets safe, try cutting a piece of rubber hose (standard irrigation hose will work) to the length of a baking stone's short edge **(1)**. Slit the tube open along one side **(2)**. Insert the stone into the slit, creating a cover for the rough edge **(3)**. To store, slide the stone into the cabinet with the covered edge on the bottom **(4)**. Remove the hose before using the stone.

BETTER BAKING MAT STORAGE

Silicone baking mats are often stored rolled, but without a way to secure them, they quickly unfurl. To improve this situation, try laying a large, clean dish towel that's at least as big as the mat on a flat surface. Place the baking mat on top. Starting at a short end, roll the towel over the mat. Tuck the ends of the towel into the tube to secure. Another option is to roll each sheet liner tightly and store it inside the tube from an empty paper towel roll. For liners of various sizes, just cut the cardboard tube to fit. For a more accessible solution, you can keep your baking mat super handy by attaching it to your fridge with a magnetic clip

CONTAINING PLASTIC LIDS

Borrow from your office to organize the disarray of plastic lids in your kitchen cabinet. A magazine box keeps reusable container lids in one place for easy retrieval. (Depending on the height of your cabinet, you may have to lay the box flat on its long side.)

2.1 A PLACE FOR EVERYTHING

TWO WAYS TO KEEP COVERS UNDER CONTROL

A. Many cooks store their pans and lids in a single drawer. To keep the lids from sliding around and under the pans, install a slender expansion curtain rod at the front of your drawer. The lids stand up straight between the front of the drawer and the curtain rod, always within sight and reach.

B. Rather than installing custom cabinet dividers, try this low-cost solution for storing cookware lids: Place a metal file sorter inside the cabinet and load the lids into each compartment. Now, instead of searching through a disorganized heap for the right top to a pot, you can quickly grab exactly what you need.

FILING YOUR CUTTING BOARDS AND BAKING SHEETS

If you're loath to waste kitchen storage space by laying cutting boards and baking sheets flat, try this solution from your local office supply store: An inexpensive metal vertical file holder is ideal for storing cutting boards and baking sheets. They not only take up less space, but are also easy to grab when you need one.

CUTTING BOARD HIDEAWAY

Conserve cabinet space by attaching two wooden napkin holders, spaced as far apart as your longest cutting board, to the underside of an upper cabinet. The napkin holders act as brackets, holding multiple stacked cutting boards.

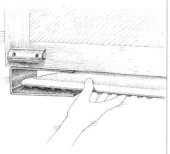

KEEPING THE KEYS TO BAKING IN EASY REACH

Many cooks keep measuring cups and spoons in a drawer, where they can get buried deep among other utensils. For greater visibility and accessibility, try mounting a simple key holder near your workspace and, instead of using it to safeguard keys, hang your measuring spoons and cups from it.

RACKING UP THE CUPS

Try storing metal measuring cups on a magnetic knife strip. Not only are the cups easy to access but each measurement is visible, unlike when the cups are nested together in a stack.

MEASURING SPOON ROUNDUP

Measuring spoons often come with flimsy rings that end up breaking. Transferring them to a simple "split" key ring keeps spoons together no matter how many times they go through the dishwasher.

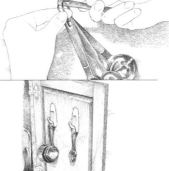

BAKING GEAR HOOKUP

To ensure that measuring spoons and cups are always in plain view, attach adhesive hooks to the inside of your cabinet and hang the tools on these handy posts, ending the game of hide-and-seek once and for all.

MEASURES AT THE READY

To make sure that you always have dry measures on hand for baking projects and the like, buy a new set of measuring cups and divide your old set among your dry ingredient canisters. With the ½-cup measure right in with the flour, for instance, you'll never want for a clean, dry measure.

MEASURING ON THE LEVEL

To measure dry ingredients accurately, teaspoons and tablespoons should be leveled off with a straight edge. Instead of hunting for a butter knife or other leveling tool in the middle of a recipe, try keeping a built-in level right in with your ingredients: the flat spout of a baking powder canister.

1. Transfer a frequently used ingredient, such as salt, to a clean baking powder canister.

2. When measuring, scrape the spoon against the level edge of the opening.

2.1 A PLACE FOR EVERYTHING

A PERFECT FIT FOR YOUR THERMOMETER

Keep your thermometer within easy reach by slipping it into your knife-storage block.

1. Use a drill to create a hole in a wooden knife block.

2. Slip in your thermometer for easy storing.

FIXING A TEST-Y PROBLEM

To keep metal cake testers from getting lost in crowded drawers, insert them into the holes of a dedicated saltshaker, where they are in plain sight and close at hand when you need them.

KEEPING OVEN MITTS AND DISH TOWELS WITHIN REACH

If you can never find your oven mitt or dish towel when you need it, try this simple way to keep them in sight: Hang the mitt or towel from a shower curtain hook placed on the oven door's handle.

REACHING BEYOND YOUR GRASP

To grasp lightweight items that are just out of reach, sidestep the stepstool in favor of another kitchen tool—a pair of tongs. They're great for grabbing things like bags of pasta, cereal boxes, or spices from the top shelves of the cupboard or pantry.

NO-SLIP DISH TOWEL

The oven door handle is a convenient place to hang dish towels, but a smooth bar offers little traction and the cloths often slip off and fall to the floor. For a simple fix, try this easy trick.

1. Cut a sheet of nonslip shelf liner about 5 inches wide and long enough to wrap around the handle of your oven.

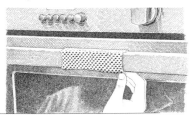

2. Wrap the liner around the oven handle and secure it with double-sided tape; hang the towel over the liner.

THINKING OUTSIDE THE BOX FOR YOUR BAGS

Many home kitchens sport a drawer filled to the gills with crumpled plastic bags. To reclaim your drawer, try one of these tricks.

A. Instead of discarding a box of wine after finishing the last glass, remove the wine bag and spout and then fill the empty box with plastic bags. When you need one, pull it through the hole in the front of the box.

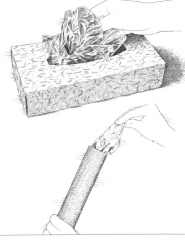

B. Stuff reusable bags into an empty tissue box. A box will accommodate many bags, which are then easy to remove one at a time when needed.

C. For a storage solution with a smaller footprint, you can also use an empty paper towel roll to store bags; one tube will fit about 20 bags.

SIX-PACK SUPPLY STORAGE

The boxes containing plastic sandwich bags, rolls of aluminum foil, plastic wrap, and the like can use up a lot of drawer space. Solve this problem by storing the boxes upright in the slots of a cardboard six-pack beer bottle or soda container in a cabinet under the counter.

2.2 HACKS FOR THE SMALL KITCHEN

INSTANT EXTRA SPACE

Envious of kitchens with miles of counter space and pullout cutting boards? Hack your own by placing a cutting board or cookie sheet over an opened drawer. Use it as a surface for prepping ingredients or for supporting bowls. No matter the size of the kitchen, a little extra space for resting bowls, platters, or cooling racks never hurts. (We don't recommend this tip for households with young children running about.)

IRONING OUT AN AREA FOR KITCHEN PREP

Not every apartment has ample kitchen counters, but most do have an ironing board. Hello, automatic prep space. Ironing boards are easily moveable, adjustable for height, and they provide several extra feet of space for cooling baked goods or holding bowls as you work.

EXTENDING A COUNTER

Home cooks who lack the luxury of ample counter space often have a problem finding room for wire cooling racks when baking cookies. To extend counter space, try setting the racks directly over the sink, which has the added benefit of making it easy to clean up the crumbs that fall through the rack. (We don't recommend this tip for households with young children running about.)

A STAND-IN FOR COUNTER SPACE

Cooks in small kitchens with limited counter space often don't have a place to rest a pot lid while they stir a soup or stew. Here's a solution: Place the pot lid on a sturdy plate stand, which takes up far less space than the lid does when lying flat and holds the lid (including larger crock pot covers) upright and out of the way.

OVEN-SPACE EXPANDER

When keeping food warm, it's all too easy to run out of oven space. Create an extra rack in an electric oven with a concealed heating element by placing a wire rack on the floor of the oven. Note: While the rack allows air to circulate and keeps the bottom pan from scorching, food placed there should be checked frequently.

AN EXTRA STORAGE RACK

To keep utensils, pots, and pans out of cluttered drawers and cabinets and at the ready, mount a large piece of plastic-covered grating (available at home improvement and discount stores) on the wall in a convenient spot. Then simply use S-hooks to hang all kinds of kitchen gear from it. If you would rather not mount the grate permanently, just set one edge on a counter and lean the grate against the wall. This way, it can be moved easily as the need arises. For a more compact solution, use a cooling rack instead of the plastic-covered grating.

MAXIMIZING CABINET SPACE

Kitchen equipment stored in the back of deep cabinets can be difficult to reach. Rather than emptying out the front of the cabinet to reach items in the back, try placing cookware on a rimmed baking sheet on the bottom of the cabinet; then you can pull the sheet out to access hard-to-reach items.

SECRET CORNER STORAGE

SHOE-IN SOLUTION FOR SMALL PANTRIES

In a small kitchen, it can be hard to find enough room for pantry goods. For quick and easy access to spices, herbs, canned goods, and other staples that frees up counter, cabinet, and drawer space, keep your stash in the pockets of an over-the-door organizer designed for shoes. Organizers with clear plastic pockets work best, providing quick, easily visible access to all of the small items that might normally take up room on a shelf.

Wall- or ceiling-mounted racks and railings are a great storage solution for pots and pans, but not every kitchen can accommodate them. Convert a corner cabinet into a catchall for your cookware by removing the shelves and attaching hooks to the underside of the cabinet's top. Lids stack neatly beneath the hanging pots and pans.

2.3 UPCYCLED ORGANIZATION

A SLICK NEW USE FOR OLIVE OIL TINS

Rather than purchase a caddy to keep cooking utensils within reach on the countertop, try repurposing an empty gallon-size olive oil tin by removing its top with a can opener. An added bonus: Its metal front holds a magnetized kitchen timer.

KNIFE STORAGE FOR WINE LOVERS

Try this ingenious new way to store knives.

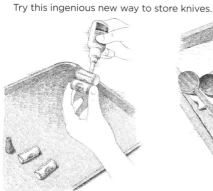

1. Glue wine corks together, side by side, and place the strip in a drawer.

2. The knife blades rest in the crevices between the corks, which keeps them upright and protected.

FINGER SAFETY FIRST

Fondue forks, paring knives, corn holders, skewers, and all manner of small, sharp objects can present a danger when tossed haphazardly into a kitchen drawer: The next time you reach into the drawer, you're likely to get poked. Try securing all those pointy tips in leftover wine corks, which not only protects hands but also keeps sharp edges from getting dull.

THE GRATE-EST PROTECTION

A rasp-style grater can nick fingers when it is left unprotected in a drawer. Store your grater safely by slipping it into an empty paper-towel tube before sliding it into the drawer.

A NEST OF MEASURING CUPS

Stacking glass measuring cups can result in chipped and broken edges. A small square of wax or parchment paper placed between the cups prevents them from chipping and makes them easier to separate when needed.

SEPARATING STUCK GLASS

Glass measuring cups and drinking glasses sometimes get locked together, with one cup stuck tightly inside the other. Rather than risk breaking the glass, try this novel way to release the seal.

1. Fill the top measuring cup or glass with ice cubes, then place the bottom cup in a bowl of warm tap water.

2. The contrast in temperatures between the cups will cause the seal to loosen, so the cups can be gently pulled apart.

A CLEAR WINNER FOR DISH PROTECTION

Wrap dishes in plastic before boxing them for moving; unlike newspaper, which can stain, plastic wrap keeps the dishes clean. Crumpled newspaper or bubble wrap can be used to pad the box and keep plastic-wrapped dishes and glassware safe. This wrapping solution also works for storing dishes on open shelving in your home, where they might get dusty between uses.

NO-FUSS WRAPPER STORAGE

Opened boxes of aluminum foil and plastic wrap often catch on the kitchen drawer frame, causing it to jam. Avoid this annoyance with this simple tip: When you return a box of foil or plastic wrap to its storage drawer, turn the box lid side down. The next time you open the drawer, there won't be any lids to stick up and prevent the drawer from opening.

2.4 AN OUNCE OF PREVENTION

STRING BEHIND THE SCENES

When tying meat with kitchen twine, it can be hard to avoid contaminating the entire roll with dirty fingers. Instead of cutting the estimated amount needed ahead of time—and ending up with too much or too little—try this trick.

1. Place the roll of twine inside a cabinet in the corner behind the hinges.

2. Thread the twine out above the hinge and close the cabinet door. Pull the twine to tie your roast, cutting just the right amount.

KEEPING TWINE CLEAN

If you don't own a twine dispenser, try this makeshift version to keep twine clean when tying raw meat. Poke a small hole through a zipper-lock bag. Place the roll of twine in the bag and feed the twine through the hole. Seal the bag. It will protect the unused twine and can be easily wiped clean.

NONSTICK PAN TLC

Many cooks make efficient use of kitchen storage space by stacking their skillets, but stacking can be tough on nonstick finishes, with the potential to cause scratches or chips. Try placing cheap paper plates between the pans to protect the coating. The plates' round shape helps them stay in place, and they last for ages. You can also just use a double layer of paper towels, or slide the pans into large plastic zipper-lock bags (the 2-gallon size for 10-inch pans and the 1-gallon size for 8-inch pans). The plastic protects the nonstick surface.

NO MORE SCRAPES

Instead of using a metal knife to loosen cakes or muffins from your nonstick pans, which can mar the nonstick surface, you can use a plastic "takeout" knife. Store it in your utensil drawer within easy reach, so you're not tempted to grab something sharp.

CLEAN SHAVE FOR BURNT SPATULAS

A plastic spatula is a must with a nonstick pan in order to prevent scratches. Over time, however, no matter how careful you are, the tool's edge will melt into an uneven, rough lip. To keep your pans safe, use a vegetable peeler to shave off the singed plastic and restore an even edge.

SCRATCHLESS STEAMING

Avoid scratching your nonstick saucepan with the metal legs of a steamer insert by protecting the pan with parchment paper.

1. Cut a piece of parchment to fit the inside of your saucepan. Fill with 1 inch of water.

2. Place the steamer insert on top of the parchment. Bring to a simmer and steam your food, being careful not to let all the water evaporate.

EASIER STEAMING

Many vegetable steamer baskets have short legs that allow only a small amount of water to be added beneath their bases. For vegetables that take a while to cook through, try this ingenious tip that eliminates the need for replenishing the water during steaming. Place three crumpled balls of aluminum foil in the pot and then place the steamer basket on top of the foil. The foil elevates the steamer basket, creating room for extra water.

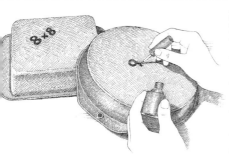

KEEPING TRACK OF BAKEWARE SIZES

With manufacturers' indications of size on baking pans often being either illegible or non-existent, you may want to take matters into your own hands and use ovensafe metal paint (available at hardware stores) to mark pan bottoms, noting dimensions or capacity.

TURNING THINGS AROUND IN YOUR FRIDGE

When a refrigerator is packed with food, it's easy to forget about items that are lingering in the back until they're long past their expiration dates. Avoid this problem by placing a rotating lazy Susan on one of your fridge shelves. Now everything is visible (and accessible) with a quick spin.

DIVIDE AND CONQUER

Group similar products in your fridge in their own labeled storage bins. Wide, shallow shapes work well. For instance, all the jams and jellies go into one container, all the Asian sauces and condiments in another, and all mustards, ketchups, and relishes in another. This is especially convenient if you are preparing, say, a stir-fry sauce that calls for several items likely to be kept in the same container. This system also limits messes on refrigerator shelves from sticky jars.

SIX-PACK CHILLIN'

If you don't have enough space in your refrigerator to store bottled beverages upright, here's a clever way to store them horizontally, without them rolling around: Fasten a large binder clip around two wires of one of the shelves (from below) and stack the drinks next to it in a pyramid. The clip holds everything in place, and it can easily be moved right or left to support more or fewer bottles.

LABELING PROTOCOLS

Keep your refrigerator neat and organized by keeping a permanent marker and masking tape handy. Every time a new bottle or jar is opened or leftovers are packaged up, write the date on a piece of tape and stick it to the side of the container in a highly visible spot.

LABEL HELPER

Here's a great tool for labeling containers of leftovers in the fridge: blue painter's tape. It comes off easily without leaving any adhesive behind, and you can rip just the right-size piece. You can even print reheating instructions on the tape.

THE MAGIC EXPANDING FRIDGE

Finding room for a large dish in a cramped refrigerator is a familiar challenge for many cooks. Here's one space-saving solution: Create an extra "shelf" by stacking a baking sheet on top of the casserole dish and then place smaller items on the baking sheet.

PROTECTING RECIPE INGREDIENTS

To keep your family or roommates from using ingredients reserved for use in a recipe, use brightly colored stickers to mark them as soon as you unpack the groceries. Make it known that anything with a sticker is off-limits and you'll be saved repeated trips to the grocery store to replace recipe ingredients.

EASY-BAKE SET

If you're tired of fumbling through your cabinets for all your basic baking ingredients, try keeping a plastic container stocked with the staples: vanilla extract, baking powder, baking soda, cinnamon, and so on. When it's time to bake, you can simply retrieve all the necessary items in one fell swoop.

INSTANT LABELING

Here's a tip to help avid bakers with multiple kinds of flour on hand keep track of which type is which: Try cutting the labels out of the flour bags and taping them to the outsides of the plastic storage containers. Now there's no second-guessing about whether you're grabbing cake, bread, or all-purpose flour.

REDUCING THE FOOTPRINT OF CANNED GOODS

Canned foods can quickly occupy most of your pantry, even when stacked, but these staples take up much less real estate if stored on their sides. Try corralling them in a magazine file (at least 5 inches wide). Its sides prevent the cans from rolling, and its slim profile frees up shelf space.

2.5 MANAGING YOUR FRIDGE AND PANTRY

TWO SIMPLE RACKS FOR SPICE DRAWERS

It is best to store spices away from heat and light (not on the counter in a spice rack), but if your chosen storage spot is a drawer, then you have to either label the lids or lift up the jars to determine their contents. Here are some options for spice racks that fit right into a kitchen drawer. These racks hold spice bottles at an angle so their labels are visible at a glance.

A. For a Wide Drawer

For a wide drawer of 24 inches or more, fit two or three expansion curtain rods into the drawer and lean the spice bottles against them.

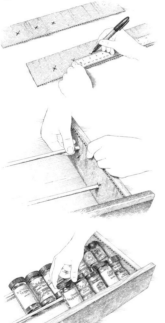

B. For a Narrow Drawer

For a drawer that is too narrow to fit an expansion curtain rod, try this trick:

1. Cut three pieces from a ¼-inch-diameter wooden dowel to the width of the drawer. Cut two pieces of corrugated cardboard to the depth and length of the drawer, then cut three small X's in each, at 2½-inch intervals, to hold the dowels in place.

2. Place one piece of cardboard against each sidewall of the drawer. Position the dowels across the drawer and insert them into the small X's.

3. Lean the spice bottles against the dowels in the drawer, with the labels facing up.

SPICE BASKETS A TO Z

Tired of playing hide-and-seek with spices stored in your kitchen cabinet? Here's a simple way to keep them organized: Arrange the spices in labeled rectangular baskets alphabetically or according to type, so you can quickly identify their location and retrieve whatever you need by pulling down the appropriate basket.

HOMEMADE KNIFE BLOCK

To keep an assortment of knives on the countertop for easy access and shield them when not in use, try this creative fix: a tall plastic container filled with rice. The rice creates a "slotless" universal system that accommodates a range of different-size knives. (Dried beans also work.)

HANDS-FREE THERMOMETER

Holding a thermometer over a steaming pot of water or oil can be a little tricky, not to mention dangerous. By attaching a large metal binder clip to the side of your pot and slipping the thermometer through the loop at the end, you can create an impromptu thermometer stand.

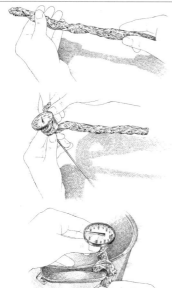

HOMEMADE CLIP-ON THERMOMETER

If you want to deep-fry a batch of doughnuts and can't find the clip for your thermometer to attach it to the side of the pot, here's a solution.

1. Crumple a 12-inch sheet of aluminum foil into a rope.

2. Wrap one end of the foil rope around the probe, directly under the face of the thermometer.

3. Add oil to the pan. Before heating it, secure the other end of the foil to the pot's handle so that the probe is stable and submerged at the desired level in the oil. (Make sure that the tip of the probe does not touch the bottom of the pot.)

INSTANT GRIP FOR INSTANT-READ THERMOMETER

The sheaths that house many instant-read thermometers are designed for use as holders so that cooks can keep their hands safely away from hot liquids when measuring their temperatures. But if you are like us, it's not long before the sheath disappears into the kitchen junk drawer, never to be seen again. In the absence of a sheath, try inserting the thermometer through one hole of a slotted cooking spoon and then simply hold onto the spoon handle to dip the thermometer tip into the liquid.

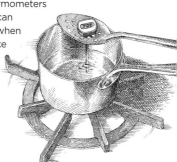

Molten Chocolate Cake for Two

✓**WHY THIS RECIPE WORKS:** These individual cakes are cooked in coffee mugs in the microwave for a nearly instant dessert, no need for ovens or pans. Microwaving the cakes at 50 percent power is the key to gentle cooking, and stirring halfway through ensures even cooking. If you're using a compact microwave with 800 watts or fewer, increase the cooking time to 90 seconds for each interval. The bittersweet chocolate is added at two points. This recipe makes 2 cakes.

- 4   tablespoons unsalted butter
- 1   ounce bittersweet chocolate, chopped, plus 1 ounce broken into 4 equal pieces
- 2   large eggs
- ¼   cup (1¾ ounces) sugar
- 2   tablespoons unsweetened cocoa powder
- 1   teaspoon vanilla extract
- ¼   teaspoon salt
- ¼   cup (1¼ ounces) all-purpose flour
- ½   teaspoon baking powder

1. Microwave butter and chopped chocolate at 50 percent power, stirring often, until melted, about 1 minute. Whisk eggs, sugar, cocoa, vanilla, and salt into chocolate mixture until smooth. In separate bowl, combine flour and baking powder. Whisk flour mixture into chocolate mixture until combined. Divide batter evenly between 2 coffee mugs.

2. Place mugs on opposite sides of microwave turntable. Microwave at 50 percent power for 45 seconds. Stir batter and microwave at 50 percent power for 45 seconds (batter will rise to just below rim of mug). Press 2 chocolate pieces into center of each cake until chocolate is flush with top of cake. Microwave at 50 percent power for 35 seconds (cake should be slightly wet around edges of mug). Let rest for 2 minutes. Serve.

MAKESHIFT SPLATTER SCREEN

Many cooks are turned off from sauté-ing because of the greasy mess that can spread around the stovetop, especially when browning meat. For those who don't own a splatter screen, try simply inverting a large-mesh strainer over the skillet during the splattering phase of cooking, and the mess will be significantly reduced.

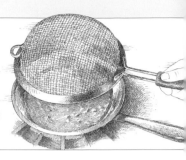

INSTANT COVERS

Many skillets are sold without covers, yet it is occasionally useful to have one on hand. Instead of buying a cover separately, which can be expensive, try a creative alternative, such as a large heatproof plate or an inexpensive 12- or 16-inch pizza pan.

IMPROMPTU PAN LID

When you find yourself short on lids to fit your skillets and sauté pans, try this clever stand-in. Cover a splatter screen with two layers of aluminum foil, then place it on top of the pan.

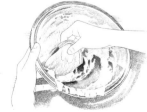

ALTERNATIVE HANDLE POTHOLDER

A silicone garlic peeler is a great stand-in for a handle potholder. The tube slides right over the handle of most pots, and the silicone protects your hand just as well as a bulky mitt does.

MAKE YOUR OWN KITCHEN SCRAPERS

A flexible plastic scraper is useful for scraping dough from bowls or scooping chopped vegetables for transfer from cutting board to pan. Make your own extra-flexible version at home with these easy instructions.

1. Draw a line along the edge of a plastic lid, such as one from a cottage cheese container, and cut along the line, leaving one-third of the edge intact for stability. You can also use an old plastic cutting mat—just cut it into 4 by 3-inch rectangles.

2. Use this homemade tool as you would a store-bought plastic scraper.

ROLL OUT THE BOTTLE

Give your pie or cookie dough a taste of the oenophile lifestyle by using an unopened bottle of wine as a rolling pin. It has just the right weight and shape for rolling out dough. Here's a bonus for white wine lovers: Refrigerate the bottle beforehand and the cold temperature of the bottle will help keep the butter in the dough chilled.

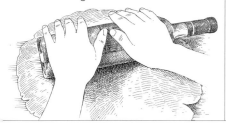

IMPROVISATIONAL MORTAR AND PESTLE

Most cooks don't need a mortar and pestle very often. Instead of buying a heavy, expensive set for infrequent use, you can use a sturdy, shallow, diner-style stoneware coffee mug and a heavy glass spice bottle next time you need to grind something.

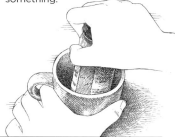

PAPER TOWEL HOLDER WITH A SECRET IDENTITY

A heavy meat pounder with a tall handle, which probably doesn't get used every day in your kitchen, can fill a different role when not in use: It makes an ideal base for a roll of paper towels. The weight of the pounder stabilizes the towels so they can be ripped off easily.

DIY ICE PACKS, THREE WAYS

A. Try making your own ice pack out of the empty liner from a box of wine, which is made of thick, durable plastic. Start by squeezing out any residual air and wine from the bag and rinsing it out. Then fill the bag halfway with water and lay it flat in the freezer to freeze. (Be sure the valve is closed when in use.)

B. You can also make your own ice packs with simple zipper-lock bags. Fill 1-quart or 1-gallon zipper-lock bags to within 2 inches of the top with water. (That way they won't burst when the water expands as it freezes.) Then place the bags in the freezer, letting them lie flat so they can be stacked. When they're frozen they can slide easily into a crowded cooler.

C. Flexible freezer packs are convenient, since they can be wrapped around containers to quickly chill the contents. Make your own by placing 2 cups water and ⅓ cup rubbing alcohol (the alcohol will prevent the pack from turning rock-solid) in a heavy-duty zipper-lock bag. Secure that bag inside a second zipper-lock bag. Freeze overnight before use; store in the freezer.

Magic Vanilla Ice Cream

⌀**WHY THIS RECIPE WORKS:** Making ice cream at home is a fun and delicious undertaking, but it has one giant drawback: It requires a bulky, kitchen-cluttering ice cream maker. In order to find a way to make ice cream at home without that technology, we had to figure out how to replicate the taste and texture created by the machine. The magic ingredients turned out to be sweetened condensed milk and folded-in whipped cream; these kept our ice cream light but velvety even after freezing. We also added a surprising ingredient—sour cream—for richness and tartness to counter the sweetness of the condensed milk. This recipe makes 1 quart.

- ½ **cup sweetened condensed milk**
- 1 **ounce white chocolate chips**
- ¼ **cup sour cream**
- 1 **tablespoon vanilla extract**
- **Pinch salt**
- 1¼ **cups heavy cream, chilled**

1. Microwave sweetened condensed milk and white chocolate in large bowl until chocolate melts, stirring halfway, about 30 seconds. Let cool. Stir in sour cream, vanilla, and salt.

2. Using stand mixer fitted with whisk, whip cream on medium-low speed to soft peaks, about 2 minutes. Whisk one-third of whipped cream into white chocolate mixture. Fold remaining whipped cream into white chocolate mixture until incorporated.

3. Place in airtight container and freeze until firm, at least 6 hours or up to 2 weeks. Serve.

CHAPTER 3

FOOD PREP HACKS

The Straight Dope on How-To from A to Z

ALCOHOL–APPLES

JUST ENOUGH BOOZE FOR COOKING

Some recipes call for just a small amount of liquor or wine. Rather than buying large bottles of a specialty alcohol or uncorking a whole bottle of wine for these occasions, try keeping small bottles on hand. For hard alcohol, try the nip-size bottles sold by the register. They usually contain 50 ml, about 3½ tablespoons each. For wine, solve the problem by keeping four-packs of miniature bottles of red and white wine in your pantry.

EASY-OPEN WINE

Whenever you need to open a bottle of wine, set the bottle on a folded dish towel placed in the kitchen sink. It's easier to insert the corkscrew when the bottle's at a lower level and the extra space provides additional leverage for uncorking, making the task a snap.

QUICK FREEZE FOR WHITE WINE

Forgot to chill that bottle of white wine and now dinner is almost ready? Fear not! There's a hack for that. Wrap the bottle in a wet dish towel and place it in the freezer. Since cooling occurs when heat is transferred away from an item, the water in the towel—a much more efficient conductor of heat than the air—will quickly freeze, dropping the temperature of the wine to 50 degrees in only 30 minutes. (Note: When you remove the bottle from the freezer, the towel will be frozen solid. To release it, place it briefly under warm running water.)

PERFECTLY MEASURED APPLE CORING

Come fall, many cooks like to use fresh-picked apples and pears in crisps, cakes, and other desserts. One well-known trick for coring and seeding the halved fruit is to use a melon baller. Of course, that doesn't mean all cooks have one at the ready when they need it. What they're more likely to have is a sturdy, rounded metal ½-teaspoon measure, which works beautifully.

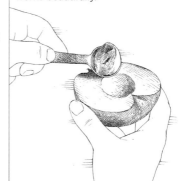

RIDDING ARTICHOKES OF THORNS

The sharp thorns at the tops of artichoke leaves can make this fancy vegetable hard to eat. Remove the thorns quickly and easily by holding the artichoke upside down (by the stem) and passing it quickly through the flame of a gas burner. The sharp points of the thorns will burn off almost instantly.

WHEN THE PIT STICKS TO THE KNIFE

In the test kitchen, we remove the pit from a halved avocado by inserting a knife into the pit and twisting the base of the fruit to release it. But what's the best way to remove the speared pit from the knife without causing injury to yourself?

A. One way is to place your thumb and forefinger on either side of where the top of the pit meets the blade, as if giving the blade a pinch. With a little downward pressure from your fingers, the pit falls right off.

B. A firm tap of the pit against the cutting board also works— the pit splits right in two. Problem solved.

(CORK)SCREWING AROUND WITH AVOCADOS

Our favorite way of pitting an avocado calls for inserting a chef's knife into the stone of the halved fruit and twisting the avocado's base to remove the pit. If you're wary of the knife's sharp blade, however, try a waiter's corkscrew instead. The tool securely (and safely) hooks into the pit and it can then be easily pulled out.

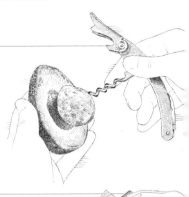

A SEPARATE PIECE

Here's an easy way to separate strips of bacon stuck together in a shrink-wrapped package.

1. Roll the package lengthwise into a cylinder, then flatten it out again.

2. Open the package and remove the desired number of strips, which are now less tightly packed.

Oven-Fried Bacon

✓ WHY THIS RECIPE WORKS: Most of us cook bacon by frying it in a pan, but controlling the temperature of a pan on the stovetop takes patience and constant attention, and even then it sometimes seems impossible to avoid getting raw and burnt spots. Oven-fried bacon is just as good, and it even has a couple of advantages. The oven offers a larger margin of error than the frying pan for perfectly cooked bacon. It also cooks the bacon more consistently, and the only tending needed is rotating the pan halfway through cooking. A large rimmed baking sheet is important here to contain the rendered bacon fat. If cooking more than one tray of bacon, switch their oven positions when you rotate them. You can use thin- or thick-cut bacon here, though cooking times will vary. This recipe makes 4 to 6 servings.

12   **slices bacon**

Adjust oven rack to middle position and heat oven to 400 degrees. Arrange bacon slices in single layer in rimmed baking sheet. Cook bacon until fat begins to render, 5 to 6 minutes. Rotate sheet and cook until bacon is crisp and brown, 5 to 6 minutes for thin-cut bacon, or 8 to 10 minutes for thick-cut bacon. Transfer bacon to paper towel-lined plate, let drain, and serve.

Maple-Glazed Oven-Fried Bacon
When bacon has reached golden brown shade and is almost done, pour off most of grease and drizzle maple syrup over each strip. Then return tray to oven and continue cooking for 2 to 3 minutes, or until maple syrup begins to bubble.

TIPS FOR OVEN-FRIED BACON

Here are two tricks for making our favorite oven-fried bacon recipe even better.

A. Minimize cleanup by lining your baking sheet with wide (18-inch) aluminum foil, covering the entire surface, including the sides. Then cook and drain the bacon, as per recipe instructions, and allow the baking sheet and any remaining grease to cool completely. Cleanup is easy: Just roll up the soiled foil and discard.

B. Once you've started lining your baking sheet with foil for easy cleanup, you can take things a step further by fashioning a makeshift rack from the foil. Crimp the foil at 1-inch intervals before placing the bacon horizontally across the crimps. This technique elevates the strips so that grease drips into the foil crevices during cooking, ensuring a crispier result.

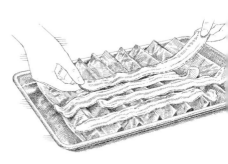

HASSLE-FREE BACON CHOPPING

Make slippery bacon a cinch to mince with the following tip.

1. Wrap the bacon in plastic wrap and freeze for 15 minutes.

2. The bacon will harden just enough so that, using a chef's knife, it can be chopped as fine as needed with nary a slip.

A BANANA'S BUILT-IN CUTTING BOARD

To avoid dirtying a cutting board when slicing bananas for a morning bowl of cereal, try this trick: Partially peel the banana, leaving a strip of peel running down its length. Then place the banana skin-side down on a work surface and cut the banana into slices.

SORTING DRIED BEANS

It is important to pick over dried beans to remove any stones or debris before cooking. Try this easy way to accomplish the task: Arrange the beans in a single layer on a rimmed baking sheet. Sort through the beans, pushing the "checked" beans to one side of the sheet and discarding debris as you go. Rinse the beans before cooking them.

BETTER BEET PEELING

To keep hands stain-free when prepping beets, grasp the cooked (and slightly cooled) beets with a plastic bag, such as one used for produce. Then, working from the outside of the bag, you can rub the skins right off.

THREE TIPS FOR BUTTER HANDLING

Butter can be a tricky thing to measure, especially once the wrapper gets discarded. Here are a few tricks for simplifying the process.

A. When unwrapping a new stick of butter, cut it into tablespoons (using the markings on the wrapper as a guide) before placing it in a butter dish. Now you can grab as many tablespoons as you need without stopping to cut them when you're busy cooking. Plus, if a recipe calls for softened butter, the smaller pieces will soften faster. Precut butter also ensures that any new or inexperienced cooks in your home will get the right measure of butter without having to cut it themselves.

B. For a less decisive trick, lightly mark all 8 tablespoons with a knife before unwrapping a stick of butter, so you're always able to easily measure out the amount that you need.

C. For a long-term solution, make yourself a cheat sheet. Staple a clean butter wrapper around an index card and use that to measure small portions of unwrapped butter from the butter dish.

A.

B.

C.

BETTER BUTTER CUTTING

Cutting cold butter with a chef's knife can be a slippery proposition. When you're cutting butter straight from the refrigerator, try using the sharp edge of a metal bench scraper to cut it into uniform pieces instead of a knife.

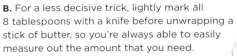

EGG-CELLENT BUTTER CUBES

Use an egg slicer to quickly and precisely cut butter into small pieces for pie dough and biscuits.

1. Place up to 4 tablespoons of butter in an egg slicer and push down on the slicing blades to create planks.

2. Rotate the butter a quarter turn, then push down on the slicing blades to create small pieces.

SOFT BUTTER AND ANGER MANAGEMENT IN ONE

Need soft butter for baking but don't have time to wait? Place the cold butter in a plastic bag and use a rolling pin to pound it to the desired consistency in a matter of seconds.

SPREADING COLD BUTTER

If you want butter for your toast but you forgot to leave it out to soften, a vegetable peeler will cut a thin ribbon that's easy to spread on hot toast.

BUTTER COOLING SHORTCUT

When preparing a recipe that calls for melted butter cooled to room temperature, speed up the process with this method: Melt three-quarters of the desired amount of butter on the stovetop or in the microwave. Off the heat, whisk the remaining one-quarter cold butter into the melted butter. The unmelted portion will help lower the warm butter's temperature in less time than it takes to heat and then cool the full amount.

DOTTING WITH BUTTER

From sweet potato casseroles to seasonal fruit pies to rich gratins of potato or other root vegetables, many recipes direct the cook to dot the surface of a dish with butter just before putting it in the oven. To keep soft, sticky pieces of butter from clinging to your fingers, try using frozen butter and a vegetable peeler for this task. Shaving thin curls off the surface of a frozen stick of butter is infinitely neater—and easy, too. You can also try grating the frozen butter over the large holes of a flat grater directly onto the dish.

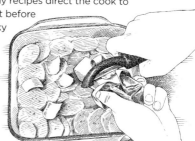

THE GREAT CAPER STRAINER

Rather than use a large colander to drain brine-packed capers, try a tea strainer. The tool, which fits inside a teacup, is ideal for an ingredient usually measured out in small quantities, and its tight weave prevents the tiny capers from falling through.

CLUMP-FREE CAPER CHOPPING

Tiny, slippery capers are difficult to chop when they roll around on the cutting board. Use the following technique to stabilize them.

1. Spoon the capers onto a double layer of paper towels, fold over the towels, and push down firmly on them to flatten.

2. Transfer the dry, flat capers to a cutting board for chopping.

QUICKER CARROTS JULIENNE

Cutting carrots into julienne— ⅛-inch-thick by 2-inch-long strips—is painstaking work, even for cooks with advanced knife skills. Save time by starting with a bag of uniformly cut and peeled baby carrots from the supermarket.

1. Cut each carrot lengthwise into quarters.

2. Cut each quarter lengthwise into ⅛-inch thick strips.

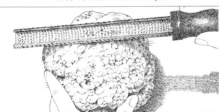

A FACELIFT FOR YOUR CAULIFLOWER

Even the freshest head of cauliflower can have minor blemishes. Rub a rasp-style grater over discolored areas until they disappear for flawless cauliflower.

CUSHION YOUR CUTTING

Sometimes it's handy to cut a smaller piece from a large chunk of hard cheese. Because hard cheese is difficult to cut through, cooks often place one hand over the top of their knife blade and the other over the handle to put their weight into the cut. When using this technique, add an extra measure of safety and comfort by putting a folded dish towel between your hand and the blade.

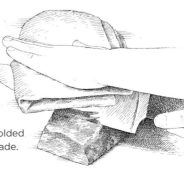

CHEESE–CHERRIES

NEATER CHEESE GRATING

Next time you need to grate some cheese, try using a large, clean zipper-lock bag to hold both grater and cheese. The bag lets you grate with clean hands and eliminates flyaway bits. Leftover grated cheese is ready for storage in a handy bag.

STICK-FREE SHREDDING

It's easy to shred semisoft cheeses such as mozzarella or cheddar in the food processor—until, of course, a big chunk sticks in the feed tube or gums up the shredding disk. Avoid this problem by spraying the feed tube, disk, and workbowl of your food processor with a light coating of vegetable oil spray before you begin.

SOFTENING CREAM CHEESE WITH EASE

When you need room-temperature cream cheese to make frosting and don't have time to wait, speed things up by submerging the foil-wrapped package in a bowl of warm water. It should only take about 10 minutes for the cheese to soften.

PITTING CHERRIES FOUR WAYS

Cherry pitters, though they work well, are oddball kitchen gadgets. Not every cook will have one on hand, which leaves many of us searching for alternative methods. Here are a few suggestions. Make sure you work over a bowl to catch the cherry juices when necessary.

A. Push the cherries down firmly onto the pointed, jagged end of a pastry bag tip. Take care not to cut your fingers on the points as they pierce the fruit.

B. Use a pair of well-cleaned needle-nose pliers. All you do is pierce the skin at the stem, spread the pliers just enough to grasp the pit, and pull it straight out.

C. Push a drinking straw through the bottom of the cherry, forcing the pit up and out the top.

D. Place a cherry over the mouth of a clean, empty glass bottle (choose one with a small mouth, such as a wine or soda bottle). Using the blunt end of a chopstick, pierce through the center of the cherry, pushing the pit through the flesh and skin and into the bottle.

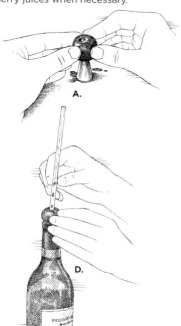

SLICING CHICKEN CUTLETS SMOOTHLY

To turn chicken breasts into cutlets, hold a sharp chef's knife parallel to the cutting surface and slice through the center of the breast horizontally. To keep your knife from skipping and tugging in the process, mist or rub the blade with water before cutting, which lubricates the knife and makes it slide easily through the meat.

SLIPPERY CHICKEN SOLUTIONS

Cutting raw chicken is a slippery proposition, especially if you're halving chicken breasts to form thin cutlets. For a safer method, try the following approach: Using tongs, hold a chicken breast that has been frozen for 15 minutes perpendicular to the cutting board. Cut through the chicken to make two even cutlets. In general, you can also give yourself a firmer grip on raw, thawed chicken by using a folded wad of paper towels to hold the meat in place as you cut.

TWO WAYS TO FLATTEN CUTLETS

Recipes often advise pounding cutlets between sheets of plastic wrap, parchment, or waxed paper, all of which can easily rip or tear. Here are two alternative solutions that will keep your counters and your chicken safer.

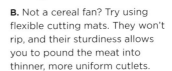

A. Use the plastic bags from inside cereal boxes. Place cutlets of meat in the empty bags before pounding to shield the counter and cutting board from contamination. The cereal bags are sturdier than plastic wrap and less likely to tear.

B. Not a cereal fan? Try using flexible cutting mats. They won't rip, and their sturdiness allows you to pound the meat into thinner, more uniform cutlets.

CHICKEN

SCORING CHICKEN SKIN

Cutting slashes in chicken skin with a
knife to help render fat during cooking
is a slippery job that often results in the
meat being scored as well, leading to
a loss of juices and drying out the meat.
Here's a better way: Pinch the chicken
skin with one hand, then use kitchen
shears in the other to snip the skin
two or three times.

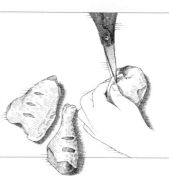

GETTING UNDER THE SKIN

Seasoning a whole chicken or turkey under the skin using your fingers
can be tricky, since it's hard to distribute the salt evenly without tear-
ing the skin. Here's a long-handled solution: Try an iced-tea spoon,
which also works to loosen the skin first.

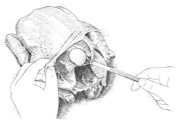

1. Pry the skin from the bird with
an iced-tea spoon.

2. Place salt on the spoon
and reach under the skin to
distribute it evenly.

REFINED TRUSSING

If you find yourself out of kitchen twine
to truss a chicken but you've recently been
celebrating with some bubbly, try grabbing a leftover champagne cage for the
job instead. Insert the legs in the cage,
twist the wire to tighten, and the chicken is
ready for roasting. (Note: The metal will
get hot in the oven, so use caution when
removing the cage.)

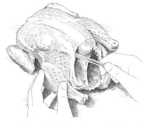

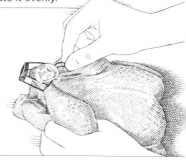

VERTICAL ROASTER
STAND-INS

While we like vertical roasters
because they let poultry cook
evenly and get the skin crisp
all over, many cooks don't own
one. A 16-ounce beer can is a
suitable substitute, but for a non-
alcoholic stand-in, try your Bundt
pan or tube-pan insert. Once
the chicken has been seasoned,
slide it onto the center post of
the pan, legs facing down, so the
chicken stands upright.

MAKESHIFT ROASTING RACKS

Next time you're preparing to roast a bird and find yourself without a V-rack, build your own using one of these tricks.

A. Aluminum Foil + Stovetop Grates

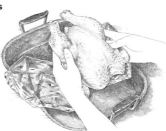

1. Wrap two light-gauge stovetop grates with foil and use a paring knife or skewer to poke large holes in the foil so that juices can drip down into the pan as the bird roasts.

2. Place the grates in the roasting pan, resting them against the sides of the pan so that the bottoms of the grates meet to create a V-shape. Roast the chicken (or turkey) as directed.

B. Aluminum Foil Cylinders

1. Roll three pieces of foil into tight cylinders and place them 2 inches apart across the middle of the roasting pan.

2. Position the chicken so that it sits evenly atop the cylinders. After cooking, cool the foil rolls and discard.

C. Cookie Cutters

Place several open-style metal cookie cutters in the bottom of the roasting pan. Put the item to be roasted on the cutters, suspending it above the bottom of the pan.

FRIED CHICKEN SHORTCUT

Save time and eliminate mess when frying chicken: Combine the bread crumbs and vegetable oil in a large bag, seal the bag, and toss to coat the crumbs. Then, one by one, carefully add all of the egg-coated chicken pieces and press the crumbs onto them through the sides of the bag. Remove the chicken pieces with pair of tongs to keep your hands clean.

TAKING THE STING OUT OF CUT CHILES

Mincing fresh chiles can lead to hand burns that last for hours. Here are some tips for avoiding that unpleasantness.

A. Protect yourself with a grater and a zipper-lock bag. Using the bag as a glove, hold the chile and grate it along the surface of a box or rasp grater. This method doesn't allow you to remove the seeds, so you will get maximum heat from chiles prepared this way.

B. For those times when you need to chop a little more carefully, coat one hand with oil (not the hand you use to hold the knife), and then cut the chiles, making sure to touch them only with your oiled hand. When you're done, wash your hands with hot, soapy water.

EASY CHILE MINCING

For a quick way to season your dips and sauces with chipotle chiles or pickled jalapeños, simply put a small amount of chile into the well of a garlic press and squeeze.

SEEDING CHILE PEPPERS

Using a knife to remove the seeds and ribs from a hot chile pepper takes a very steady hand. Here's a safer and equally effective alternative.

1. Cut the chile in half with a knife.

2. Starting opposite the stem end, run the edge of a small melon baller scoop down the inside of the chile, scraping up seeds and ribs.

3. Cut off the core with the scoop.

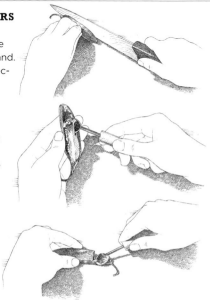

SEEDING SMALL CHILES

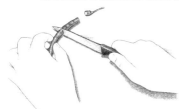

1. To easily seed very small chiles before slicing them, remove the stem and halve the chile crosswise.

2. Roll the chile gently, breaking the ribs off and forcing them, and the seeds, out the cut end. The seed-free chile can be sliced into rings.

SEEDLESS JALAPEÑO RINGS

To make neat rings of jalapeños without the seeds or spicy ribs for garnishing nachos and the like, employ a vegetable peeler.

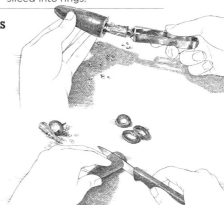

1. Cut off the stem end of the jalapeño with a knife, then insert the peeler down into the chile. Using a circular motion, core the chile and pull out the ribs and seeds.

2. Shake any remaining seeds out of the chile, then slice it into rings.

ROASTING CHILES

It is tedious and inefficient to hold small chiles over a flame with tongs to roast them. Try this method for roasting multiple chiles at a time. Place the chiles on a wire rack and lay the rack flat on top of the burner. You can easily shake the rack, and therefore turn the chiles, by grasping at the outer edge with an oven mitt or tongs.

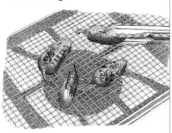

EASIER STUFFED CHILES

Poblano chiles are good for stuffing and baking, but their long, tubular shape can make filling them a challenge. Get help from a drinking glass. After cutting off the poblano's top and removing its seeds, set it into the glass, which holds it upright and stable while it's stuffed.

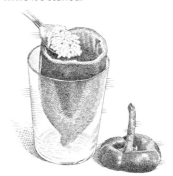

KEEPING CHIVES IN CHECK

Prepping a bunch of chives can be tricky; the slender herbs roll all over the cutting board, making them difficult to chop. Try securing the chives with a rubber band to keep the leaves together.

POWDER-FREE CHOPPED CHOCOLATE

When chopped into chunks for cookies or bars, chocolate often shatters, leaving behind shavings and powder. Use your microwave to solve the problem.

1. Place the chocolate bar on a microwave-safe plate and microwave on the lowest setting for about 1 minute, turning the chocolate halfway through microwaving. When the chocolate softens and begins to melt at the corners, remove it from the microwave. (If the chocolate bar is very thick, it may take longer to soften.)

2. Place the warm chocolate on a cutting board and chop it into chunks.

EASIER CHOCOLATE CHOPPING

Most home cooks don't own a fancy chocolate fork for breaking up large blocks of chocolate into more manageable pieces. Here's a way to improvise one: Using the sharp two-tined fork from your meat-slicing set and a secured cutting board, press straight down into the chocolate. The chocolate breaks into neater pieces than when cut by a knife, and a lot less effort is required.

CREATING PERFECT CHOCOLATE CURLS

The secret to perfect shaved chocolate curls is warming the chocolate.

1. Wrap a chocolate bar in plastic wrap and then rub the palm of your hand against the edge of the bar until it is warm.

2. To make curls, remove the plastic and run a vegetable peeler along the chocolate bar toward you. Repeat the warming process as needed.

GADGETLESS CHOCOLATE MELTING

Many recipes call for melting chocolate in a homemade double boiler, which is created by suspending a heatproof bowl over a pot of simmering water. If your bowl is too small for your pot, try this clever solution.

1. Place a heatproof colander in a pot of simmering water (the perforations should be above the level of the water).

2. Set a heatproof bowl with the chocolate inside the colander. Using an oven mitt to avoid a steam burn, stir the chocolate with a spatula until it melts.

BEAT THE CITRUS-JUICING BLUES

Next time you find yourself with a lemon, lime, or orange to juice and no fancy juicing equipment on hand, try one of these alternative tools that you probably already have laying around.

A. Fork

1. For just a little bit of juice, slice the fruit in half and poke the flesh a few times with a fork.

2. Then stick the fork in the citrus and twist, just as you would with a citrus reamer.

B. Kitchen Tongs

For a more extensive juicing job, reach for a pair of kitchen tongs. Holding the tongs closed, stick the pincers into the halved fruit and use a twisting motion to extract the juice.

C. Mixer Beater

Another unusual kitchen utensil that makes an excellent stand-in for a missing juicer is one of the beaters from a handheld mixer. Simply take the beater in your hand and use it as you would a citrus reamer.

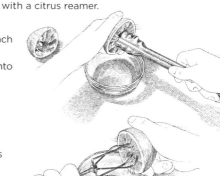

CITRUS

AN EASIER SQUEEZE

Pressing all the juice from a piece of citrus can be tricky. To ensure you get every last drop, try one of the following techniques.

A. Using a paring knife, cut the lemon peel from pole to pole, making four ¼-inch-deep slits. Next, cut the lemon in half crosswise. Place the lemon half in the juicer and squeeze to remove all of the juice.

B. Place quartered citrus in the hopper of a potato ricer and squeeze the handles together. Juicing a quarter is not only easier than juicing a half, but it also yields more juice.

C. Place quartered fruit pieces in the bowl of a stand mixer fitted with the paddle attachment. Cover the top of the workbowl with plastic wrap, turn on the mixer at low speed, and muddle the fruit to extract the juice (about 2 minutes). After the fruit pieces release their juices, strain the mixture through a fine-mesh strainer set over a large bowl, pressing on the fruit to extract as much juice as possible.

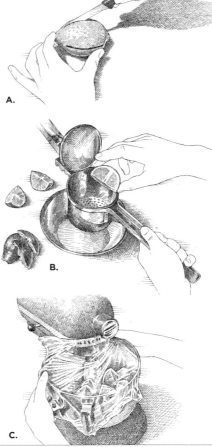

A.

B.

C.

NEATER LEMON WEDGES

The thick strand of white pith along the center ridge of a lemon wedge can cause the juice to squirt out in all directions during squeezing.

1. To make sure the juice lands in your teacup (and not in your eye), use a paring knife to remove the tough pith from wedges.

2. The resulting wedges will squeeze neatly into food and drinks.

SERIOUSLY COOL ZEST SHORTCUT

If citrus fruits are really soft or your grater is dull, removing the zest can be a chore. Here's one way to make zesting easier. First, place the whole fruit in the freezer until it is partially hardened, about 30 minutes. Then remove the fruit and rub it against the holes of a box or rasp-style grater.

COLLECTING ZEST NEATLY

Tired of watching citrus zest fly off your rasp-style grater and all over your work surface? Try inverting the whole operation. When you turn the grater upside down, so that the teeth face down and the fruit is under the grater rather than above it, the shavings collect right in the trough of the grater.

EASY ZESTING

Try this alternate zesting technique to keep precious citrus zest from getting stuck in the teeth of your box grater: Cover the fine holes of a box grater with a piece of waxed paper before grating, then grate the citrus to remove the zest. The zest will remain on top of the waxed paper rather than clogging the grater's teeth. You can easily brush off the paper after grating to collect all the zest.

THIS COOL TIP IS (COCO)NUTS

Opening the hard shell of a fresh, whole coconut is only half the battle: You then need a sharp knife and steady hand to pry the meat away from the shell. Freezing the whole coconut makes the shell pop away from the flesh as soon as you crack it open.

1. Freeze the coconut overnight.

2. Whack the frozen fruit around its equator with the dull side of a cleaver and then peel the shell off of the meat. An additional benefit: The coconut water inside will be frozen, making it easy to remove without any spillage or waste.

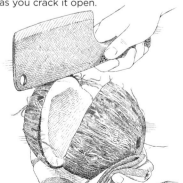

QUICK-PREP COFFEE

Instead of tracking down a measuring cup every morning to make coffee, try premeasuring the coffee into individual coffee filters. Stack the coffee-filled filters back into an empty coffee can or another airtight container and store in the freezer. All you have to do in the morning is grab one of the filters from the freezer and pop it into the coffee maker.

DIY SINGLE-CUP COFFEE FILTER

Instead of buying special coffee filters in order to brew a single cup, try this creative alternative using a funnel.

1. Fit an appropriately sized plastic funnel over a mug and place a cone-shaped filter inside the funnel. Fill it with the desired amount of ground coffee (the test kitchen prefers 2 tablespoons of coffee for 6 ounces of water).

2. Pour just-boiling water into the funnel and let the coffee "brew" into the mug.

FRESH COFFEE, RIGHT ON TIME

Wake up to a fresh pot of coffee even if your coffee maker lacks a built-in timer. Rather than spring for a new model, purchase an inexpensive appliance timer (the kind that turns lights on and off when you go on vacation) at the local hardware store. You can set the brewing time before you go to bed and also set a time for the machine to turn off, so you'll never worry that you left it on.

SOUNDPROOF COFFEE GRINDER

Nothing is better than waking up to the smell of fresh-brewed coffee, but no one likes to be jolted from sleep by the loud whirring of the coffee grinder. To muffle the noise, place an oven mitt over the grinder before turning it on.

NUKE-AND-SHAKE CORN HUSKING

Husking corn is no one's favorite job, but you can make it much easier with this trick: Start by cutting off the stalk end, 1 inch above the last row of kernels. Place the corn on a plate and microwave for 2 to 4 minutes. The microwave creates just enough steam between the kernels and the husk to separate the two. Grab the corn by the uncut end and shake it and squeeze at the same time, and the corn will slide out silk-free and husk-free

LIFTING CORN ON THE COB FROM BOILING WATER

Without a pair of tongs, removing corn on the cob from a pot of boiling water can be quite a challenge. Next time you find yourself in that predicament, reach for a potato masher, which both cradles and drains the corn beautifully.

DRAINING HOT BOILED CORN

Boiled corn on the cob is a backyard summer staple, but how to drain all those bulky ears at once when a colander is too small? Rather than juggling ear after ear in a cramped colander, try putting all the corn into a clean, empty dish rack as you remove it from the pot. The rack accommodates many more ears than a colander.

CORN ON THE KEBAB

Grill cooks who like pieces of corn on the cob on their kebabs know how difficult it can be to impale them on the skewer. To make things easier, start by running a corkscrew through the pieces before skewering them. The puncture makes it easier to skewer the corn, and the coiled hole helps ensure a snug fit.

STEAMED CORN FOR A CROWD

Here's a trick for steaming a lot of corn without a giant pot.

1. Cut two medium onions into 1-inch-thick slices, separate them into rings, and arrange them on the bottom of a large roasting pan. Fill the pan with 1 inch of water and place ears of shucked corn on top of the onions. Cover the pan with aluminum foil and seal tightly.

2. Set the pan over two burners and steam over high heat until tender, about 10 minutes.

CLEVER WAYS TO CUT KERNELS

Here are several tips for the tricky job of taking corn kernels off the cob.

A. Place a clean dish towel over a rimmed baking sheet. Cut the ears in half crosswise and then stand the half ears on their cut surface on the sheet and cut. The fabric will catch the kernels as they fall and keep them from jumping every which way.

B. After setting a mandoline to ¼-inch thickness and placing a pie plate underneath to catch the kernels, grip the corn with a dish towel for safety, then strip each ear in four quick sweeps down the blade.

C. Place a small bowl upside down inside a larger bowl. Steady the wide end of a corn cob on top of the overturned bowl and slice downward to remove the kernels. The smaller bowl elevates the cob so you can get a clean slice, and the larger bowl catches the kernels.

HOMEMADE MICROWAVE POPCORN

Instead of buying expensive, unhealthy microwave popcorn at the supermarket, make your own with these simple instructions.

1. Place ¼ cup bulk popcorn in a 4-quart microwave-safe bowl with 1 teaspoon vegetable or olive oil. Cover the bowl tightly with microwave-safe plastic wrap, poke a few holes in the surface, and microwave. The popcorn will take between 2 and 6 minutes to pop. Check its progress frequently.

2. When the majority of the kernels have popped, use potholders to remove the bowl from the microwave and place it on a clean, dry surface—it will be extremely hot. Toss with melted butter and salt, if desired.

CUCUMBER PREP MULTITASKER

Removing the seeds from cucumbers is a vital step toward avoiding soggy salads. Instead of dirtying a spoon, use the curved blade of the swivel-style peeler that you just used to peel the cucumber. After halving the cucumber lengthwise, use the tip of the blade to gently scrape out the seeds.

HOW TO SKIN AN EGGPLANT

Removing the charred skin from a roasted eggplant can be frustrating and time-consuming. You can use plastic wrap to make quick work of this job.

1. After roasting the eggplant over a direct flame or under a broiler until completely soft, let it cool to room temperature, then wrap it in two layers of plastic wrap. Cut off the top inch of the eggplant at the stem end.

2. Holding the plastic wrap as you would a tube of toothpaste, squeeze out the eggplant flesh, leaving the skin attached to the inside of the plastic wrap.

FOOLPROOFING UNWANTED EGG ROLLS

Try these tips for putting an end to wobbly eggs on your kitchen counter (and their occasional accidental trips to your kitchen floor).

A. Use a recycled egg carton both as a container to keep the eggs from rolling off the counter and as a receptacle for the empty shells. Trim the top and the flap from the carton, then cut the base into three sections, each able to hold up to four eggs. While measuring the other ingredients of a recipe, safely store the eggs in one section and return the spent shells to the container as you use them.

B. Here's a quicker fix when only one or two eggs need to be corralled. Simply nest the egg inside of a thick rubber band.

C. Steady eggs with the help of a small piece of rubber shelf liner mat. Its tacky surface keeps the eggs in place.

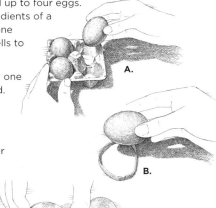

A.

B.

C.

A CLEANER BREAK

Rather than crack eggs on the edge of a bowl or countertop and risk dripping the raw contents on the work surface, break each egg on a flat, rimmed surface, such as a large plate or plastic container lid. It not only offers easy cleanup but also prevents any uncracked eggs from rolling away and holds broken shells before they're discarded.

TEACUP EGG DUMP

When frying or poaching eggs, it is important to get all the eggs into the pan at the same time. In order to do this efficiently and neatly, crack the eggs into small cups with handles, like a teacup. You can have one or two eggs in each cup. When the pan is ready, lower the lip of each cup into the pan at the same time and then tip the eggs into the pan.

PICK UP (CHOP)STICKS

Keep a pair of chopsticks on hand in case you accidentally drop a piece of shell into the pan while cracking eggs into a hot skillet. When it happens, quickly remove the pan from the heat and use the chopsticks to carefully extract the shell.

EGGSHELL MAGIC

Trying to remove small bits of stray yolk or eggshell from freshly cracked eggs can test the patience of any cook. Try solving the problem with the egg itself.

A. Dip an eggshell half into egg whites to scoop out bits of yolk. The eggshell acts as a magnet, attracting the wayward yolk.

B. An eggshell half can also be used to attract pieces of shell that fall into cracked eggs.

SEPARATING EGGS

Many baking recipes call for bringing eggs to room temperature before they are separated, but this can be a tricky business, as warm egg yolk can easily leak into the white. We have found that we have much better luck when we separate the eggs while they are still chilly from the fridge. Yolks are more taut and less apt to break into the whites when cold. If a recipe calls for the eggs to be brought to room temperature, simply separate the eggs while cold, cover both bowls with plastic wrap (make sure the wrap touches the surface of the eggs to keep them from drying out), and let them sit on the counter to warm up.

A PEELING EGG IDEA OR TWO

Hard-cooked eggs can be difficult to peel, especially when the shell shatters into tiny pieces. Here are some techniques to help.

FOR FRESHLY HARD-COOKED EGGS

A. Tap with a Spoon

1. Tap the surface of a cooked egg with the back of a teaspoon to crack the shell.

2. Slip the spoon under the shell at the egg's base, then continue to move along the curve to remove the rest of the shell.

B. Jostle in the Pot

1. After draining the hot water from the pot used to cook the eggs, shake the pot back and forth to crack the shells.

2. Add enough ice water to cover the eggs and let cool. The water seeps under the broken shells, making peeling easy.

FOR DAY-OLD HARD-COOKED EGGS

After sitting in a cold refrigerator for a day or two, eggs are even harder to peel. Try this method to make the shell release more easily.

1. Submerge the hard-cooked eggs in hot water for 1 minute.

2. Transfer the eggs to ice water for 1 minute for easy peeling.

MIXING JUST A FEW EGG WHITES

If you want to use your handheld mixer to whip just a few egg whites for a recipe, you may find that the volume of whites is too small for the beaters to work. Solve this dilemma by transferring the whites to a smaller bowl and then removing one of the beaters from the mixer. The single beater is a perfect fit for the smaller bowl, and you will be able to whip the whites easily.

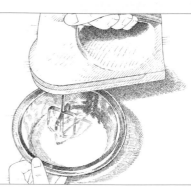

POACHED EGG FOR ONE

Try using the microwave for an easier way to cook up your poached egg in the morning.

1. Add 1½ cups of water, 2 teaspoons of distilled white vinegar, and ¼ teaspoon of table salt to a 2-cup liquid measuring cup and microwave the mixture on high until it reaches a rolling boil. Stirring the mixture in a circular motion, slip in an egg and continue to gently stir for 3 seconds.

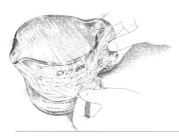

2. Cover the measuring cup with plastic wrap or a plate and let the egg stand for 4 minutes before removing with a slotted spoon.

PICTURE-PERFECT FRIED EGGS

It's always disappointing when you cook a perfect fried egg only to tear it while transferring the egg from the skillet to a plate. Avoid this mishap by applying vegetable oil spray to the spatula, which allows you to gently slide the cooked eggs onto the plate.

NEATER EGG SLICING

Slicing hard-cooked eggs can be messy because the yolk tends to crumble and stick to the blade of the knife. Solve the problem by spraying the knife with vegetable oil spray. The eggs can now be neatly sliced. Respray the knife blade as needed.

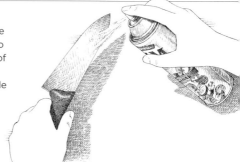

CRUMBLING HARD-BOILED EGGS EXTRA FINE

If you have trouble chopping hard-cooked eggs as fine as you like for garnishes, try pressing the eggs through a sieve for extra-fine, evenly crumbled egg.

REMOVING PINBONES FROM FISH

Locating the pinbones in a side of fish, or a couple of fillets, and removing them can be tricky. Running your fingers along the flesh is one way to locate them, but we've found an even better method. Invert a size-appropriate mixing bowl on a counter and drape the fish over it, flesh side up. The curvature of the bowl forces the pinbones to stick up and out, so they are easier to spot, grasp with pliers, and remove.

A BETTER WAY TO MINCE ANCHOVIES

Tired of the scent anchovies leave on your hands after mincing? Try the following approach to eliminate direct contact with the fillets.

1. With a fork, remove an anchovy from its tin and place it on a cutting board. Use the fork to anchor the anchovy as you cut the fillet crosswise into pieces, your hands at a safe distance away.

2. Use the side of the knife to gently smear the anchovy pieces against the cutting board. Rock the knife back and forth to finely mince the fillets.

EASY FISH TRANSFER

Grilling a large fillet or a whole fish can prove a challenge when it comes to turning the fish or removing it from the grill without having it fall apart. For a simple solution, try enlisting some extra support. Once the fish is done, slide two metal spatulas under the belly to give it proper support, lifting gently to make sure the skin is not sticking to the grill. Quickly lift the fish and place it on a nearby platter.

TWO WAYS TO AVOID "FISH STICKS" ON THE GRILL

A superclean, superhot, oiled grill grate should prevent grilled fish steaks, fillets, or kebabs from sticking to the grate. But some cooks like a little extra insurance, such as using one of the following methods to prevent sticking.

A. Place a few thin slices of lemon, lime, or orange (whatever best complements the flavor of the fish) on the cooking grate, and place the fish on the slices. Though you may sacrifice the grill marks on the fish, it will still pick up a great grilled flavor (as well as extra flavor from the citrus), and it will not stick to the grate.

B. When oiling a cooking grate, the oil vaporizes almost immediately, leaving behind a black, web-like residue. As the oil heats up, its fatty-acid chains form polymers (that is, they stick together), creating that crisscross pattern over the surface of the metal. A single layer of those polymers won't prevent sticking, but applying and heating oil repeatedly will build up a thick layer of them and make the surface "nonstick." Use tongs to rub oiled paper towels over the heated grate five to 10 times. When the grate is black and glossy you know you've built up a sufficient layer of polymers. The proteins in the fish will no longer be in direct contact with the cooking grate and therefore cannot bond with it. (Note that this effect is temporary and the grill must be reseasoned every time you want to cook fish.)

CLASSY CRAB CAKES

You can use an adjustable measuring cup to form tidy, uniform crab cakes worthy of an upscale restaurant.

1. Set the cup to the desired cake size, lightly coat the inside with oil, and load it with the filling.

2. Invert the cake onto a plate. This trick also works with other patties, including hamburgers and veggie burgers.

RIPENING ROCK-HARD FRUIT

Climacteric fruits (including apples, apricots, avocados, bananas, mangos, nectarines, peaches, pears, plums, and tomatoes) ripen off the plant once their ethylene—a colorless, odorless gas—content reaches a certain level. Hasten ripening by storing unripe fruit in a brown paper bag with ripe fruit that is already producing copious amounts of ethylene, such as bananas.

SLICING AND DICING DRIED FRUIT

Using a regular knife to cut dried fruit can leave a sticky residue on the blade, making it hard to cut the fruit evenly. You can improve this process by spraying a thin film of vegetable oil spray onto the blade of the knife just before you begin chopping. For a less oily solution, try a pair of kitchen shears dipped in hot water. Simply shake off any excess water before cutting the fruit.

A SWEET SOLUTION TO BROWN FRUIT

Most people toss cut apples and other fruits prone to browning in lemon juice. Here's another way to keep fruit fresh: Toss it in honey water. We diluted 2 tablespoons of honey with 1 cup of water, added one apple cut into slices, and left it to soak. Unlike untreated apple slices, which began to brown after a few minutes, the soaked slices were bright for more than 24 hours. Even better: The fruit needed only a 30-second dunk in the same solution to inhibit browning for a solid 8 hours. (Incidentally, honey seems to work just as well at stopping browning in vegetables such as potatoes.)

AVOIDING SOGGY FRUIT

Fresh-cut fruit, especially watermelon, can exude a lot of juice. Left in a bowl, the fruit at the bottom inevitably turns mushy. You can avoid this problem by storing chopped fruit in a salad spinner, where the juice can drain from the spinner's basket into the surrounding bowl. (A strainer set in a bowl also works well.)

JUICING FRUITS FOR JAM

When making jams and jellies from fresh summer fruits such as grapes, cherries, and plums, it's usually necessary to juice some of the fruit. Make quick work of juicing by fitting your food processor with the short plastic dough blade. It breaks down the fruit without nicking the seeds or pits, which, when cut, release bitter flavors into fruit.

Raspberry Refrigerator Jam

✔ **WHY THIS RECIPE WORKS:** The traditional canning process requires time, plus ingredients and equipment that the average cook might not have on hand. This simplified recipe offers pure fruit flavor in a small batch that takes just 30 minutes and three ingredients. The jam can be kept in the fridge for up to three weeks. This recipe makes 2 cups.

- 1 **pound raspberries**
- ¾ **cup sugar**
- 2 **tablespoons lemon juice**

1. Place metal spoon in freezer to chill. Combine raspberries, sugar, and lemon juice in large saucepan. Bring to boil over medium-high heat, then reduce heat to medium. Mash fruit with potato masher until fruit is mostly broken down. Simmer vigorously until fruit mixture thickens to jam-like consistency, 15 to 20 minutes.

2. To test for proper thickness and consistency, remove saucepan from heat, dip chilled spoon into jam, and allow jam to run off spoon. Jam should slowly fall off spoon in single thickened clump. If jam is runny, return to medium heat and simmer 2 to 4 minutes before retesting. Transfer finished jam to jar with tight-fitting lid, let cool to room temperature, then cover and refrigerate.

Strawberry Refrigerator Jam
Substitute 1½ pounds strawberries, hulled and cut into ½-inch pieces (3 cups) for raspberries. Increase sugar to 1 cup and lemon juice to 3 tablespoons.

Blueberry Refrigerator Jam
Substitute 1 pound blueberries for raspberries and leave fruit whole. Reduce sugar to ¾ cup. In step 1, simmer mixture for 8 to 12 minutes.

A-PEELING GARLIC POSSIBILITIES

There are a number of different ways to peel garlic cloves. One effective method is to crush them using the broad side of a knife blade. While this method is perfectly safe if you treat the knife blade with care, some cooks would rather skip the knife altogether. Here are some other options.

A. Here's a method that's particularly useful if you want to end up with whole, intact cloves: Place the garlic cloves on a microwave-safe plate in the microwave and cook on high power for 10 to 20 seconds. Rub the skins gently to remove.

B. If crushed cloves aren't a problem, try whacking the clove with the bottom of a can. The weight helps crush the clove, and the lip at the bottom of the can keeps it neatly in place on the counter.

C. Cover the garlic clove with the concave side of a wooden spoon and press down hard. The cup of the spoon prevents the garlic clove from shooting out across the counter.

STICKING IT TO GARLIC

Home cooks often shy away from hand-mincing garlic because it can be sticky stuff. If a recipe leaves you no alternative, try this helpful tip.

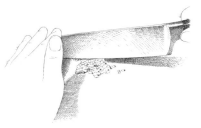

1. Sprinkle a few drops of olive or vegetable oil over the garlic.

2. Proceed to chop or mince; the oil coats the garlic and keeps it from sticking to either the knife or your hands.

SYNCING GARLIC AND HERB CHOPPING

When you are making a recipe that calls for both garlic and herbs, you can combine the tasks and make both of them easier. When chopping garlic by itself, the garlic often sticks to the knife, riding up on the sides of the blade. If you chop the garlic and herbs together, the garlic sticks to the herbs, rather than to the knife.

HASSLE-FREE GARLIC PASTE

Making garlic paste with the blade of a chef's knife (where the flat edge of the blade breaks down the minced garlic) takes practice. Sidestep the knife work with this easy method.

1. Coarsely chop garlic cloves and sprinkle with a pinch of salt.

2. Using the flat, unglazed underside of a small ramekin, press the garlic against the cutting board, smearing it to make a smooth paste.

EASY PUREED GARLIC

In addition to grating nutmeg, citrus, and hard cheese, a rasp-style grater is an ideal tool for producing finely pureed garlic, shallot, or onion. For recipes such as Caesar salad or aïoli, peel a clove of garlic and grate it on the grater before adding it to the recipe.

ROASTED GARLIC PASTE

Roasted garlic cloves are great for spreading on bread or stirring into soups and stews for extra flavor, but it can take some time and patience to extrude the roasted cloves from their papery skins. Here's one way to streamline the process: After dry-toasting individual garlic cloves on the stovetop, pass the unpeeled cloves through a garlic press. This creates a perfectly smooth paste, and the garlic peel is easily removed from the press.

GETTING AHEAD WITH GARLIC

When making bean soup, vegetable soup, or another such dish, you can boost and deepen the garlic flavor by adding a whole head. Just rub the papery outer layer of skin off an intact head of garlic, cut about ½ inch off the top to expose the flesh of the cloves, and throw the head into the soup pot. When the soup is done, remove the garlic head and either discard it or squeeze the softened garlic into the soup to further flavor and thicken it.

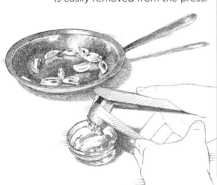

GINGER-GREEN BEANS

GREATER GRATED GINGER

When you're grating ginger on a rasp grater, a brief stint in the freezer helps firm it up and keeps it from disintegrating.

1. Place peeled ginger in a zipper-lock bag and freeze for 30 minutes.

2. The ginger can then be neatly grated.

SAFER GINGER GRATING

It can be tricky to grate a small knob of fresh ginger without your knuckles skimming dangerously close to the grater. To avoid scraping yourself, stick a fork into the peeled piece of ginger and rub it over the grater, using the fork as a handle.

EASY MINCED GINGER

Mincing large quantities of fibrous ginger can be a chore. Freezing the peeled root before mincing helps, but slicing the frozen ginger and giving the pieces a spin in a rotary grater completes the task in no time.

A NONSTICK SOLUTION FOR CHOPPING CANDIED GINGER

The sticky interior of candied ginger makes chopping it a challenge: What doesn't cling to the knife clumps together on the cutting board. To fix this problem, try storing your candied ginger in a zipper-lock bag in the freezer. When you need a bit for cooking, pull out the brittle frozen ginger and break it into pieces with a meat pounder.

SNIPPING GREEN BEANS

Here's a timesaving technique for trimming green beans. Gather three or four beans with the stem ends together in one hand. Use kitchen shears to trim the ends from the beans.

PERFECTLY DRY SALAD GREENS

Even a salad spinner may not get salad greens perfectly dry. To make sure that the greens are as dry as possible before dressing them, toss the spun greens in a large bowl with a few sheets of paper towel, each of which has been torn into quarters. The paper towels wick away the last traces of moisture. Or just throw the paper towels into the salad spinner with the greens and spin them all together. In either case, be sure to pick out all of the towel pieces before dressing the salad.

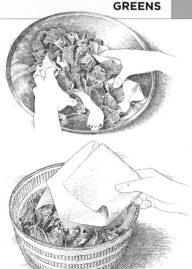

RINSING GREENS FOR ONE

When you need to prepare just a handful of greens or herbs, here's how to avoid hauling out the salad spinner.

 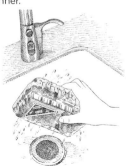

1. Place the greens inside an empty perforated plastic clamshell container (like those used for strawberries) and give them a quick rinse.

2. Close the container and shake vigorously to drive off water from the leaves.

TWO WAYS TO DRY COOKED GREENS

Sometimes even steamed greens have too much water, and when preparing a dish it's often important to remove all the excess moisture for the best results. Try one of these easy ways to squeeze extra water from cooked greens.

A. Place the cooked greens on a dinner plate and put a second plate on top of them. Squeeze the plates together over the sink (or a bowl, if you're reserving the liquid) until the greens are dry.

B. Put the cooked greens in a collapsible basket steamer and fold the sections shut to squeeze out the water, which escapes through the holes.

Quick Microwave Kale Chips

✓ **WHY THIS RECIPE WORKS:** If you've somehow missed that kale chips are a "thing," trust us: Tossing torn leaves of kale with oil and salt and baking them until crispy is a worthwhile endeavor. But the standard oven approach isn't perfect: It's hard to get the leaves evenly browned; plus, it's difficult to drive off enough moisture so that the chips stay crispy for more than a few hours. We found that the microwave dehydrates the leaves evenly and thoroughly, so they stay crispy longer—and the chips cook a whole lot faster. For the best texture, we prefer to use flatter Lacinato kale. Collard greens also work well, but don't use curly-leaf kale or Swiss chard, which turn crumbly when crisped. Make sure to dry the kale thoroughly and spread the pieces out evenly on the plate before microwaving to avoid any arcing, or sparking, of the kale. This recipe makes 2 servings.

5   **ounces Lacinato kale or collard greens, stemmed and torn into 2-inch pieces, washed, and thoroughly dried**
4   **teaspoons vegetable oil**
   Kosher salt

1. Toss kale with oil in large bowl.

2. Spread roughly one-third of leaves in single layer on large plate and season lightly with salt.

3. Microwave at full power for 3 minutes. If leaves are crispy, transfer to serving bowl; if not, continue to microwave leaves in 30-second increments until crispy. Repeat with remaining leaves in 2 batches. Store chips in airtight container at room temperature for up to 1 week.

EASIER HERB WASHING

Use a salad spinner to wash herbs. Once the herbs are clean, simply lift the basket with the herbs out of the dirty water, discard the water, fit the basket back into its base, and spin the herbs dry.

SHEAR BRILLIANCE

Plucking the individual leaves from fresh herbs like parsley and dill can be time-consuming, especially when you need a large amount. Here's a quicker method: Hold the bunch with one hand and, using a downward stroke, shave what you need from the stem. (Be sure to discard any large, woody stems that get cut off before proceeding with the recipe.)

FRESH HERBS, FAST

Fresh herbs are the finishing touch to countless recipes, but carefully plucking the leaves from a bunch of parsley or cilantro can be tedious. You can use some everyday kitchen utensils to streamline the job.

A. Put a Fork on It

1. Holding a bunch of clean, dry parsley or cilantro in one hand, use the other hand to comb the tines of a dinner fork through the herbs to pull off the leaves.

2. Pick through the leaves to remove any remaining stems.

B. A Hole New Way to Pluck

Thread the stems of your tender herbs through your colander (starting from the inside and pulling through) to make quick work of this task—plus, the bowl of the colander collects the leaves for you!

WHOLE HERB HELPERS

In recipes that call for thyme or rosemary, instead of stripping leaves off the branches and mincing them, simply throw the whole branch into the pan. Remember to remove the spent branch, as you would spent bay leaves, before serving. Rosemary is very strong, so you may want to keep it in the pot for only 15 minutes or so.

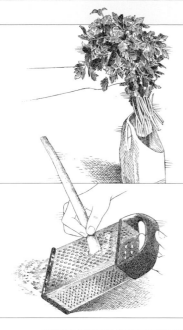

BETTER VASE FOR HERBS

A good way to store fresh herbs such as basil or parsley is stems down in a water-filled glass, with the leaves covered by a plastic bag. But the leaves and the bag make the setup top-heavy and prone to tips and spills in the refrigerator. You can make a more stable container from a one-quart or half-gallon plastic milk jug.

GRATING LEMON GRASS

Mincing a tough, fibrous stalk of lemon grass with a chef's knife can be a painstaking job. Make it a cinch by freezing the lemon grass stalk until firm (about 1 hour) before grating it on a rasp-style or box grater to create fine shards.

THIN MEAT SLICING SIMPLIFIED

Many recipes call for thinly slicing a boneless cut of meat, such as a chicken or pork cutlet. Of course, fresh meat can be slippery and hard to grasp, which can make cutting thin slices a challenge. To make the job a little easier, place the meat in the freezer for about 20 minutes. The meat will firm up but not freeze, making it easier to slice or trim. Alternatively, if the meat has already been frozen solid, slice or trim it before it has thawed completely.

DEGREASING PEPPERONI

Straight from the package, pepperoni often leaves unsightly puddles of grease when baked atop a pizza. Here's one way to prevent this problem.

1. Line a microwave-safe plate with a double layer of paper towels, place the pepperoni on top, then cover with two more paper towels and another plate to keep the meaty disks flat.

2. Cook for 30 seconds in a microwave on high, carefully remove the hot plate from the microwave, and uncover.

3. Place the degreased pepperoni on the pizza and bake according to the recipe.

USE SALT TO PREVENT FLARE-UPS

Fat sputtering up from a broiler pan can cause dangerous flare-ups. To prevent these flames, spread a generous amount of kosher salt on the bottom of the pan.

1. Cover the bottom of the broiler pan with aluminum foil and 2 cups of kosher salt.

2. Place the perforated rack on top. The salt layer catches any grease and prevents flare-ups.

DOUBLE-DUTY POT LIDS

Most stews start with browning the protein component, which is then removed from the pan so other ingredients can be browned, and is added back later to finish cooking with the cover in place. Try the following shortcut to avoid dirtying extra dishes. Instead of transferring the browned meat to a bowl, invert the lid of the pan in which you're cooking over a bowl or another pot. The lid, which you would have to wash anyway, now serves as both a spoon rest and receptacle for the sautéed food.

A WARMER REST

Resting meat before carving is key to getting the juiciest slices, but a chilly cutting board can make the temperature of the meat plummet. To keep heat loss under control, warm your cutting board under hot running tap water for a few minutes.

STEAK ELEVATOR

Most recipes call for resting steaks after cooking to allow the internal juices to redistribute. Inevitably, some of these juices leak out, ruining the nice crust. Try using a bowl to elevate the meat up and out of its juices. Place a small bowl in the center of a plate, and prop the steak on top. Once the steak is done resting, pour the collected juices into a pan to make a sauce.

RIB-RACK STAND-IN

A barbecue rib rack is a specialized tool that lets you barbecue twice as many slabs of baby back ribs at once. However, you probably already own a kitchen tool that could be used as a rib rack. If placed upside down on the grill grate, any fixed V-rack used for roasting easily serves as a rib rack, holding up to six slabs of baby back ribs.

STANDING (UP) RIB ROASTS

Some standing rib roasts aren't so great at the "standing" part, especially smaller roasts, which have a tendency to tip over during cooking. Avoid this problem by turning a skewer into a support bar.

 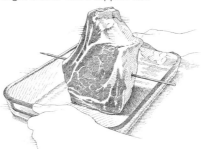

1. Run a skewer through the roast. (If using a wooden skewer, first soak it for about 20 minutes.)

2. Rest the ends of the skewer on the sides of the roasting pan and cook the roast. When ready to carve, simply remove the skewer.

TAKING THE PLUNGE WITH DRIED MUSHROOMS

Dried mushrooms are so light that they often bob to the surface of the water being used to hydrate them. This can cause the pieces to soften unevenly. To keep the pieces evenly submerged, try one of these tips. (These can also be used with dried tomatoes.)

A. Anchor the ingredients by nesting a 1-cup liquid measuring cup inside a 2-cup vessel. The 2-cup measure holds the liquid and mushrooms, while the 1-cup measure (a small bowl would work, too) ensures that the mushrooms stay below the surface while they soak.

B. Use a pot with its own steamer insert. Place the liquid and the ingredients to be hydrated in the pot and then position the steamer insert over them to keep the mushrooms submerged in the liquid. Make sure the water level rises above the holes in the bottom of the steamer insert.

C. Use a French press coffee maker. Place the mushrooms in the clean carafe and fill with water. Use the press to submerge the ingredients.

C.

CLEANING AND DRYING MUSHROOMS

Some batches of fresh mushrooms are so dirty that a cloth won't adequately clean them. Washing the mushrooms is a must, as is drying them. Pull out your salad spinner to perform both tasks.

1. Place the mushrooms in a salad spinner basket and spray with water until the dirt is removed.

2. Quickly fit the basket into the salad spinner and spin the mushrooms dry.

LESS-MESS NUT CHOPPING

Chopping nuts on a cutting board can send projectiles flying across the kitchen. Solve this problem with one of these tricks.

A. **B.**

C. **D.**

A. Swap out your chef's knife for a serrated bread knife instead. Its scalloped edge grabs and keeps the nuts in place better than a straight edge does. (Note: A bread knife doesn't rock like a chef's blade, but it's still faster to use one than to chase nuts around the cutting board.)

B. If you're still using a chef's knife to chop, keep nuts corralled on the cutting board with a towel. Wet a dish towel, grasp both ends, and twist them in opposite directions to form a tight rope. Place the rope on the cutting board in a ring around the nuts. Leave enough room in the center of the ring to fit the knife, and chop away.

C. For a neater alternative to a knife, try an apple cutter: Pressing the tool straight down chops the nuts into pieces while keeping them in place.

D. Try using a sharp-edged pastry blender to chop soft nuts like walnuts or pecans in a mixing bowl.

NOT FULL OF HOT AIR

Here's a reason to dust off that old hot-air popcorn popper: to toast nuts. Place ¼ cup of nuts in the popper and turn on the contraption for about 1 minute, until the nuts turn golden brown.

MICROWAVE-TOASTED NUTS AND SEEDS

When you need to toast nuts or seeds and your stovetop and oven are unavailable, try the microwave.

1. For fragrant, browned results, place ½ cup of seeds or nuts in a microwave-safe bowl and microwave at full power for about 2 minutes, checking and stirring every 30 seconds, until the seeds or nuts are golden brown.

2. Spread the seeds or nuts on paper towels to cool and absorb oils. This technique works best for cashews, almonds, pine nuts, hazelnuts, and sesame seeds.

DE-SALTING NUTS

Here's a way to make salted nuts usable in recipes that call for the unsalted variety.

1. Rinse the nuts in a strainer under cool water.

2. Spread the nuts evenly on a rimmed baking sheet and cook at 350 degrees for about 6 minutes, or until the nuts are dry and slightly toasted.

A HARD NUT TO CRACK

Try this crackerjack method to shell stubborn, barely open pistachios. Holding the nut in one hand, insert the tip of another pistachio shell half into the opening. Twist the shell half 90 degrees in either direction, or until the closed nut pops open. If that doesn't work, try using a garlic press:

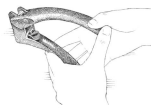

1. Put a single unopened pistachio in the chamber of the garlic press. Apply gentle pressure until the shell of the nut cracks open.

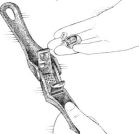

2. Remove the pistachio and discard the broken shell.

Chocolate-Hazelnut Spread

⌀ **WHY THIS RECIPE WORKS:** This homemade version of Nutella uses toasted hazelnuts and cocoa powder as its backbone, while a food processor and some oil bring it together. Mix in confectioners' sugar, vanilla, and salt, and you'll never go back to the jarred stuff. Try one of our other tips for skinning hazelnuts (see page 114) if you don't have two bowls of the same size. This recipe makes 1½ cups.

2	cups (8 ounces) hazelnuts
1	cup confectioners' sugar
⅓	cup unsweetened cocoa powder
2	tablespoons hazelnut oil
1	teaspoon vanilla extract
⅛	teaspoon salt

1. Adjust oven rack to middle position and heat oven to 375 degrees. Place hazelnuts in single layer on rimmed baking sheet and roast until fragrant and dark brown, 12 to 15 minutes, rotating sheet halfway through baking. Transfer nuts to medium bowl. When hazelnuts are cool enough to handle, place second medium bowl on top and shake vigorously to remove skins.

2. Process nuts in food processor until their oil is released and they form a smooth, loose paste, about 5 minutes, scraping bowl often.

3. Add sugar, cocoa, oil, vanilla, and salt and process until fully incorporated and mixture begins to loosen slightly and becomes glossy, about 2 minutes, scraping down bowl as needed.

4. Transfer to jar with tight-fitting lid. Store at room temperature or refrigerate for up to 1 month.

NAKED HAZELNUTS IN NO TIME

For a trick to peel toasted hazelnuts without the mess of rubbing them in a dish towel, try a mesh strainer. Dump the freshly toasted nuts into it and, once they've cooled slightly, rub them back and forth against the rough mesh. Most of the skins sift through the strainer, and it's easy to extract the skinned nuts from the remaining loose skins. Alternatively, try using a wire cooling rack: Place the nuts on a wire rack set in a rimmed baking sheet, then lightly toast them in a 350-degree oven for 10 to 15 minutes. Once the hazelnuts are cool enough to touch, rub them against the rack, letting the skins fall onto the pan below.

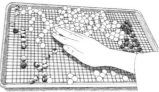

BLANCH YOUR OWN ALMONDS

If you're making a recipe that calls for blanched (skinned) almonds but you can only find whole, skin-on almonds at your supermarket, try this simple technique to remove the skins.

1. Place 1 cup of almonds in a medium heatproof bowl and cover with 2 cups boiling water. Let the almonds stand for 2 minutes, then drain and rinse them under cold running water.

2. Press each almond between your thumb and index finger to slip off the skin.

3. To dry and lightly toast the skinned nuts, place them on a baking sheet in a 350-degree oven for 7 to 10 minutes.

PREVENTING OIL SPILLS

Pouring olive oil often results not in a drizzle but a deluge. You can remedy this situation by transferring the oil to a maple syrup dispenser. Its quick-closing spout gives complete control over the pour. (Since the container is clear, be sure to store it in a dark cabinet to keep the oil from going rancid.)

JUST A SPLASH OF OIL

Pour spouts are a great way to
mete out just the right amount
of oil for a sauté or a salad, but
what do you do if you don't have
enough spouts, or if you don't
have cupboards tall enough to fit
both the bottles and the spouts?
Here are a few ways to get just
a splash of oil from the bottle
without a spout.

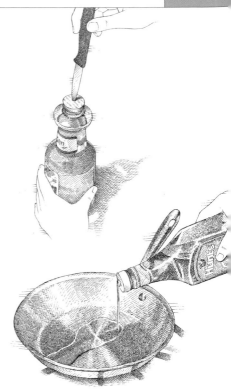

A. Build a Solution into the Bottle

1. Remove the cap from a newly
purchased bottle of oil and poke
a small hole through the safety
seal with a paring knife. Replace
the cap and store as usual.

2. When you need a little oil,
just remove the cap, invert the
bottle, and give it a squeeze or
a shake.

B. Squeeze Out a Solution

Try this one-handed plan: Pour
the oil into an old ketchup bottle.
Now whenever you need a splash
of oil, just flip the top and squirt
it into the pan.

SLOW-FLOW OIL

A drizzle of highly flavored oil
like truffle oil or toasted sesame
oil can add character and
complexity to a dish, but if too
much accidentally gushes from
the bottle, it can also ruin it.
To prevent this, hold a chopstick
across the bottle opening with
its tip pointed toward the food
as you pour—the oil travels along
the length of the chopstick in a
thin stream, making it easier to
control the flow.

QUICK-MEASURE OIL

When you're at the stove, instead
of digging around for a tablespoon, you can measure cooking
oil with the lid of the bottle. The
lids on most bottled oil hold
about that amount, and cleanup
is as easy as wiping the cap.

OLIVES

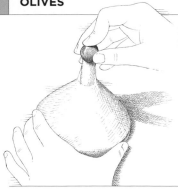

PITTING OLIVES THE FUN(NEL) WAY

The most common way to remove pits from olives without an olive pitter is to smash them on a cutting board. For a more elegant—and equally effective—alternative, place a funnel upside down on the counter, stand one end of the olive on the spout, and press down, allowing the pit to fall through the funnel.

SMARTER OLIVE RETRIEVAL

Here's an easy way to extract capers and olives from their narrow jars. Use the small scoop of a melon baller to retrieve capers and the larger scoop for olives. As a bonus, the excess brine drains through the scoop's perforations.

EASY OLIVE SLICING

If you're making nachos or another dish that requires lots of sliced olives, individually cutting each olive can be tedious. An egg slicer speeds up the process.

1. Depending on the size of the olives, set two or three in the egg slicer and push down to slice.

2. If a coarse chop is desired, turn the olives 90 degrees and slice again.

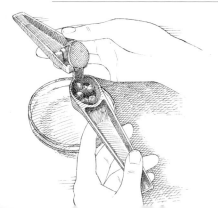

INSTANT OLIVE PASTE

Next time you need a few spoonfuls of very finely minced olives, capers, or sun-dried tomatoes, pull out a garlic press. Place two or three pitted olives, a teaspoonful of capers, or two oil-packed sun-dried tomatoes in the hopper of a garlic press and squeeze. The pastes can be used to flavor salad dressings, dips, and sauces or be used as a pasta topping or sandwich spread.

CANDLELIT ONIONS

We tested every which way to staunch the tears that flow when chopping onions. The most practical method turned out to be chopping near a flame from a lit gas burner (if you have a gas stove) or a candle (if you have electric burners). So we figured that if one candle was good, three or four would be better. To make a cheap, easy candle holder, put about two cups of kosher salt (sugar would be fine, too) in a bowl and plant the candles right in the salt, which keeps them upright and stable. (Another effective way to protect your eyes is to wear goggles, since they form a physical barrier that keeps the irritating vapors away from your eyes. So if you don't mind looking a little silly, you can instead put on a pair of ski goggles to keep the tears at bay next time you need to chop some onions.)

GETTING A GRIP ON ONION SLICING

Try this tip to make dicing or slicing onions even easier. After trimming the top of the onion and halving it pole to pole, follow the steps below.

1. Carefully peel the outer layers from each half down to—but not all the way off—the root end.

2. When you have diced or sliced most of the onion, hold on to the outer layers to stabilize the root end as you finish cutting.

SWEETER ONIONS

Many people enjoy onions in their salads but find their flavor harsh when raw. Temper them with the following method: Place the onion slices on a microwave-safe plate, cover with plastic wrap, and microwave on high power for 15 to 30 seconds. Once they're cool, toss the mellowed onions into your salad.

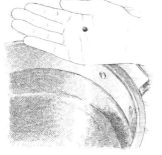

SALTED WATER REMINDER

If you have trouble remembering whether you've salted the water you're bringing to a boil for pasta or vegetables, try this trick: Every time you add the salt, also put one whole black peppercorn in the water as a reminder.

MAKING SURE TO SEASON

If you don't like to add salt to pasta water before it comes to a boil for fear of pitting your pots but want to make sure that by the time it does come to a boil, you're not too preoccupied with the rest of the meal to remember to add the salt, try this tip. Add the salt to the opened box of pasta (we recommend 1 tablespoon of table salt per pound of pasta), then simply dump the contents into the boiling water.

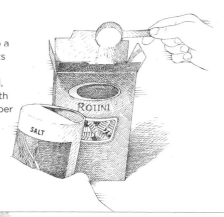

PROTECTING DRAINED PASTA

We noticed that every time we drained pasta into a shallow colander, the hot water would back up into the pasta before it had a chance to empty down the drain, creating a risk of contamination if the sink wasn't perfectly clean. We now steady the colander on an upside-down cake pan before draining. This elevates the colander and pasta above the basin.

IMPROMPTU COLANDER

You can use a salad spinner to drain pasta rather than digging out a colander. After cooking the pasta, pour it into the salad spinner insert and drain.

A REMINDER TO RESERVE PASTA WATER

In that last flurry of activity before saucing the pasta and getting dinner on the table, it's easy to overlook small details. It's no wonder, then, that many cooks forget to save a bit of pasta cooking water to thin the sauce when the recipe recommends it. For a foolproof reminder, place a measuring cup inside the colander in the sink before cooking the pasta. It's sure to nudge your memory at the appropriate moment.

GIVING GNOCCHI THEIR RIDGES

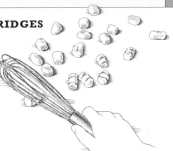

When making gnocchi, it is customary to give each piece distinct ridges using a butter paddle or the tines of a fork. For a quicker process, use a whisk for that job. Simply line up the gnocchi pieces on the counter and then roll the whisk over them to create deep, even ridges.

IMPROMPTU RAVIOLI WRAPPERS

Store-bought wonton wrappers make a great substitute for home-made pasta when making ravioli.

1. Lay one wrapper on counter; place your homemade filling on top.

2. Brush the edges of the dough with water and cover with another wrapper. Use the tines of a fork to seal the edges of the ravioli.

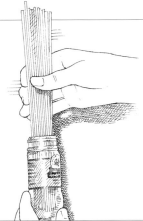

SPICE-JAR SPAGHETTI MEASURING

Judging the correct amount of spaghetti to cook for two people can be tricky, especially if you try to do so by eye. Take the guesswork out by saving a clean empty spice jar (with a 1-inch diameter opening) and using it to measure out just the right amount for two servings. Simply halve this amount when you want to measure spaghetti for one serving.

PAINLESS PITTING

Removing a split pit from a soft peach half can lead to mashed fruit. For foolproof removal, use a grapefruit spoon. The serrated edge of the spoon can easily cut out the stone without damaging the delicate flesh.

HALVING PEACHES AND NECTARINES

If you're tired of wrestling with peaches and nectarines to remove the pit, try this method, which guarantees an unbroken pit.

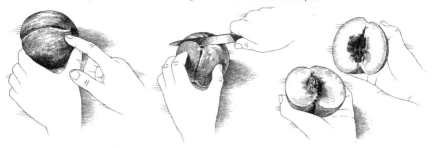

1. Locate the crease on the fruit that marks the pointed edge of the pit.

2. Position the knife at 90 degrees from the crease and cut the fruit in half, pole to pole.

3. Grasp both halves of the fruit and twist apart to expose the pit, which can then be popped out easily.

STABILIZING STUFFED PEPPERS

Here are several methods for dealing with a common problem: how to keep stuffed peppers upright in the pan as they cook.

A. Trim the lobes on the bottom of the pepper to create a flat surface so the pepper stands upright. Then drop the trimmings into the pepper cavity to plug up any holes created by cutting and fill the pepper with stuffing.

B. Place each pepper in an individual ovensafe ramekin. This is also a great system when you want to cook only a couple of peppers, instead of a whole batch.

C. Reserve the tops of the peppers, which you have cut off in order to stuff them, and insert them between the stuffed peppers in the pan for added stability.

D. Instead of cooking the peppers in a baking dish or roasting pan, put them in a tube pan. The snug fit makes the peppers sit right up. Alternatively, try using the cups of a muffin tin.

PUTTING A LID ON ROASTED PEPPERS

After roasting peppers, we usually place them in a bowl and cover them with plastic wrap, which loosens their charred skin and makes them easier to peel. You can also use a tightly covered pot. The tight seal of the lid creates the same sauna-like effect, with no wasted plastic.

SEEDING PEPPERS

Use a grapefruit spoon to scrape the seeds and veins out of peppers. The spoon's serrated edge pulls the veins from the inner core and walls, and its rounded sides glide around the chile or bell pepper more easily than a knife.

JUDGING PINEAPPLE RIPENESS

Because pineapples do not continue to ripen once they're picked, you want to make sure you're getting a ripe one. Use this trick to choose ripe pineapples at the grocery store. With one hand, gently tug at a leaf in the center of the fruit. If the leaf releases with little effort, the pineapple is ripe. If the leaf holds fast, choose a different pineapple. (Conversely, avoid pineapples with dried-out leaves and a fermented aroma—the fruit may be overripe.)

PINEAPPLE (PREP) EXPRESS

After you remove the rind from a pineapple, the hard, dark bits, or "eyes," remain attached to the flesh. Using a paring knife to trim the eyes is time-consuming and can result in a good deal of waste. Here are two easy and efficient solutions.

A. Use a small melon baller to quickly and neatly scoop out the eyes.

B. Use a strawberry huller to remove the spiny eyes from a pineapple. The tool's prongs pluck out the fruit's tough spots with minimal effort.

POTATOES

POTATO PEELING TRICK

Peeling raw potatoes can be a challenge, since the peeled flesh makes the potato slippery and difficult to grasp. This is particularly true of smaller spuds. Avoid this problem by creating a handle for the potatoes with a corkscrew. Just lodge the corkscrew firmly in the potato as if it were a cork and hold the potato by the corkscrew handle.

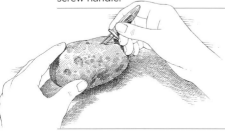

SAFER POTATO PIERCING

Forks and knives sometimes get stuck when piercing raw potatoes to allow steam to escape during baking, but there's a better tool for the job. Prick the skin of the potato with the sharp tip of a corncob holder.

HOT POTATO HANDLING

When potatoes are destined for mashing, we prefer to boil them with their skins on to keep them from getting waterlogged (drier potatoes are able to absorb more melted butter and cream). There is no doubt, though, that peeling just-boiled potatoes is a painstaking job. Here in the test kitchen we hold the potato with a fork and use a paring knife. If you have a ricer, you can avoid even this inconvenience by cutting each potato in half and then quickly placing each half cut side down in the ricer. This way the flesh is forced through the holes while the skin remains in the hopper. (Note: The discarded skins need to be cleaned from the hopper after each press.)

IMPROMPTU POTATO RICER

For making mashed potatoes without a potato ricer, try using a sturdy metal colander with fine perforations. Press the potatoes through the colander with a stiff rubber spatula.

IMPROVISED MASHER

If you ever find yourself without a potato masher, you can use the beaters from a handheld mixer to mash potatoes. Never mash potatoes in the electric mixer itself: The motorized beaters will overwork the potatoes and turn them gluey.

REALLY FAST FRIES

By using an apple slicer, you can get spuds cut and ready for the fryer in no time.

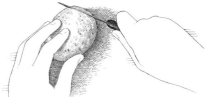 

1. Slice one end of the potato to create a stable base. Set the potato cut side down on the cutting board.

2. Push the apple slicer down over the potato, sectioning it into steak fry–size wedges. Cut the center cylinder in half lengthwise before cooking.

HASH BROWNS, SIMPLIFIED

Preparing hash browns can occupy a lot of kitchen real estate: counter for grating, sink for rinsing, clean towels for wringing out and drying—and that's all before the potatoes make it to the frying pan. Trim the preparation by placing the grated potatoes directly in the basket of a salad spinner. From here, you can rinse them and then spin away the moisture.

QUICK-MEASURE SALAD DRESSING

Rather than dirty your measuring cups, spoons, and whisk every time you want to make your favorite vinaigrette, try this practical solution. Separately measure out the oil and vinegar (we like a 3:1 ratio) and then pour them into a clear plastic bottle, using a permanent-ink pen to mark the level of the mixture after you've added each ingredient. As long as you keep the bottle, you'll never again have to dirty a measuring cup or spoon for these components. Add any solid ingredients (such as garlic, herbs, or mustard), close the bottle, and shake it until the dressing is thoroughly mixed. The bottle can be washed and reused for easier mixing next time.

NO-WASTE DRESSING

You can prepare vinaigrettes in a child's "sippy" cup and use the cup as a tool for dressing salads as well. The dressing is released slowly from the small spout, making it nearly impossible to waste vinaigrette or overdress a salad.

1. Add all the dressing ingredients to the cup and secure the lid.

2. While holding one finger securely over the spout, shake the cup vigorously to incorporate. Remove your finger from the spout and sprinkle the dressing over the salad.

Instant Aged Balsamic Vinegar

✓ **WHY THIS RECIPE WORKS:** Traditionally produced balsamic vinegar, labeled *tradizionale*, is aged for a minimum of 12 years for results that are intense, complex, and incredibly expensive—up to $60 an ounce. Fortunately, in the test kitchen we've found a way to reproduce some of its flavor qualities without having to visit a specialty food store or a loan officer. To imitate aged balsamic, start with decent supermarket balsamic vinegar. When reducing the ingredients, be sure to keep the heat low; vigorous boiling will destroy nuances in the vinegar's flavor. This reduced balsamic has a strong, fruity flavor and it should be used in the same way as tradizionale balsamic: drizzled over fresh fruit, ice cream, or grilled meats and fish for a major—but much less expensive—flavor boost. This recipe makes about ¼ cup.

⅓　**cup balsamic vinegar**
1　**tablespoon sugar**
1　**tablespoon port**

Combine ingredients in shallow pan and slowly reduce over extremely low heat. Mixture should be barely simmering. Continue until mixture is reduced to half its original volume. Let cool to room temperature and use immediately.

EASIER VINAIGRETTE

To evenly dispense oil when making a vinaigrette or mayonnaise, measure the oil into a squeeze bottle first. The squeeze bottle is easy to hold and makes adding the oil in a slow, steady stream effortless.

GETTING SAUSAGES STRAIGHT

Grilled sausages make a great summer sandwich, but fitting a curved link into a flat bun can be downright frustrating. Here's a perfect solution.

1. Insert bamboo skewers (that have first been soaked in water) lengthwise into each sausage prior to grilling. The skewers keep the sausages from curling during cooking.

2. When the sausages are done, pull out the skewers before fitting the straight links perfectly into their buns.

SAUSAGE CASING SOLUTION

When eating hard sausage or salami, it's a nuisance to peel off the sticky white casing from each individual slice. If the casing won't peel off the whole sausage easily before slicing, use a vegetable peeler to quickly remove the casing in advance. Alternatively, you can try this trick:

1. Slit the paper casing lengthwise with a paring knife, taking care not to cut into the sausage itself.

2. Run the sausage under warm water for 15 to 20 seconds, then pat it dry.

3. Pull the casing off in one piece.

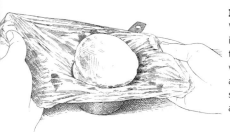

MESS-FREE SHORTENING

When measuring messy, malleable ingredients like shortening, line the measuring cup with plastic wrap, scoop in the shortening, and level it off. To retrieve it, simply lift out the plastic liner and the contents come with it.

SIMPLIFIED SHORTENING MEASURING

Use this handy trick to measure shortening by displacement.

1. For shortening amounts less than 1 cup, fill a 2-cup liquid measuring cup with 1 cup of cold water and spoon the shortening into the cold water.

2. Add or remove shortening until the water level equals the desired amount plus 1 cup (i.e., for ¼ cup of shortening, the water level should be at 1¼ cups).

EFFICIENT SHRIMP BATTERING

It's tedious to individually dip shrimp in batter before deep-frying, and the cooked shellfish are also hard to pick up and eat when their tails are covered in batter. Here's an ingenious technique that keeps the tails clean and gets the job done quickly: Tuck the ends of three shrimp (shelled and deveined but with the tails left on) between the fingers of one hand, form a loose fist around the tails, and dip all three shrimp at once into a bowl of batter.

EASIEST SHRIMP PEELING

Between pulling off all the little legs and prying open the shells, peeling shrimp can be a tiresome chore. Over the years, though, we've perfected an easy two-step method.

1. Holding the tail end of the shrimp with one hand and the opposite end of the shrimp with the other, bend the shrimp back and forth and side to side to split the shell.

2. Lift off the tail portion of the shell, then slide your thumb under the legs of the remaining portion and lift it off as well.

SHRIMP–SPICES AND SEASONINGS

SNAZZIER-LOOKING SHRIMP

Deveining usually creates a large, unsightly slit on the outer curve of shrimp. Here's a technique for more attractive results.

1. Insert one tine of a dinner fork into the shrimp, pass the tine beneath the vein, and hook it under.

2. Draw the vein out through the very small hole you've created, leaving the shrimp looking virtually untouched.

SHRIMP DEVEINING AID

Once removed from a shrimp, the vein can stick tenaciously to the tip of a paring knife, nail scissors, fork, or other deveining tool of your choice. Instead of fighting to remove each vein from your utensil (as it fights to stay right where it is), try this method: Place a sheet of paper towel flat on your work surface. Once you have freed the vein with the tip of the paring knife, just touch the knife to the paper towel and the vein will slip off the knife and stick to the towel. When you are through, toss the dirty towel into the trash.

THE PERFECT GRIND

Measuring fresh-ground pepper for a recipe can be tricky. A coffee grinder works, but, if you're like us, you end up grinding much more than you need. Solve this problem by counting the number of grinds your pepper mill requires to produce ¼ teaspoon of pepper and then marking the number on a piece of tape affixed to the mill.

MESS-FREE PEPPER GRINDING

Try this trick for a way to catch your pepper mill's loose grinds and make neat work of measuring fresh-ground pepper.

1. Grind the pepper into a cupcake liner.

2. Bend the liner edges to pour the pepper into a measuring spoon.

3. Discard any extra pepper and store the mill and liner inside a ramekin.

QUICK HOMEMADE FUNNELS

The filler opening of many pepper grinders is so small that the only way to fill them is by using a funnel. But even that trick has its problems, as peppercorns can easily catch in the neck of the funnel and block it. To avoid this problem, try one of these solutions:

A. Coffee Filter

1. Cut off the bottom ¼ inch of the filter. Fold the filter in half and separate the layers to create a funnel.

2. Insert the narrow end of the funnel into a pepper mill and add peppercorns.

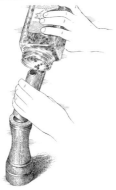 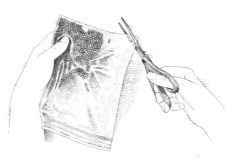

B. Rubber Garlic Peeler
A rubber garlic peeler is both wide and malleable, so it's perfect for this job.

C. Plastic Storage Bag
Place the peppercorns in a zipper-lock bag and snip off one corner. Position the snipped corner in the grinder to fill.

D. Envelope

1. Snip the sealed corner from an envelope to create a funnel of the desired width.

2. Crack open the envelope, insert the funnel into the container, and pour in ingredients.

SPICES AND SEASONINGS

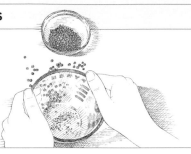

CRUSHING PEPPERCORNS

You can use a Pyrex measuring cup to crush peppercorns. The cup is heavy enough to crush the peppercorns, and its clear glass bottom allows you to gauge your progress as you work.

SPICES, STAY PUT

We like to grind our own spices with a mortar and pestle, but we find that some spices, like peppercorns, tend to fly out of the mortar in the process. Here's a tip: Put the spices in the mortar and cover it tightly with plastic wrap. Then make a tiny slit in the wrap and poke the pestle through. Even though the slit will end up stretching as you grind, as long as the wrap seals the edges, the spices will stay put.

SPICE GRINDING SOLUTION

Here's a clever way to grind whole spices without a spice grinder: Purchase peppercorns in glass jars with removable grinding mechanisms, which can be found in the spice section of the supermarket. After reserving their contents for later use, fill the now-empty jars with cumin, coriander, or fennel seeds; red pepper flakes; and more. The spices can now be ground as needed.

HANDS-FREE SEASONING

Keep your hands clean when seasoning chops, steaks, or cutlets with this tip.

1. Sprinkle a plate or other flat surface liberally with salt and pepper (or other seasonings), then use a pair of tongs to lay the meat on the plate.

2. Season the top side of the meat.

3. Use the tongs to transfer the meat to the stovetop or grill.

SHAKER FOR SPICE RUBS

Use empty store-bought spice jars to store homemade spice rubs.

1. Gently pry the perforated lid off the jar, refill with your favorite homemade spice rub, and snap the lid back in place.

2. The spices can now be applied more evenly to the meat.

KOSHER SALT SHAKER

When sprinkling kosher salt on foods such as steak, it can be hard to get an even coating using your hands. But the holes on a salt shaker are too small to allow the large grains to pass through. Try storing your kosher salt in a clean spice jar with a shaker top. The holes are the perfect size to dispense the large grains.

POP SECRET SEASONING

Sprinkling popcorn with table salt usually results in a pile of salt at the bottom of the bowl—and a bland snack. Clingy superfine popcorn salt is available for purchase, but it's easy to make your own.

1. Pulse salt in a spice grinder for about 30 seconds (its texture should be very fine). Pour the pulsed salt into an empty spice jar fitted with a perforated shaker lid.

2. Season the popcorn in a very large bowl, carefully stirring to evenly distribute the salt.

EFFICIENT SPINACH DRAINING

Removing excess water from thawed frozen spinach by pressing it against a colander or squeezing it by hand or in a towel inevitably leaves little green bits everywhere. Here's a neater approach: Puncture the bag a few times with a fork and set it inside a bowl to defrost. Once the spinach has thawed, squeeze the bag; water drains out through the holes without mess or waste.

SPINACH–STRAWBERRIES

WELL-PRESSED SPINACH

Squeezing cooked spinach dry is a tedious but necessary step before incorporating it into a recipe. Here's a very effective method for doing so: Place the waterlogged spinach in a colander in the sink and position a slightly smaller glass bowl on top. Then squeeze the two vessels together, pressing out the unwanted liquid.

QUICKER BLANCHED SPINACH

When a recipe calls for blanching spinach, it means boiling lots of water for a mere 30-second plunge. Speed things up by heating the water in a teakettle and pouring it over the spinach, placed in a colander. Boil 4 to 6 cups of water in a teakettle. Place 1 pound of cleaned and stemmed spinach in a colander set in the sink. Pour the boiling water over the spinach in a steady stream to wilt. Shock the spinach with cold running water, squeeze out the excess moisture, then use as directed in the recipe.

STRAWBERRY SPOON

The serrated tip of a grapefruit spoon is a better tool than a paring knife for removing the green crown from strawberries. It's faster, easier to maneuver, and wastes less fruit.

FASTER STRAWBERRY HULLING

Many cooks do not own a strawberry huller. However, they may have a drinking straw, which makes the perfect replacement tool. Pushed through the bottom up to the top, a straw cores and hulls whole strawberries quickly and easily.

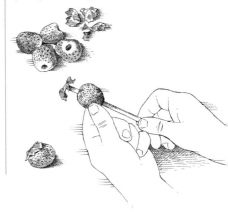

MAKING PERFECT DIPPED BERRIES

Here's a quick way to solve the problem of uneven-looking chocolate-dipped strawberries. Rather than laying them on waxed paper once they've been dipped, try following this procedure: Use scissors to trim the edges from an empty egg carton. Trim the tall center divider from the egg carton. Then place the strawberries, dipped side up, in the egg holes of the trimmed carton.

QUICKER TOFU PREP

Pressing tofu dry prior to cooking improves its texture and allows for better browning, but it's a time-consuming process. Next time, try this shortcut.

1. Drain the tofu and cut it into pieces of the desired size.

2. Place the tofu on a coffee filter set on a plate; microwave on medium power for 4 to 6 minutes or until the coffee filter is damp.

PEELING TOMATOES— THERE'S THE RUB

Even after you blanch and shock tomatoes or stone fruits, a knife can still sometimes fail to remove the skin effectively. When your paring knife fails you, try placing stubborn fruits in a dish towel and rubbing lightly.

PEELING JUST ONE TOMATO

Blanching tomatoes (or peaches) in a pot of boiling water is a great way to remove their skins, but when you need to peel just a single piece of fruit, try this shortcut.

1. Microwave 1⅓ cups of water in a 2-cup liquid measuring cup for 1 to 2 minutes, until simmering.

2. Cut a shallow X into the bottom of the fruit, drop it into the hot water for 30 seconds, and then transfer it to ice water for 30 seconds.

3. The skin pulls right off.

TAKE SEEDS FOR A SPIN

Removing the seeds from one tomato is a snap, but this task becomes time-consuming when a recipe calls for several pounds of tomatoes. Here's a shortcut.

1. Core the tomatoes and cut them into pieces.

2. Spin the chopped tomatoes in the basket of a salad spinner until most of the seeds are released. Repeat the spinning process as necessary to remove excess seeds.

TOMATO SCOOP

Use the serrated edges of a grapefruit spoon to cut out the seeded portion of tomatoes after quartering them. It's more effective than using a regular spoon—and less messy than using your fingers.

QUICKER TOMATO CORING

A. Use a large star tip from a pastry bag to core tomatoes. Pierce the tomato at the stem scar with the pointed end of the tip, give it a twist, and use the tip to cut out and remove the core.

B. You can employ a similar technique with an apple corer inserted halfway into the tomato.

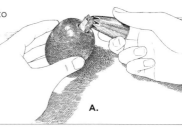

A.

NO-MESS CHOPPING

Instead of chopping whole canned tomatoes on a cutting board and ending up with tomato juice all over the counter, cut them up right in the can with a pair of kitchen shears.

TOMATOES: THIS SIDE UP

Place unwashed tomatoes stem end down at room temperature. We've found that this prevents moisture from escaping and bacteria from entering through the scar, prolonging shelf life. If the vine is still attached, though, leave it on and store the tomatoes stem end up.

PERFECT TOMATO SLICES

1. Core the tomato. Working from pole to pole, use the tines of a fork to pierce the skin gently along one side of the tomato.

2. Using the tine marks as guides, cut the tomato into even slices.

SPLATTER-FREE TOMATOES

When a recipe calls for crushing whole tomatoes by hand, things can get messy. For a neat solution, pour the tomatoes and their juice into a bowl. Submerge the tomatoes under the juice and then use your hands to crush them, one at a time, keeping the juices contained.

CRUSHING FRESH TOMATOES

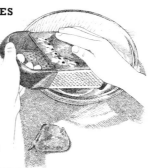

Sweet and juicy crushed fresh tomatoes are perfect for a quick sauce when in season. This method delivers all the pulp while leaving the skins behind. Slice the tomatoes across their equators and grate the cut side of each tomato half on the large holes of a box grater until all the flesh has been pressed through and only the skin remains.

STEADY STUFFED TOMATOES

Stuffed tomatoes have the tendency to slip and slide all over the pan when they're being transferred in and out of the oven. Here are two resourceful solutions.

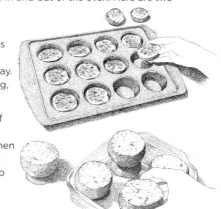

A. Use a muffin tin to prevent wobbling. Place tomato halves in the cups of a muffin tin sprayed with vegetable oil spray. Top the tomatoes with stuffing, then bake.

B. Slice the blossom end off of each tomato and arrange, cut side down, in a baking dish. Then place the stuffed tomatoes on the blossom-end slices to keep them in place during baking.

SHOPPING THE SALAD BAR

While some cooks enjoy the Zen of chopping vegetables for stir-fries or pizza toppings, others consider the task a necessary evil—time-consuming and tedious. For those in the latter camp, here are the magic words: salad bar. Many supermarkets feature salad bars where cooks can pick out a wide variety of ingredients, cleaned and chopped, in just the quantities they need.

VEGETABLE SCRUBBER

If you grow lots of fresh vegetables in your home garden, try using body-scrubbing/loofah gloves from the dollar store to clean carrots, leeks, potatoes, and any other sturdy root vegetables. Used in a bowl of water, these gloves make quick work of scrubbing the vegetables clean.

ICELESS ICE BATH

Part of the routine for blanching vegetables is to stop the cooking process by transferring the vegetables from boiling water into a bath of ice water, which is called "shocking." To shock when you have no ice in the freezer, try using frozen ice packs—the type used to chill foods in a cooler—in place of the ice cubes.

SHOCKING DISCOVERY

If you run out of ice to shock vegetables after blanching them, reach for a chilled ice cream maker insert and fill it with cold tap water. After the vegetables are finished cooking, shock them in the cold water in the insert. The water remains cold for at least one batch of vegetables.

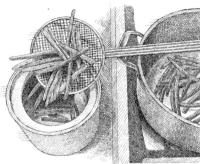

SPACE-SAVING INGREDIENT PREP

Recipes often call for adding a variety of vegetables and other ingredients at different points during the cooking time. Instead of placing each prepared ingredient in its own smaller bowl or into piles crowded onto a cutting board, you can save both space and dirty dishes by layering the ingredients in a single large bowl and separating the layers with sheets of waxed paper or plastic wrap. (Make sure that the ingredients are in the right order, with the one you'll need first on top.)

VEGETABLE WEIGHT

In the test kitchen, we extract as much liquid as possible from salted raw vegetables destined for a salad or slaw by pressing down on them with a weight. One quick and easy way to do this is to place the salted vegetables in a colander, then set a 1-gallon zipper-lock bag filled with pie weights on top of the vegetables.

PREVENTING THE VEGETABLE VANISHING ACT

Cooks who have a garbage disposal installed in their sink often peel and pare vegetables and fruit right over the sink. Of course, this likely means they have at some point also dropped the item they were paring and watched in dismay as it vanished down the drain hole into the disposal. Avoid this problem by positioning a small funnel in the drain hole. The funnel catches the desirable pieces of food, especially things like new potatoes, kiwis, and strawberries.

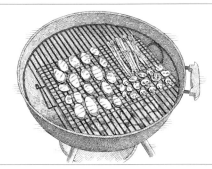

GRILLING VEGETABLES

Grill cooks know the pain of watching perfectly grilled vegetables slip through the grate and scorch on the hot coals below. Protect your vegetables with this tip. Place a wire cooling rack perpendicular to the grate bars. Heat for about 5 minutes, then rub the rack lightly with oil before grilling.

GRILL-MARKING ZUCCHINI ON BOTH SIDES

Grill marks enhance both the appearance and the flavor of grilled vegetables. Here's a way to get that tasty marking on both sides of squash and zucchini on the grill.

1. Cut a zucchini (or yellow summer squash) in half lengthwise and run a cheese plane or Y-shaped vegetable peeler over the skin side a couple of times. This exposes some flesh and flattens the squash for stability on the cooking grate.

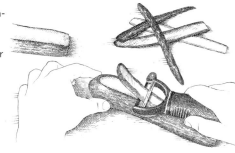

2. The extra exposed flesh allows for grill marks on both sides of each squash half.

CHAPTER 4

HACKING THE BASICS

Smarter Skills for Everyday Kitchen Tasks

BURN BLOCKER

For a simple way to protect yourself from still-warm burners on the stove, keep a kettle on the stove and place it over the hot burner after turning it off to shield the surface while it cools. (To prevent the bottom of the kettle from burning on the hot surface, make sure it has some water in it.)

FIGHTING FIRE WITH...SALT?

According to authorities, most home fires are started in the kitchen. You should always have a kitchen fire plan. If you feel a fire is quickly growing out of control, your first instinct should definitely be to get out of your house and alert the fire department. However, many small stovetop fires can be safely smothered by placing a lid over the pan and turning off the burner. Salt or baking soda, if handy, will also put out the flames. Most important, never use water to douse a grease fire. The safest course is to keep a portable ABC-type fire extinguisher within easy reach of your stove.

MAKE YOUR PAN EASIER TO HANDLE

Many recipes call for an ovensafe skillet that can move from the stovetop to the oven and back again. However, just because the pan is safe to go in the oven, that doesn't mean it will be safe for your bare hands when it comes out. You'll probably remember to use an oven mitt to pull the skillet out, but it's all too easy to forget that the handle is still hot as you continue to work with the pan on the stovetop. As a reminder, leave a potholder, folded kitchen towel, or oven mitt over the hot handle.

PREEMPTIVE FIRE EXTINGUISHING

It is not unheard of for a kitchen fire to start from a casually extinguished match that was tossed into the trash. Make doubly sure to avoid this potential disaster by holding the head of the extinguished match under a running faucet (or dipping it into a water-filled dish in the sink) to douse it before putting it in the trash.

BEATING STUBBORN LIDS

Next time you're fighting with a difficult jar lid, give your hands a rest and try one of these tips.

A. | **B.**

C. | **D.**

A. Invert the jar so that it rests lid-down in about ½ inch of hot tap water in a shallow bowl or pie plate. After 30 seconds or so, the heat will break the vacuum seal and the lid will unscrew easily.

C. Grab an old computer mouse pad. Its rubber bottom—engineered to anchor it to a desk—creates a good grip that helps budge stubborn lids.

B. Try a thin metal spoon. Use the spoon as a lever and slide its tip between the lid and the jar—avoiding the lid's notches. Gently press down on the handle until the seal releases. This will also work with a church key.

D. Rubber wristbands and bracelets can do more than promote a favorite team, charity, or cause. Wrapping the wristband around the lid helps you gain traction as you twist.

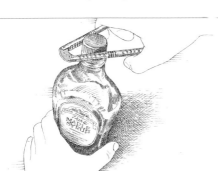

BOTTLE OPENER AID

When the small lid to a bottle of syrup, ketchup, Worcestershire or soy sauce, vinegar, salad dressing, or the like sticks and won't unscrew easily, try enlisting the services of a nutcracker to help the lid release.

PREVENTING JARRING PROBLEMS

The lids of jars with sticky contents such as jelly, honey, or molasses often stick as if they were cemented in place. Instead of struggling with sticky lids, try one of these two tips.

A. Cover the tops of these jars with plastic wrap before screwing on the lids. The plastic prevents any serious sticking, so the lids always unscrew easily.

B. Dip a small piece of paper towel (or your impeccably clean fingertip) into a bit of vegetable oil and wipe the threads of the jar. The bare film of oil prevents the lid from sticking to the jar the next time you open it.

MAGNETISM IN THE KITCHEN

When you're using a manual can opener, the lid sometimes drops into the can. Don't dirty a butter knife to fish it out. Instead, reach for a handy tool hanging right on the refrigerator—a decorative magnet. Place a magnet over the can and the lid will come right out, with no mess.

DITCHING CLINGY INGREDIENTS

When a rubber spatula is too big to use to scrape clingy bits of tomato sauce or paste from emptied jars and cans, try this trick: Add a tablespoon or two of liquid to the container, swirl it around to wash the bottom and sides, and then empty it into the pot. A bonus: Rinsing with a splash of wine or broth adds extra flavor.

STRIPPING PRODUCE STICKERS

It's easy to puncture thin-skinned produce like plums and tomatoes when peeling away the produce sticker. To keep them blemish-free, use one of these tricks.

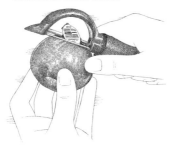

A. Gently pry the sticker away with a vegetable peeler—the blade catches the paper's edge and lifts it off without damaging the skin.

B. Dip the corner of a paper towel in vegetable oil. Rub the oiled towel over the sticker and let sit for about 5 minutes. You should now be able to peel off the offending sticker without marring the fruit's skin.

UNWRAPPING PLASTIC WRAP

Here's a clever way to find the beginning of a roll of plastic wrap that has torn and stuck to itself: Hold a clean vegetable brush or toothbrush parallel to the roll of plastic wrap, rotating the roll and rubbing the bristles along the surface of the plastic until the hidden edge loosens and the plastic can be unwrapped.

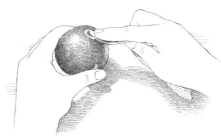

SECOND LINERS

If you run out of liners when baking cupcakes or muffins, try this easy substitute.

1. Cut 5-inch squares from a sheet of parchment paper and firmly press them over the base of an inverted drinking glass to shape them.

2. Place the shaped liners into the muffin cups. Fill and bake as directed.

MAKING EXTRAWIDE SHEETS OF ALUMINUM FOIL

When you have an especially large item to cover with foil, follow this procedure to fashion a double-width sheet:

1. Place a length of foil flat on the counter, then place a second sheet directly on top of it.

2. Fold one long edge of the two sheets over on itself twice.

3. Starting from the opposite edge (which has not been crimped), open the sheets as you would a book.

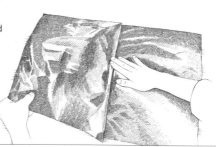

PUTTING PARCHMENT PAPER IN ITS PLACE

Some parchment paper comes in handy precut sheets, but most doesn't. In roll form it comes with one big drawback: It curls into a scroll the second it is cut. Here are some simple solutions.

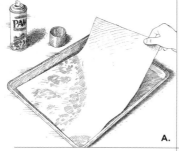

A.

B.

C.

D.

A. Spray the pan with a light coating of vegetable oil spray and lay the parchment sheet down on the sticky surface.

B. Lightly crumple the sheet of parchment paper, then unfold it and smooth it flat. The folds will help keep it from curling.

C. Cut the parchment paper into lengths to fit a baking sheet. Store the sheets of paper in the baking sheet, weighing them down with a second baking sheet. Now you have perfectly flat, perfectly sized sheets ready to go when you want them.

D. Grab four refrigerator magnets and place one over each corner of the parchment. Make sure to return the magnets to the fridge before putting the baking sheet in the oven.

FANCY KNIFEWORK FOR FRUITS AND VEGETABLES

Here's a collection of our best tips for the trickiest parts of slicing, dicing, and chopping fruits and vegetables in your kitchen.

A. Cut Slicing Time in Half

Individually halving cherry tomatoes, grapes, or freshly pitted cherries can be time-consuming. Here's a way to speed things along.

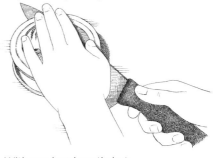

1. Place a medium-size plastic lid on a surface with the lip side up. Place a single layer of the food to be sliced in the lid and a second lid, lip side down, over the food,

2. With one hand gently but firmly holding the top lid and the other hand holding a sharp chef's or serrated knife, slice horizontally between the lids, cutting the food in half.

B. To the Very End

Slicing to the very end of oblong foods like zucchini, cucumber, and salami can be dicey work. To save your fingers, spear one end of the food with a corn holder just deep enough for the prongs to get a good grip. Then grasp the corn holder, leaving your fingers out of harm's way as you slice all the way to the end.

C. Knifeless Slicing

Instead of trying to slice radishes and carrots thinly and evenly enough for salad with a chef's knife, enlist a vegetable peeler. The sharp blade makes it easy to cut wafer-thin slices.

PAPER ROUTE FOR KNIVES

Even the best knives dull quickly with regular use. To determine if your knife needs sharpening, put it to the paper test. Hold a sheet of paper by one end and drag your knife, from heel to tip, across it. If the knife snags or fails to cut the paper, it needs to be honed. If the knife still fails the test after you hone it, run it through a sharpener.

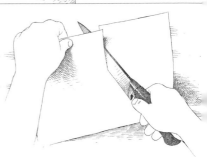

4.3 MAKING THE CUT

IN-A-PINCH KNIFE SHARPENER

If you find yourself with a dull knife but without a knife sharpener, you can use the unglazed bottom of a ceramic mug to sharpen small knives. Applying moderate pressure, hold the knife at a 20-degree angle and carefully draw the entire length of the blade across the rough surface.

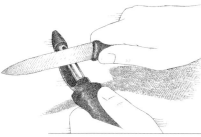

SHARPENING VEGETABLE PEELERS

To bring back the edge on a dull vegetable peeler, run the back of a paring knife along the blade at a 45-degree angle. The metal spine of the paring knife acts as a hone, aligning the tiny metal "teeth" of the blade.

NONSKID CUTTING BOARDS

Nonskid shelf liner is a perfect tool for keeping cutting boards in place while chopping—just cut it to the same dimensions as your cutting boards. When the makeshift mats are not in use, just roll them up and store them neatly in a kitchen drawer.

BETTER SPREADERS

A butter knife is a serviceable utensil for spreading nut butters and preserves, but for even better spreading, take a cue from cake decorating and reach for a mini offset spatula. Just as it aids in frosting cupcakes, the tool's wider blade allows you to scoop more from the jar at once and spread with ease.

NO-SLIP MIXING

If you like to keep one hand free for adding ingredients to the bowl when using a handheld mixer, you can keep the bowl from sliding around by placing it on a rubber shelf liner or silicone baking sheet liner. The mixing bowl sticks to the liner and stays stable.

LUMP-FREE THICKENING

Adding cornstarch to liquid ingredients when making pudding or pastry cream can result in lumps. Use the following method to smoothly blend the thickener into the liquid.

1. Instead of adding the cornstarch by itself to the liquid, mix it with the sugar from the recipe.

2. Slowly add the cornstarch-sugar mixture to the liquid. The sugar will help the cornstarch to dissolve without creating any lumps.

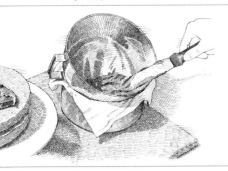

STABLE SCOOPING

Angling a mixing bowl can make it much easier to dig in while scooping out cookie dough or cake frosting. To stabilize your bowl at the perfect angle while keeping your hands free for scooping, place the mixing bowl in a pot lined with a dish towel. The now-secure bowl can be tilted in any direction.

BLENDING NATURAL BUTTERS

Fans of natural peanut butter (without sugar or other stabilizers) on their PB&Js, as well as other nut butters and tahini, know that the butter often separates into a dense, solid mass beneath a layer of oil that has risen to the surface. Before spreading, the oil and solids have to be reblended. A spoon makes a mess of everything, but there is an easier way. Simply turn the sealed jar upside down and allow the oil to rise to the top. As the oil passes thorough the butter, the solids will absorb some oil and become soft enough to spread. Flip the jar right side up, and the butter is ready to use.

4.5 THE DEPARTMENT OF WEIGHTS AND MEASURES

A HANDY RULE OF THUMB

The length between the thumb's knuckle and its tip is almost exactly 1 inch, so you can use your thumb as a guide for measuring and chopping the first few pieces during ingredient prep and then use those pieces as guides for the remaining cuts. (For some people, the distance between the second joint of the pointer finger and its tip is closer to 1 inch. Measure both your thumb and your pointer finger with a ruler to see which is more accurate.)

MAKING THE GRADE(S)

To avoid having to drag out a ruler every time you want a precise cut, use a permanent marker to mark measurements right on your cutting board.

1. On one edge of a wooden cutting board, make marks for ¼ inch, ½ inch, ¾ inch, and 1 inch.

2. Place an item against the guide to check your knife work.

ELEVATED MEASURING

Resting a liquid measuring cup with its contents on a flat surface is essential to obtaining an accurate measurement. To avoid having to crouch down to read the measurement from a cup sitting on a counter or table, try this tip: Invert a large mixing bowl on the counter and place the measuring cup on the bowl.

STANDARD YOGURT MEASUREMENTS

If you find yourself in a kitchen without a set of measuring cups, you can substitute cleaned yogurt containers: the 4-ounce size for ½ cup, the 6-ounce size for ¾ cup, and the 8-ounce size for a full cup.

HALVE OR HALVE NOT

Here's an ingenious way to accurately measure ½ cup of liquid with a 1-cup dry measuring cup: Fill a straight-sided 1-cup measuring cup with liquid approximately halfway and tilt the cup diagonally. When the liquid touches the brim on one side of the cup and the edge of the flat bottom on the opposite side of the cup, you have measured exactly ½ cup. Use the same method to measure ¼ cup from a ½-cup measure, ⅛ cup from a ¼-cup measure, and so on.

SOLVING STICKY SPOONS

When measuring small amounts of sticky liquid like honey or corn syrup, run the measuring spoons under hot water before using them. A heated spoon keeps the sticky liquid runnier, which helps it release more easily.

MEASURING BY THE SPOONFUL

Dipping a measuring spoon into a dry ingredient, then sweeping across the top with a knife to level it off, is the best way to get an accurate measurement. But it can also be a messy proposition. Here are two ways to tidy things up.

A. Coffee Filter

1. Holding a cone-shaped coffee filter in one hand, pour in a generous amount of the spice. Dip the measuring spoon into the spice, using a straight edge to level it off.

2. Holding the coffee filter at an angle and pinching one corner, carefully pour the excess back into the spice container.

B. Masking Tape

Run a double strip of masking tape across the opening of the container. Scoop up a heaping spoonful of the ingredient and level it off by scraping it against the tape.

KITCHEN SCALE PERCH

Bulky containers, large roasts, and the like can obscure the display on a digital scale. Here's a clever way around the problem: Steady a lightweight cake stand on the scale, and set the tare at zero. The cake stand, which is wide enough to accommodate large pans and big cuts of meat, elevates items so that the display is visible.

4.5 THE DEPARTMENT OF WEIGHTS AND MEASURES

A FLEXIBLE WAY TO WEIGH

Pouring dry ingredients from a bowl into a running stand mixer usually results in a messy counter. Try setting a silicone cake pan on the scale and measuring the dry ingredients in it instead. The pan easily bends, so you can add to the mixer without a mess.

A CLEAN STREAM

Some liquid measuring cups have itsy-bitsy pouring spouts that can make a big mess if you pour too quickly—the liquid will leak and run down the cup, not into your bowl. For a mess-free pour, follow this easy procedure: As you pour, hold a butter knife (blade up) in the spout at an angle. The liquid will follow the knife and stay in a steady stream.

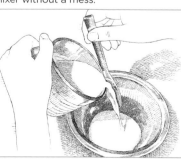

BROWN-BAG FLOUR POWER

Many bakers weigh out their flour in a bowl or on a piece of parchment paper, but you may find it easier to use a brown paper lunch bag to hold the flour, particularly if the quantity is large. The bag stands open on the scale, is deep enough to hold a lot with no overflow, and pours neatly.

MUFFIN-TIN *MISE EN PLACE*

Preparing and measuring the ingredients for a dish before you begin to cook, called *mise en place*, makes a recipe go smoothly and quickly. But this can mean keeping track of many small, full bowls. Rather than chasing down individual dishes, try using the cups of a muffin tin, each fitted with a liner, to hold various ingredients. Adding the ingredients to your dish is easy and cleanup is a cinch.

SWEET PREPARATIONS

During the holidays, many bakers make multiple batches of treats. To save time and eliminate mess, measure out and label the recipes ahead of time, storing the dry ingredients in zipper-lock bags and wet ingredients in plastic containers in the refrigerator.

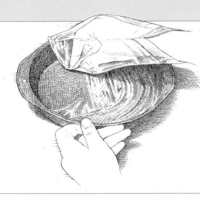

NO MORE GREASY HANDS

Keep your hands clean while greasing a pan by using a plastic sandwich bag.

1. Wearing the bag like a glove, grease the pan.

2. When finished, remove the bag by turning it inside out and neatly discarding it. No more messy paper towels!

TWO TRICKS FOR PREPPING CAKE PANS

A. The traditional method of greasing and flouring cake pans can be a bit of a nuisance. Save yourself some work by combining the greasing and flouring steps: Mix 2 parts shortening with 1 part flour and brush this paste lightly onto the cake pans. This eliminates the messy step of dusting the pans with flour.

B. Greasing and flouring cake pans prevents baked goods from sticking, but bakers often struggle with covering every nook and cranny. Instead of banging the pan on the counter to achieve an even coat, try using your turkey baster like a bellows to spread the flour evenly. (Hold the pan upside down over the sink and tap once to remove any excess flour.)

GREASE, LIGHTNING FAST

Here's a smart way to grease pans: Save empty butter wrappers in a zipper-lock bag in the freezer. Whenever a recipe calls for a greased pan, pull out one wrapper and wipe it on the pan's surface. Each wrapper is just enough to grease a pan.

MESS-FREE PAN SPRAY

Many cooks have encountered the oily film on their counter that results from using an aerosol vegetable oil spray. To avoid this problem, open the door of your dishwasher, lay the item to be greased right on the door, and spray away. Any excess spray will be cleaned off the door the next time you run the dishwasher.

QUICKER CHILLING

When you need to quickly chill a liquid—whether it's an ice cream base or a soup—recipes often instruct you to pour it into a metal bowl set in a larger bowl filled with ice water. Here's a way to speed up the process: Pour the liquid into a metal Bundt pan and then place the Bundt pan in an ice bath. More of the liquid comes in contact with cold metal in a Bundt pan than in a bowl, so the temperature nose-dives faster.

COLDER, FASTER

It's good to quick-chill meat before it goes into the freezer for long-term storage. The faster the meat freezes, the smaller the ice crystals, and smaller ice crystals translate to less cellular damage and less loss of juices during cooking. Adding salt to an ice bath lowers the freezing point of water and turns the bath into a superfast freezer. To make an ice bath for quick chilling, combine 1 pound ice, ⅓ cup salt, and ⅓ cup water. Wrap the meat in plastic wrap, place the pieces in a zipper-lock bag, and submerge the bag in the water mixture. Once the meat is frozen solid, remove the bag from the ice bath and transfer it to the freezer. You can also use a brine like this to quick-chill drinks; for every bottle of wine or three to four 12-ounce bottles of beer or soda you want to chill, mix 1 quart water with 4 quarts ice and 1 cup salt.

THE LOWDOWN ON COOLING SOUPS

For food safety reasons, soups and stews should be cooled to 40 degrees and stored within 4 hours of cooking, but placing large containers of the hot liquid directly in the refrigerator raises the appliance's temperature to an unsafe level. Here's a smarter approach: Fill a large cooler or the sink with cold water and ice packs. Place the saucepan or stockpot in the cooler or sink until the contents register about 80 degrees, 30 to 45 minutes, stirring the pot occasionally to speed the chilling process. Refill the cooler or sink with cold water if necessary.

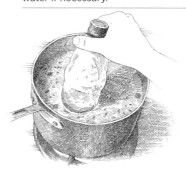

ICE IN A BOTTLE

Here's a simple way to cool down soups, stews, or stock quickly so they can be refrigerated: Fill a large, clean plastic beverage bottle almost to the top with water, seal it, and freeze it. Use the frozen bottle to stir the stock in the pot. The ice inside the bottle will cool the food rapidly without diluting it.

COOL OFF WITH CUTLERY

If you find yourself with two hot dishes or baking sheets and only one trivet, try flipping over four large spoons or dinner knives and laying them on the counter-top a few inches apart. Then you can set the hot item on top of the silverware to cool.

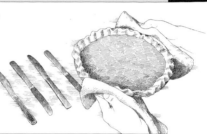

COOLING-RACK SUBSTITUTES

During holiday baking marathons, cooks may find themselves with a shortage of equipment. Here are some clever ideas for improvising.

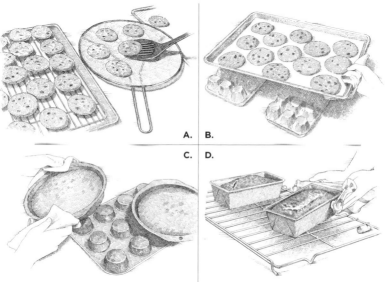

A.   **B.**

C.   **D.**

A. Next time you find yourself with a baking sheet full of hot cookies and a shortage of cooling racks, try transferring the cookies to a splatter screen to cool.

C. Set the hot pan on an overturned muffin tin. The muffin tin will also support a cake after it's been turned out of its pan.

B. You can also use cardboard egg trays for the same purpose. Set two empty inverted dozen-size egg trays side-by-side to fully support a cookie sheet or pie plate.

D. When baking in a kitchen that isn't equipped with a cooling rack, move the extra oven rack to a counter before heating the oven. You can prop up the rack with corks and then use it as a cooling rack for your finished baked goods.

LESS PAIN, BETTER STRAIN

Pushing any type of food through a fine-mesh strainer goes much faster—and requires less elbow grease—when the round bottom of a ladle is used instead of a spatula or wooden spoon. Simply press the bowl of the ladle, which follows the curve of the strainer, against the solids in a circular motion.

STRAINING ABOVE IT ALL

When draining ingredients such as grated potatoes or yogurt in a mesh strainer set over a bowl, the strained liquid can sometimes rise back into the food, ruining the effort. Solve the problem this way.

1. Place an overturned ramekin or small bowl in a larger bowl that will catch the strained liquid.

2. Rest the strainer on the ramekin to elevate the food, preventing liquid from seeping back into it.

NO-SLIP STRAINER

When straining vegetables or broths, it can be difficult to keep the lip of a fine-mesh strainer from falling into the bowl or pot you are straining into. Try wrapping a thick rubber band around the balancing loop of the strainer to create a no-slip grip that stays in place.

MAKESHIFT COLANDER

To avoid dirtying a large colander for a small cleaning job, reuse the perforated plastic containers in which small produce items such as cherry tomatoes and berries are packaged.

1. Place the items to be cleaned in an empty container and rinse, letting the water drain out through the holes.

2. Once thoroughly cleaned, transfer the items to paper towels to dry.

STRAINERLESS STRAINING

Here are some tips for situations where you might not actually have to dig out a strainer after all.

A. Use the Can

Rather than dirtying a colander to rinse and drain canned goods like beans and olives, try the following method.

1. Hold the can upside down over the sink and make three small holes at the bottom with a church key or can opener.

2. Turn the can right side up, set it over the clean drain in the sink, and then open the top with a can opener. Liquid from the can will drain through the holes.

B. Mesh Bag

If you don't happen to have the right strainer for small jobs (such as straining the juice of one or two lemons) and would rather not haul out your larger strainer, try this trick.

1. Save the leftover mesh bags from small produce items (such as shallots or new potatoes). After cleaning the bag well, drop in a lemon half.

2. Squeeze as much juice as needed. All of the seeds and pith will be trapped in the mesh bag.

C. Use the Rasp

After using your rasp-style grater to zest citrus, you can turn the grater over and use it to strain the seeds and pulp from the juice.

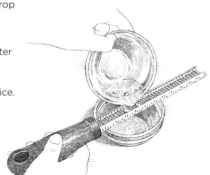

Greek-Style Yogurt

☑ **WHY THIS RECIPE WORKS:** Instead of worrying about the ingredients in commercial yogurt, you can make your own. Use the best-quality pasteurized milk and "starter" yogurt (with live active cultures). Dry milk powder thickens without adding off-flavors. Make sure to save some yogurt from one batch to start your next. Start the recipe a day ahead of time to allow time for straining. This recipe makes 2 cups.

4 cups 2 percent pasteurized
(not ultra–pasteurized or UHT) low-fat milk

¼ cup nonfat dry milk powder

¼ cup plain 2 percent Greek yogurt

1. Adjust oven rack to middle position. Place fine-mesh strainer over large glass bowl, then set in larger bowl filled with ice water. Heat milk in large saucepan over medium-low heat (do not stir), until it registers 185 degrees. Remove from heat, gently stir in milk powder, and let cool to 160 degrees, 7 to 10 minutes. Strain milk through prepared strainer and let cool, stirring occasionally, until milk registers 110 to 112 degrees; remove from ice bath.

2. Gently stir ½ cup warm milk into yogurt until smooth. Stir yogurt mixture back into remaining milk. Cover tightly with plastic wrap and poke several holes in plastic. Place bowl in oven and turn on oven light, creating a warm environment of 100 to 110 degrees. Let yogurt sit until thickened and set, 5 to 7 hours. Transfer to refrigerator until completely chilled, about 3 hours.

3. Set clean fine-mesh strainer over large measuring cup and line with double layer of coffee filters. Transfer yogurt to strainer, cover with plastic, and refrigerate until about 2 cups of liquid drain out, 7 to 8 hours. Transfer strained yogurt to jar with tight-fitting lid, discarding drained liquid. Yogurt can be refrigerated for up to 1 week.

SKIMMING TIPS FOR SOUPS, STEWS, AND STOCKS

Defatting is a key step in making a perfect soup, stew, or stock, but it can also be difficult, messy, and frustrating. Try these tips for better skimming and degreasing.

A. Shift the Heat

Skimming fat from a simmering pot of soup or stock often means chasing it around a bubbling surface. To make this task easier, move the pot to one side of the burner so that only half has contact with the heat. The simmering bubbles on the heated side push the fat to the cooler side, making it easier to skim.

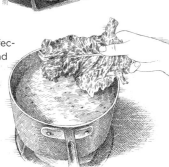

B. Lettuce Helper

Using a gravy separator to defat liquids is effective, but, admittedly, it's sometimes a pain and requires a special tool. And forget about using one to defat a chunky stew. But there's an easy alternative method that uses something you probably already have on hand. Just place a large lettuce leaf on the surface of the liquid in the pot; it will absorb excess fat, and then you can remove and discard it.

C. Cheesecloth Cleanup

Spooning fat off of cooled stocks or broths can be tricky if the fat layer is thin and breaks into tiny pieces. Use cheesecloth to solve the problem.

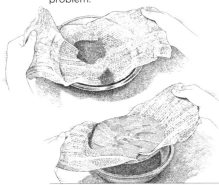

1. Cut a single layer of cheesecloth (or paper towel) to fit over the container of cooling stock or broth, with enough excess to drape over the sides. Place the cheesecloth so that it lies directly on top of the liquid and doesn't sink more than ¼ inch below the surface.

2. Refrigerate. Gather the edges of the cheesecloth and carefully lift to remove the hardened fat.

SPOONING OFF THE FAT

After sautéing sausage or bacon, it's often necessary to spoon off the fat before proceeding with the recipe. To get rid of the fat without removing the meat from the pan, use a pair of metal tongs to prop up one side of the skillet. Push the meat to the elevated part of the skillet and let it sit for a few moments so that the fat collects in the lower portion, where it can be easily spooned away.

EASY DEFATTING FOR PAN DRIPPINGS

No one looks forward to spooning that thin layer of liquid fat off the drippings from a roast before making a pan sauce or gravy. Yet if the fat remains, the sauce will be greasy. Here's a method that makes the process much faster and easier.

1. Deglaze the roasting pan, fat and all, and scrape up and dissolve the browned bits from the bottom of the pan, but stop short of reducing the liquid. Pour the brown, fatty liquid into a small mixing bowl (metal works best because it reacts quickly to changes in temperature), and set the bowl in an ice water bath.

2. After a few minutes, as the liquid cools, small bits of fat will solidify and rise to the surface. If you rock the inner bowl very gently to create a small wave of liquid moving around its perimeter, the fat will collect around the upper inside edge of the bowl, where it will be easy to remove.

MAKESHIFT FAT SEPARATOR

Try this novel way to remove fat from pan drippings before making a sauce or gravy.

1. Pour the pan drippings into a paper coffee cup and place the cup in the freezer. Once the fat has separated and begun to solidify on top, after about 10 minutes, poke a hole in the bottom of the cup with the tip of a skewer.

2. Let the defatted drippings run out through the hole until the fat reaches the bottom of the cup.

HEADLINING PAPER TOWEL SUBSTITUTE

Here's an economical, earth-friendly way to conserve paper towels and recycle newspapers: When you needs several layers of paper towels to absorb water or grease, spread out a few layers of newspaper and top them with a single layer of paper towels. The newspapers are wonderfully absorbent and much less expensive than paper towels.

4.10 TEMPERING AND TEMPING

CONTROL YOUR TEMPERING

Tempering—the process of gradually increasing the temperature of a heat-sensitive ingredient (such as eggs or dairy) with hot liquid to avoid breaking or curdling—usually requires a measuring cup and a steady hand. For a clever alternative, try a turkey baster. After sucking up hot liquid into the baster, you can control the speed at which it is mixed into the cool ingredient with a gentle squeeze. A baster is also easier to grasp than a full measuring cup while simultaneously whisking with the opposite hand.

POPPING THE SECRET OF OIL TEMPERATURE

Here's a trick that takes the guesswork out of determining when frying oil is hot: Simply place a kernel of popcorn in the oil as it heats up. The kernel will pop when the oil is between 350 and 365 degrees, just the right temperature for deep frying.

MESS-FREE MONITORING

When frying foods, it's important to keep an eye on the temperature of the oil. But if you use a splatter screen, it can get in the way of hooking a thermometer on the edge of the pot. Here's a solution: Poke a small hole at the edge of the screen and slip the arm of the thermometer through the hole. Now it's possible to prevent splatter and monitor the oil temperature at the same time.

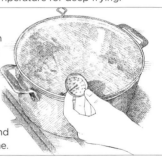

PROTECTING HANDS FROM POTS

Most instant-read thermometers come in a protective plastic sleeve with a metal clip (for clipping to aprons) that forms a loop at the very top. Use this clip and plastic sleeve to distance your hand from hot pots when taking a temperature.

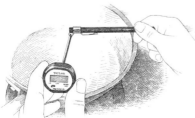

1. Slide the probe end of the thermometer into the loop at the tip of the clip.

2. Hold the end of the plastic sleeve to keep the thermometer upright, and then lower the probe into the food.

GETTING A READ ON SHALLOW LIQUIDS

Recipes with delicate or heat-sensitive ingredients often indicate the temperature at which the mixture should be taken off the heat. If you are cooking a small quantity, use this technique to get an accurate reading with an instant-read thermometer: Tilt the pan so that the liquid collects on one side, creating enough depth to get an accurate reading.

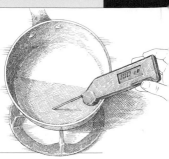

BIGGER THERMOMETER FOOTPRINT

If you have problems with your oven thermometer falling through the bars of your oven rack, try folding a sheet of aluminum foil around the base of the thermometer a few times to create a bigger "foot" so the device can sit on the rack without falling off.

DOUBLE-CHECKING YOUR OVEN

A properly calibrated oven is essential for ensuring consistent cooking results. If you don't have an oven thermometer, here's an easy method to test for accuracy using an instant-read thermometer. Set an oven rack to the middle position and heat your oven to 350 degrees for at least 30 minutes. Fill an ovenproof glass 2-cup measure with 1 cup of water. Using an instant-read thermometer, check that the water is exactly 70 degrees, adjusting the temperature as necessary. Place the cup in the center of the rack and close the oven door. After 15 minutes, remove the cup and insert the instant-read thermometer, making sure to swirl the thermometer around in the water to even out any hot spots. If your oven is properly calibrated, the water should be at 150 degrees (plus or minus 2 degrees). If the water is not at 150 degrees, then your oven is running too hot or too cold and needs to be adjusted accordingly. (Note: To avoid shattering the glass cup, allow the water to cool before pouring it out.)

RETRIEVING AN OVEN THERMOMETER

Oven thermometers are apt to fall off the rack and onto the oven floor. When this happens, use a pair of tongs to retrieve or reposition the thermometer. Tongs keep your hands a safe distance away from the hot rack while enabling dexterity that's not possible with your hand clad in an oven mitt.

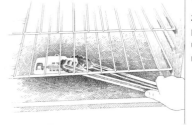

COOL CALIBRATION

It's important to calibrate your kitchen thermometer once in a while to make sure you're getting accurate readings. For dial-face thermometers, use the following technique.

1. Immerse the thermometer in a slurry of ice water (boiling temperature calibration is not necessary), being careful not to touch the container.

2. Using a pair of needle-nose pliers, adjust the screw on the underside of the dial face until it read 32 degrees.

Maple Cream

✓ **WHY THIS RECIPE WORKS:** Pure maple syrup is delicious, but sometime you want a condiment that's a little more substantial. Enter maple cream— all of the amazing flavor of maple syrup but with a thick, spreadable texture. All it takes is heat and some old-fashioned elbow grease to magically transform pure maple syrup into a thick, creamy spread. The challenge in making this treat lies in the beating of the cooled syrup, which requires strong arms, a sturdy grip, a resolute nature, and—if possible—a similarly equipped assistant to share stirring duties. Maple cream is a delicious topping for toast, biscuits, and waffles, and it's really good in a peanut butter sandwich. If your batch comes out a bit stiffer than you'd like, you can roll it into small balls and coat them with finely chopped nuts—instant confections, perfect for gift giving. Maple syrup is graded based on color. Do not use dark syrup here; it will not crystallize properly. This recipe makes about 2 cups.

3   cups maple syrup
¼   teaspoon vegetable oil (optional)
     Pinch salt (optional)

1. Set medium saucepan in bowl of ice and scatter more ice around sides of pan. Bring syrup, oil, if using, and salt, if using, to boil in second medium saucepan over medium heat and cook, without stirring, until syrup registers 235 degrees, 16 to 18 minutes. Quickly pour hot syrup into prepared saucepan and let cool, without stirring, until syrup registers 100 degrees, about 15 minutes.

2. Remove saucepan from ice bath and stir syrup vigorously with wooden spoon until it turns thick, pale, and opaque, about 30 minutes. Quickly transfer cream to jar with tight-fitting lid. Maple cream can be stored at room temperature or refrigerated for at least 2 months.

A SLICK SOLUTION FOR DOUGH

Working with high-hydration bread doughs that are extremely wet can be messy, especially when it comes to prying the sticky mass from the mixing bowl or food processor. Spraying both sides of a spatula with vegetable oil spray allows you to effortlessly scrape the dough from the container.

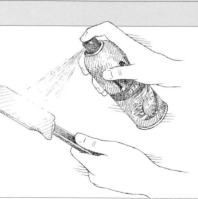

OFF THE HOOK

Lightly spraying the dough hook with vegetable oil spray before mixing bread dough prevents dough from edging up the hook and makes cleanup a breeze.

PREVENTING A STICKY SITUATION

Spraying plastic wrap with vegetable oil spray before using it to cover a bowl of rising dough is sometimes necessary to prevent sticking. But keeping the plastic from clinging to itself during spraying is a challenge. Here's one solution.

1. Drape the plastic over the bowl and spray it.

2. Quickly flip the plastic over so the sprayed side is facing the dough. Cover the bowl with the plastic.

A SOLUTION ON THE RISE

Covering dough while it rises prevents it from drying out. Plastic wrap is a standard choice, but you can also reuse bags from the produce section of the supermarket. The long bags easily cover a loaf pan, and they are food-safe.

PUTTING A LID ON YOUR DOUGH

Many bread recipes call for the rising dough to be covered with plastic wrap to prevent it from drying out and to protect it from drafts. For a more economical alternative, try a glass pot lid (tight-fitting is best, but any lid that covers the surface is fine). Just as with plastic wrap, the transparent lid allows you to gauge the dough's progress.

TRACKING DOUGH RISE

Not every baker owns a dough-rising bucket with markings for tracking the rise of dough, but any baker with a large, clear container can improvise one with this trick: After adding the dough to the container, mark its height by placing a rubber band around the container. This reference will make it easy to judge when the dough has doubled in volume.

KEEPING A RECORD OF RISES

To keep track of which step you're on when making a bread recipe that calls for several folds and rises, jot notes with a marker on the plastic wrap covering the bowl of rising dough.

BREAD SLASHER TIPS

Often when you slash the top of a loaf of bread prior to baking it, the blade will snag a bit of dough and drag it out of shape. To avoid this small annoyance, spray the blade lightly with vegetable oil spray so it will travel through the dough smoothly.

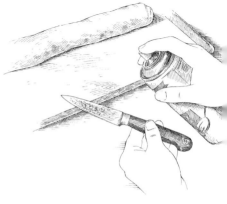

BREAD TIPS FOR EVERY CLIMATE

Changes in the weather can make it hard to get your bread dough to rise reliably. Here are some tips for adjusting your baking plan to suit your surroundings.

A. Microwave

When a chilly house makes it hard for bread or pizza to rise, look to your microwave for help.

1. Place a coffee mug filled with ½ cup water in the microwave. Run the microwave on high power for about 1 minute.

2. Open the microwave, push the cup to a back corner, and set the dough inside. Close the door and let the dough rise. (The warmed mug will keep the interior between 80 and 90 degrees for up to 90 minutes.) Remove the dough once it has doubled in size or reached the desired volume for your recipe.

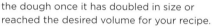

B. Dishwasher

To create a humid, draft-free environment in which bread dough can rise even in a dry, desert-like climate or a chilly house, use your dishwasher. Turn on the dishwasher for about 4 minutes, or long enough for some warm water to fill the bottom. Place the dough in a loaf pan or bowl, cover it with plastic wrap, set it on the bottom rack of the dishwasher, and close the door. Make sure to turn off the dishwasher; otherwise, the water will start to flow again once you close the door.

C. Insulated Cooler

In the winter, some kitchens get too chilly (less than 70 degrees) for bread dough to rise well. Use a cooler and this method for larger batches of bread.

1. Heat 1½ cups of water in a measuring cup in the microwave for 1 minute or until nearly simmering.

2. Place the cup of hot water and the dough in an insulated cooler. Close the lid and let the dough rise. (The hot water will keep the interior warm for up to 2 hours.) Remove the dough once it has doubled in size or reached the desired volume.

THE GOOD KIND OF BREAD MOLD

Try this trick to keep your loaves of bread in their long, narrow shape as they rise without using a mold.

1. Save the cardboard box from a spent roll of parchment paper or extra-wide aluminum foil or plastic wrap. Line the box with a lightly floured dish towel and place the shaped loaf inside, seam side down.

2. When the loaf has risen, gently roll it over onto a baking sheet or peel the towel off (keeping the bread seam side down again), then slash the loaf and bake it.

ONE PAN, TWO (OR EVEN THREE!) LOAVES

Pity the baker who owns a single loaf pan but whose bread recipe yields enough dough to make two loaves. Here's a unique—and very effective—way to bake both loaves. In testing, we found that this tip works particularly well with a Pyrex loaf pan matched with a Pyrex baking dish because their bottom edges share the same contours.

1. Place a single loaf pan across the center of a 13 by 9-inch baking dish.

2. Position one portion of shaped dough on either side of the loaf pan and bake. (You can even fill the loaf pan with a third portion of dough to bake three loaves.)

STRAIGHT-UP BREAD DOUGH

If you have trouble telling when your bread dough has properly risen inside a sloped bowl, try the following trick: Lightly spray a slow-cooker insert with vegetable oil spray. Place the dough in the insert and cover until it has risen. The straight sides and glass lid of the insert allow the baker to easily gauge the dough's progress.

WATCHING YOUR DOUGH

Baking suppliers sell special buckets that protect rising dough from drafts and have markings to show when dough has doubled in size, but these products can be expensive and difficult to find. You can use a clean, food-safe 5-quart clear plastic paint bucket from your local hardware store. It, too, has markings on the side so that you can easily track the dough's rise—and it's a fraction of the cost of a baker's bucket.

QUICK BREAD SLING

For extra assurance that your breads will release intact from their pans, try not only spraying the pan with vegetable oil spray, but also borrowing this classic technique for working with French pastry dough.

1. Make a sling for the loaf by laying long, wide strips of parchment paper across the length and width of the pan so that the paper overlaps the edges.

2. Use the overlap as a handy grip when it's time to remove the loaf from the pan.

OVERNIGHT BREAD COOLING

If you often bake bread in the evening, you may find that your loaves don't cool sufficiently before bedtime. Instead of wrapping a slightly warm loaf in plastic wrap (a method that yields a soggy crust) or leaving it out on a rack (an approach that can attract kitchen critters), take the following approach. Place the loaf on a wire rack and turn a large colander upside down over the loaf, allowing it to cool safely while preserving the crisp crust.

EASIER BREAD SLICING

Slicing a loaf of rustic bread freshly heated in the oven can be a hot and messy proposition: It's hard to get a hold on the bread, and the crumbs tend to spray everywhere. Here's a practical way to solve the problem.

1. Cut slices of bread about ¾ of the way down to the bottom crust before crisping the loaf in the oven.

2. Because the loaf is still intact, it is easy to transfer to a serving basket, and the slices can be torn apart at the table with minimal mess.

EVENLY SLICED BREAD

Slicing a boule of bread straight across like a sandwich loaf delivers smaller slices at the ends and bigger slices toward the middle. To create more even-size pieces, try cutting circular loaves in this unique pattern.

1. Slice away one end of the bread.

2. Rotate the bread one-quarter turn to the right and cut a slice.

3. Rotate the bread one-quarter turn to the left and slice again. Continue to rotate the bread after each cut.

BUILT-IN BREAD SLICING GUIDE

Try this tip for a shortcut to cutting evenly thick slices of homemade sandwich bread: Let the loaf cool on its side on an oven rack. The rack's bars leave subtle vertical indentations that act as a template for evenly spaced slices.

THE SIMPLEST WAY TO KEEP BREAD FRESH

Without preservatives to keep them tasting fresh, artisanal loaves can quickly taste stale. We've found that storing the bread cut side down on a cutting board works better than wrapping the loaf in paper or plastic. The crust will stay dry, while contact with the board will keep moisture inside the crumb.

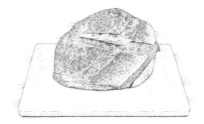

WELL-BALANCED CAKE BATTER

To ensure that you end up with equal amounts of batter in each pan when making layer cakes, use a kitchen scale to measure the weight of the filled pans.

PERFECT PARCHMENT LINING

When preparing parchment to line the bottom of a tube pan, the center tube can make it tricky to cut out that perfect "circle within a circle." Here's one foolproof technique.

1. Place the pan right side up and trace the outside perimeter.

2. Turn the pan upside down, place the parchment on top of the pan, and then place a measuring cup that fits the opening of the center hole right in the middle of traced circle, where the hole is. Use it as a guide to trace the center hole.

3. Fold the parchment into quarters and cut out the hole. Finally, cut out the circle.

COFFEE (FILTER) CAKE

To line an 8-inch cake pan when you're out of parchment paper, try a large (8- to 10-cup) basket-style paper coffee filter. Grease the pan, place the flattened filter in the bottom of the pan, spray it with vegetable oil spray, and pour in the cake batter. This substitution works perfectly, without any special trimming to make the coffee filter fit inside the pan.

EASIER CAKE REMOVAL

If you don't manage to get your cake out of its greased pan before it cools, it can be hard to coax it out. Make things easier by carefully running the cake pan over low heat on the stovetop, which melts the grease that was initially spread on the pan bottom. The cake will pop out easily when the pan is flipped over. This technique also works well for loosening stubborn Bavarians, flans, crèmes caramels, and muffins.

CAKE FLIP

Try this easy method for turning a cake out of an uncomfortably hot pan.

1. Place the cake pan on top of a large dish towel and top with an inverted plate.

2. Gather each corner of the towel and hold the ends together on the bottom of the plate. Gripping the towel tightly in one hand, lift the cake and the plate together.

3. Place your other hand on the bottom and gently invert the cake pan and plate onto the countertop. Lift off the pan to release the cake.

CRUMB-FREE CAKE LAYERS

When you cut a cake round in half for a layer cake, it can be tricky to keep the top layer intact upon removal. Here's a foolproof method to keep the layers neat.

1. Use masking tape to attach a 10-inch-wide piece of parchment paper to the nonserrated edge of a long serrated knife.

2. Cut the cake layer in half, dragging the paper through the cake as you cut.

3. Detach the tape from the knife, leaving the parchment between the cake layers. Lift up the cake to move it before frosting.

LAYERING IT ON

A rimless baking sheet easily slides between the cut halves of a cake round, allowing you to remove and then replace the delicate cake layers, unbroken, in order to frost the cake.

1. Slide the flat edge of the baking sheet between the top and bottom layers of a halved cake until the top half is fully on the sheet. Lift off the top layer and set aside.

2. Frost the bottom layer of the cake.

3. Slide the other round back on top, tilting the baking sheet and gently shimmying the cake off the flat end.

4.12 BAKING: CAKES

TIDIER CAKE FROSTING

After you line a cake pan, use the leftover parchment paper as a "bib" for protecting the cake plate when you frost the baked layers.

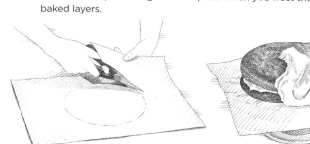

1. Use the bottom of a cake pan to trace a circle on a piece of parchment paper. Cut out the circle, to line the pan, and reserve the rest of the parchment.

2. When the cake is ready to frost, place it on a cake plate and arrange the reserved parchment around it like a bib. Discard the paper after frosting.

COOL DECORATING

Many frostings, such as butter-cream and ganache, soften as they warm up. This means that when you're piping designs with a pastry bag, warm hands can cause sloppy-looking decorations. To keep rosettes and borders perky, wear latex gloves—they'll help to insulate your hands and prevent your body heat from softening the frosting.

CONNECT-THE-DOTS FROSTING

When frosting a cake, the act of spreading can dislodge some of the crumbs, which then get incorporated into the frosting, muddying its smoothness. Here's how to minimize the problem.

1. Place large, evenly spaced dollops of frosting over the top of the cake.

2. Using an offset spatula, spread one dollop to another until the frosting is smooth and equally distributed.

CREATING A FROSTING-FILLING BARRIER

When a cake filling differs in color from the outer frosting, it often seeps through the frosting and mars the appearance of the cake. To prevent this from happening, follow this tip.

1. Fit a pastry bag with a plain round tip and fill it with the outer frosting. Pipe a circle of the frosting around the top edge of all the layers except the one that will form the top of the cake.

2. Spread the filling inside this frosting ring. The frosting ring will seal the layers of the cake together and prevent the filling from seeping out.

PERFECT CHEESECAKE IS IN THE BAG

Most cheesecake recipes call for wrapping a springform pan with aluminum foil before placing the cake in a water bath. The foil is meant to keep the water out, but sometimes water leaks in anyway and you wind up with an unappetizing, soggy crust. For a simple solution, place the filled springform pan in a large oven bag (the kind used for baking ham) and pull the bag up the sides of the pan, leaving the top surface of the cake exposed. When the wrapped pan is placed in a water bath, it's sure to stay dry.

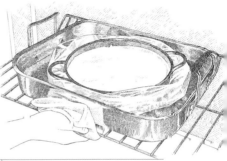

NO MORE SOGGY CHEESECAKE

After refrigerating a baked and cooled cheesecake, you may find that unwanted moisture collects on the top of the cake, ruining your creation. Fix this problem by arranging a layer of paper towels over the cheesecake before covering it with plastic wrap and refrigerating.

DRAINING A WATER BATH

Recipes for crème brûlée, cheesecake, and soufflé often call for a water bath, a technique where the ramekins or baking dish is placed in a large, shallow pan of warm water to ensure gentle, even baking. If you find that you've overfilled the pan with water, try this simple, splash-free remedy: Use a turkey baster to siphon off the excess.

TRICKS FOR PERFECT CUT-OUT COOKIES

Making rolled cookies is a holiday tradition for many cooks. Since these are often destined as gifts for friends and family, you want to make sure your goodies look their best. Here are a few tips to help you achieve cookie greatness.

A. Check for Bumps

Rolling dough to an even thickness is key. To check yours, try running a bench scraper lightly over the surface of the dough to feel for high and low points. This way, you know which area to correct with the rolling pin.

B. Roll in Place

If you like to use parchment paper to roll out your dough, try this method, which keeps the layers of parchment from moving around as you're rolling.

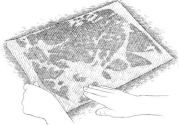

1. Sprinkle water on a clean surface and lay a sheet of waxed or parchment paper on top. The water will cling to the paper and hold it in place, creating a stick-free surface for the dough.

2. Place the dough on the paper and place another sheet on top. Roll out the dough and cut cookies; toss the paper for quick cleanup.

C. Reverse the Cut

When cookie cutters are used to create intricate shapes from a thin sheet of dough, transferring the shapes to a baking sheet with a spatula can distort or ruin their appearance. Try this clever method instead.

1. Roll the cookie dough out on a piece of parchment paper or on a nonstick baking liner, then use a cookie cutter to cut shapes. Transfer the filled parchment or baking liner to a baking sheet.

2. Use a small spatula to carefully remove the excess scraps of dough from around the shapes, leaving behind perfectly formed cookies.

SMART COOKIE SHAPING

Don't let the lack of a cookie scoop stand in the way of swiftly portioning cookie dough. Fill a quarter-cup measure (equal to 4 tablespoons) with dough and then divide it according to the desired size (e.g., halved for 2 tablespoons).

ENSURING PERFECTLY ROUND COOKIES

A. You can use cardboard paper towel rolls to store refrigerator cookie dough. Once you've formed the dough into a log, roll it in plastic wrap and slide the dough inside the cardboard (slit lengthwise) to protect it in the fridge and keep it perfectly round.

B. If you don't have a paper towel tube handy, try resting your rolled, wrapped dough on a bed of rice while chilling it in the fridge. The rice perfectly cradles the dough logs.

THUMBS-UP COOKIE SHAPING

While thumbprint cookies get their name from the digit that's used to make the jam-filled indentation, you can also use a clean rubber wine cork. It creates a perfect circle every time and keeps your hands clean.

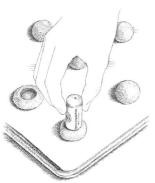

PEANUT BUTTER COOKIE SHORTCUT

Using a fork to make a cross-hatch pattern on the tops of peanut butter cookies is a two-step process. Here's a way to cut the work in half: Mark the cookies in one swipe with a perforated potato masher.

4.13 BAKING: COOKIES

SWEETER SUGAR-COATED COOKIES

Rather than rolling balls of gingersnap or sugar-cookie dough individually in sugar, fill a small plastic container with sugar, then place the dough balls in the container and secure the lid. After a gentle shake, remove the lid to reveal dough balls that are completely coated in sugar.

COOKIE REAL ESTATE RULES

Many types of cookies, including sugar cookies, spread on the baking sheet as they bake. If the balls of dough are placed too closely together on the sheet, they'll run into each other and fuse when they spread in the oven, resulting in cookies with odd shapes and soft edges. To give each cookie a little extra space without severely limiting the number of cookies baked in a batch, arrange them as follows: Instead of placing the dough balls in neat rows of three or four so that all the cookies line up, alternate the rows. For example, three cookies in the first row, two in the second, three in the third, two in the fourth, and so on.

TAKING YOUR BAKING SHEETS FOR A TWIRL

Often when you have two sheets of cookies in the oven at once, the recipe will direct you to reverse them from front to back and top to bottom. But it can be a challenge to keep track of the required movements. Simplify things by lining your baking sheets with parchment paper and marking the front edge of the paper, even indicating which pan starts on top and which on the bottom. The notation will help you keep track of which edge goes where when you reverse the pans' positions.

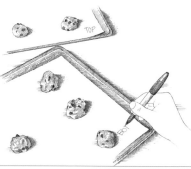

A CLEAN SLICE AND BAKE

With a roll of homemade cookie dough in the freezer, you can have warm, fresh cookies any time. Slicing through the frozen roll, however, can be a chore, as the knife often drags, making sloppy cuts and producing misshapen cookies. Minimize the sticky knife problem by dipping the blade in flour after every couple of cuts.

DROP COOKIE STOCKPILING

Stock your freezer with ready-to-bake drop cookies so you can have one or more delicious fresh cookies in just a few minutes.

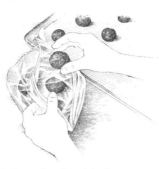

1. Scoop out or roll individual balls of cookie dough and place them on a baking sheet lined with parchment or waxed paper. Place the cookie sheet in the freezer for an hour or two, until the dough balls are completely frozen.

2. Once the dough balls are frozen hard, transfer them to a zipper-lock bag for storage in the freezer. There is no need to defrost the dough balls before baking them; just increase the baking time by a minute or two.

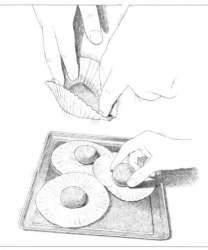

A TOAST—TO COOKIES!

Even in the middle of a hot summer, sometimes you want a freshly baked cookie. Skip the big, hot oven and the mess of baking sheets and parchment paper by scaling things down in your toaster oven with paper muffin-tin liners and cookie dough from the freezer.

1. Flatten three or four paper muffin-tin liners on a toaster-oven baking sheet.

2. Place a frozen ball of dough on each liner and bake the cookies as usual.

MAKING SUGAR STICK

Here's a trick for keeping the colored sugar from falling off your decorated holiday cookies: Using a spray bottle (a plant mister works well), spritz the cookies with a light coating of water. Then sprinkle on the colored sugar.

COOKIE DECORATING FROM THE RECYCLING BIN

After washing and drying them well, you can use yogurt containers with plastic snap-on lids to store cookie-decorating supplies such as colored sugars and sprinkles. Take their use one step further by turning them into shakers.

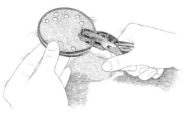

1. Punch holes in the lids with a paper hole-punch. Fill the clean containers with decorations.

2. Replace the lids and invert the containers to sprinkle decorations onto frosted cookies.

FROSTED COOKIE HIGH-RISE

A tin of colorful frosted cookies makes a nice gift around the holidays. But before the cookies can be wrapped, the frosting has to dry thoroughly, and it can be a real challenge to find enough space to spread out a few dozen cookies in a cramped kitchen. Create extra space by pressing some paper plates and cups into service.

1. Coat the rim of a small paper cup with frosting and invert it onto the middle of a paper plate. Arrange as many drying cookies around the cup as will fit comfortably on the plate. Dab the exposed rim with frosting, then make another plate in the same manner and stack it on top of the first.

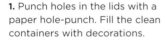

2. Repeat until you have a stack of four or five cookie-laden plates.

QUICK-DRYING BISCOTTI

Traditionally, biscotti dough is baked in a log and then cut into slices to be baked a second time, and flipped halfway through the baking time to dry both sides of each slice. Streamline this process by laying the slices on a wire cooling rack set in a baking sheet, then placing them in the oven. The rack elevates the slices, allowing air to circulate all around, drying both sides at once.

CAR CRUSH

Crushing vanilla wafers or other cookies for a recipe can get laborious if done by hand. Here's an easier way: Take the whole, unopened box of cookies and use a skewer to poke a couple of small holes through the sealed box (and the plastic bag on the inside) to release the pressure. Then drive your car right over the box and presto—instant crumbs.

SUPER SLICING SECRETS

Neatly cutting brownies or bar cookies can be tricky. Crumbs stick to the knife, the treats end up with jagged edges, and knives aren't shaped to make clean, straight cuts. Here are a few tricks for solving these problems.

A. Choosing Plastic

Instead of using a serrated or chef's knife to cut brownies, try a sturdy plastic knife. It glides easily through even the stickiest bars, picking up no crumbs.

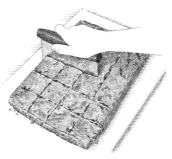

B. Scoring First

Although it might try your patience, you shouldn't cut into your brownies until they've had time to cool. To make them easier to cut, try using a sharp knife to score the bars as soon as the pan comes out of the oven. This will make it easier to cut clean, even pieces along the scored lines when the bars have cooled.

C. Going to the Bench (Scraper)

Bench scrapers are used primarily by bakers to divide masses of unbaked dough or to scrape flour and dried dough off their work surfaces. However, this tool, which is wider than most spatulas, is also very useful for cutting and neatly serving bar cookies.

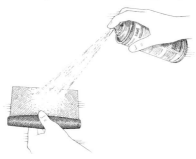

1. Spray both sides of a bench scraper with vegetable oil spray.

2. Push the blade into the brownies, spacing the cuts evenly. When all the pieces are cut, slide the wide blade under the pieces to lift them up and out.

SIMPLE CHOCOLATE-COATED SWEETS

Try this easy way to give bar cookies a chocolate topping without having to use a double boiler or the microwave to melt the chocolate.

1. When the cookies come out of the oven, lay chocolate bars directly on top of the pan contents.

2. Once the chocolate bars have melted, use a butter knife or an offset spatula to spread the chocolate.

3. Continue spreading until the chocolate makes a thin, even layer over the entire top of the cookies.

4.14 BAKING: MUFFINS

CLEANER BATTER POURING

Here's a way to prevent the gunky buildup around the lip of the liquid measuring cup used to portion pancake, muffin, and cupcake batter: Spritz vegetable oil spray along the cup's edge so batter slides out cleanly.

SPRINKLING STREUSEL NEATLY

No matter how carefully you sprinkle streusel onto a batch of muffins, you probably still end up with a mess all over the muffin tins and counter. To contain the crumbs, cut out the bottom of an empty 6-ounce yogurt container to create a funnel. The topping falls perfectly into place.

AVOIDING SOGGY MUFFIN BOTTOMS

Solve the common problem of soggy bottoms in fruit muffins by following this advice: Before adding fruit to the batter, spoon a table-spoon of plain batter into each greased or lined muffin cup. Stir the fruit into the remaining batter, then divide among the muffin cups.

GETTING A GRIP ON MINI MUFFIN TINS

Miniature muffin tins are usually fitted with a rim that is too tiny to grasp with bulky oven mitts. Avoid this struggle by leaving one corner cup empty when you fill the tin. Now you have a place to insert your thumb, allowing you to remove the tin without getting burned or squishing any of the muffins.

LIBERATING TRICKY MUFFINS

Just-baked muffins can be difficult to dislodge from the pan; they can stick or, if they are top heavy, break in half. Try tilting the muffin pan on its side and then slowly removing the muffins. They will slide out more easily and in one piece. If they still stick, try using a curved grapefruit knife to gently free the bottom of the muffin from the cup.

PASTRY BAG POINTERS

A. Pastry Bag Stand

It's always easier to fill a pastry bag when it is propped up and open. For an unusual accessory in this job, try an empty Pringles potato chips can. A Pringles can is the ideal size and shape, and if you fold an inch or two of the bag over the rim of the can, the bag remains perfectly stable. A tall beer glass will also work.

B. Backup Pastry Bag

You can easily make extra make-shift pastry bags when your canvas pastry bag is dirty or already filled.

1. Snip away one corner of a 1-gallon zipper-lock bag. (A freezer bag is preferable, as it can withstand the pressure needed to pipe the bag's contents.) Make a small cut so just the end of the pastry tip will be exposed.

2. Insert the pastry tip through the hole. Fill the bag and pipe as usual.

C. Maximum Extraction

To make sure you get every last bit out of your pastry bag, lay the bag flat on the countertop and gently press a rolling pin toward the tip, pushing the contents to the bottom of the bag where they can be easily piped.

MAKESHIFT PASTRY CUTTER

A stiff wire whisk can sub in if you don't have a pastry cutter on hand. Tilt the bowl and hold the whisk at an angle to cut the butter into the flour.

GIVING PASTRY THE BRUSH-OFF

When you're rolling out pastry dough, excess flour often clings to the dough, lending an unpleasant, floury taste and texture to the finished product. Extra flour can also make the pastry tough if it gets worked into the dough. To avoid this, use a clean pastry brush to sweep excess flour off the surface of your dough.

PIE-DOUGH SPRITZER

Anyone who makes pie dough has faced the problem of dough that is too dry and crumbly when it's time to roll it out. Mixing in more water with a spoon or spatula can overwork the dough and make the crust tough, so try using a spray-bottle full of ice water to distribute just the right amount.

TWO COOL TRICKS FOR ROLLING OUT PIE DOUGH

Pie and tart doughs can't take the heat: In order to bake up flaky, the fat in the dough must stay cool, which is problematic, since working the dough warms it up. Here are two methods for keeping it cool.

A. Chill the Counter

1. While the dough is chilling in the refrigerator, fill two 1-gallon zipper-lock bags halfway with ice and lay them on the counter for 20 minutes.

2. When ready to roll out the dough, remove the ice bags and wipe any condensation from the surface. Work quickly with the dough in the cold space as directed in the recipe.

B. Canvas the Area

1. Cut a sheet of cotton canvas (available at fabric stores) into a 16-inch square; launder and dry. Fold the canvas, place it in a zipper-lock bag, and freeze.

2. When you're ready to use it, unfold the canvas and lay it on the countertop, sprinkle it with flour, and place the dough on top to roll.

INSTANTLY FLATTER COUNTERTOPS

Tile countertops may look attractive, but they are not especially practical when it comes to baking. To avoid rumpled pie dough (not to mention a floury mess in the cracks between tiles), place a flexible cutting board over the tile countertop to create a smoother surface.

PERFECT PIE CRUST CHEATS AND SHORTCUTS

Smoothly rolling pie dough into an even circle requires deft hands and experience. Use these tricks to make the process less daunting.

A. Stop, Trace, and Roll

To make sure your dough is the right size, make a template with parchment paper and a pencil.

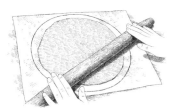

1. Place a 12-inch skillet lid on a sheet of parchment paper. Using a pencil, trace a circle around the lid.

2. Roll out a disk of lightly floured dough on the parchment, using the tracing as a guide and stopping when the dough reaches the line.

B. Put a Bowl on It

To create as perfect a circle as possible before your pie dough goes into the pan, minimizing the need for trimming in the pan, try this trick.

1. Roll the dough into an 11-inch round. Place a 10-inch-wide bowl on top and trim around the edge.

2. Finish rolling the circle into the desired size (the dough will be thin but sturdy enough to transfer to a pie plate).

C. Tape Recording

Rather than pulling out a ruler every time you roll out a pie crust during busy baking times like the holidays, use masking tape to create a 12-inch square on your countertop to use as a guide for rolling out a 12-inch crust.

D. Take It to the Mat

Try placing a nonstick silicone mat underneath the parchment paper when rolling out pie dough to keep the dough in place for smooth, stable rolling.

QUICKER DOUGH WRAPPING

While preparing batches of pie dough for the holidays, we discovered a time-saving trick that keeps our hands and the counter clean: Once the dough is mixed, transfer it directly from the bowl to a large zipper-lock bag. Shape the dough into a disk through the outside of the bag, and chill until ready to use.

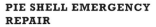

PIE SHELL EMERGENCY REPAIR

Rather than throw away pie dough trimmings, save the scraps for patchwork. If there are any cracks or holes after prebaking a pie shell, patch them with the leftover dough, pressing it into place, and then finish baking according to the recipe.

IN-A-PINCH PIE PLATE

If you find yourself short a pie plate, a seasoned cast-iron skillet can make the perfect alternative. (Make sure the skillet is 9 or 10 inches in diameter to keep the volume and baking times consistent with the recipe.)

PERFECT PIE CRUST FOR JUST PENNIES

We prefer ceramic or metal pie weights to those old standbys, rice and beans. If you don't have any of these, you can improvise by emptying the contents of your penny jar into an aluminum foil liner. The pennies lie flat and conduct heat beautifully.

SUPER-EFFICIENT PIE WEIGHTS

To streamline your pie-baking process, store your pie weights (or beans or rice used for the same purpose) in a doubled-up ovensafe cooking bag that can be used again and again. Because the bag can be lifted in and out of the pie plate, there's no need to line it with foil or transfer the weights from their storage container to the pie plate and back again.

A NEW USE FOR COFFEE FILTERS

When you need to blind-bake a pie shell, try using a large basket-type coffee filter to contain the pie weights.

LAZY COOK'S LATTICE

If you need a little help making clean, even strips for your lattice-top pie, try this foolproof tip.

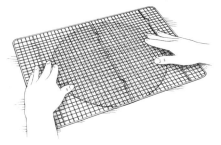

1. Roll out the dough and then lightly press the top of a cooling rack into the dough.

2. Use the indentations as a guide to cut the dough into 1¼-inch strips with a pizza wheel.

FOOLPROOF LATTICE TOP TRANSFER

Fragile strips of dough for lattice pies or tarts often break when they are transferred from the counter to the pie. Here's a way to make this delicate task easier.

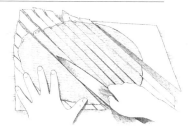

1. Transfer the dough, still on parchment paper, to a cutting board. Using a sharp knife or a pizza cutter, cut through the dough and parchment paper to form strips. (If the dough is too soft to cut, place it in the freezer until firm, about 5 minutes.)

2. Using the parchment paper to lift the dough, transfer the strips to the top of the pie, gently pulling the paper away.

REMOVING TART PAN RINGS

To free a baked tart from the ring of its pan, set a wide, stout can, such as a 28-ounce tomato can, on a flat surface and set the cooled tart and pan on top of the can. Hold the pan ring and gently pull it downward—the can will support the pan base with the tart as you remove the ring.

NO MORE SHRINKING PIZZA DOUGH

Try this clever trick to keep pizza dough from shrinking back as you roll it out.

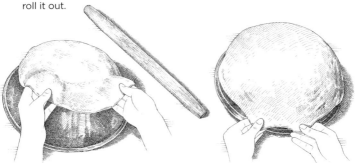

1. Roll the dough into a 6-inch disk and place it on an over-turned mixing bowl that has been lightly dusted with flour.

2. Gently pull the edges of the dough downward, stretching it over the bowl until it is the desired size.

DUSTING WITH BREAD CRUMBS

If you run out of cornmeal while making pizza, you can dust the surface of your pizza peel with finely ground bread crumbs, which work just as well: They keep the dough from sticking, do not burn, and have a neutral flavor.

HANDLING GRILLED PIZZA EASILY

Once the toppings on a grilled pizza are heated through, it is important to remove the pizza from the grill swiftly to make sure that the crust does not burn. For many grill cooks, though, that is more easily said than done, as the pizza can be difficult to maneuver intact with tongs or a spatula. Here's a trick that helps: Using a splatter screen or rimless baking sheet as a pizza peel. Don an oven mitt on one hand to hold the "peel" and use tongs or a spatula with the other hand to slide the pizza onto the peel.

THE BEST SLICE

If you crave the long, foldable slices typical of New York City pizzerias, not the 6-inch-long pieces produced by making multiple cuts through the center of a round pizza, you can achieve floppy perfection with a few quick adjustments.

1. Instead of forming a 13-inch round on the pizza peel, stretch the dough into an oblong shape. Bake as directed.

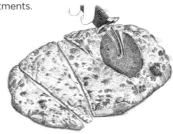

2. Slice the pizza using a zigzag pattern across the width of the pie.

SOAK-AHEAD WOOD CHUNKS

Try this trick to make sure soaked wood chunks are always ready when you are. Soak as many chunks as you like at the same time. Drain the chunks, seal them in a zipper-lock bag, and store them in the freezer. When ready to grill, place the frozen chunks on the grill. They defrost quickly and impart as much flavor as freshly soaked chunks.

WOODEN SKEWERS AT THE READY

Soak wooden skewers ahead of time and store them in the freezer so you can have them on hand and ready to go when you want to throw them on the grill.

CHARCOAL PREP

Hoisting a huge bag of charcoal to pour some into a chimney starter can be messy and difficult, especially when you are dressed nicely for a summer dinner party. To get around this sloppy situation, try this tip.

1. When you first bring home the sack, divide the briquettes into smaller bags, about 4 quarts (50 briquettes) to a bag.

2. When you need to build a fire, just cut a hole in the bottom of a small bag, and the charcoal flows right into the chimney.

USING THE EMPTY CHARCOAL BAG

Instead of using old newspapers to light a chimney starter, save the empty bags from your charcoal briquettes to light your next fire.

1. Cut or tear the bag (separating the layers of paper) into pieces small enough to fit in the bottom of a chimney starter.

2. Stuff a few pieces of the bag in the bottom of the chimney and light. The charcoal residue on the bag will help it stay lit.

HOT TIPS FOR GRILL LIGHTING

Lighting up a charcoal grill can be a tricky business, even with a chimney starter to help you. Here are a few tips for getting your charcoal grill started quickly and efficiently in a variety of circumstances.

A. Egg Carton

For a quick light, use a cardboard egg carton. Place the empty carton in the kettle, stack up to 3 quarts of briquettes on top of it, and then light the cardboard to start the flame, adding more briquettes once the first batch is lit. The coals light quickly and evenly, without the need for a chimney. Rearrange the hot coals as needed.

B. Potato Chips

Here's a grill-lighting method that is also a great way to use up stale potato chips. Arrange 2 cups of plain potato chips in a coffee filter and place the filter in the bottom of a charcoal grill. Place a chimney starter on top of the chips, fill the chimney with charcoal, and light the chips. The greasy chips burn slowly, igniting the charcoal with ease.

C. Self-Starting Charcoal

A chimney starter is practically foolproof, but just to make absolutely sure that it will get the job done on a cold or windy day, try the following trick. Place four or five briquettes of self-starting charcoal at the bottom of the chimney, then fill the balance with hardwood charcoal. By using just a handful of self-starting briquettes, you're guaranteed both a quick start and food without the acrid taste that comes from using self-starting charcoal exclusively.

D. Paper Towel Roll

Use your recycling to help light a chimney starter on a blustery day.

1. Place wads of crumpled newspaper underneath the chimney starter and set the chimney starter on the grill grate. Hold an empty paper towel roll in the center of the chimney starter and surround it with briquettes.

2. Light the newspaper. The paper towel roll encourages air to flow up through the briquettes, carrying the flames upward for efficient ignition.

WINDPROOF FIRE STARTING

Anyone who enjoys grilling well into autumn knows how frustrating it can be to light a grill or chimney full of charcoal on a blustery fall day. Instead of using a match or lighter, you can get the fire going with a small butane torch (the kind used for caramelizing crème brûlée).

REMINDER TO TURN OFF THE GAS

Make sure you remember to turn off the gas tank after grilling with this simple trick. Jog your memory by slipping a rubber band around the knob of the gas tank. When you turn the tank on, place the rubber band around your wrist, and only remove it when you turn the tank off. As long as you're wearing the rubber band, you know that the tank is on.

A BETTER WAY TO GREASE THE GRILL

If you find yourself out of paper towels, you can use standard coffee filters to oil your grill grate. The sturdy filter paper is less apt to tear or leave behind fuzz, and—since it's less absorbent than paper towels—you can get the job done using less oil.

RAKED ACROSS THE COALS

Arranging lit coals in a grill with a pair of long-handled tongs requires patience: The tongs can only grasp one or two coals at a time. Try using a handheld metal garden rake to arrange the coals as desired.

KEEPING GRILL PLATTERS WARM

When you're barbecuing on a gas grill, the flat lid of the grill is an ideal spot to warm a serving platter. The heated platter can then be used for serving foods right away or for keeping meat warm as it rests before carving. Make sure to handle the platter with potholders.

CHECK YOUR LEVELS

It's a huge pain to run out of propane halfway through grilling. If your grill doesn't have a gas gauge, use this technique to estimate how much gas is left in the tank. Boil a cup of water and pour it over the side of the tank. Feel the metal with your hand. Where the water has succeeded in warming the tank, it is empty; where the tank remains cool to the touch, there is still propane inside.

CHAPTER 5

HACKS
IN AND OUT OF THE
KITCHEN

Supervision May Be Required!

TURBO-POWERED PEPPER GRINDER

At one time or another, many cooks face the task of seasoning a huge quantity of meat with salt and ground black pepper while preparing for a large dinner party or big outdoor barbecue. Instead of wearing out your arm peppering 16 pounds of beef with a hand-operated grinder, try using a cordless power driver/drill to motorize the pepper mill. Two tips make the whole operation run smoothly: First, make sure the driver/drill is scrupulously clean. Second, use only the slower driver settings—the higher speed settings might overheat the pepper mill.

1. Unscrew the finial at the top of the mill to reveal the tip of the square shaft that runs down the center.

2. Insert the shaft into the chuck of a power driver/drill and off you go. Changing the tension in the connection between shaft and driver/drill controls the grind size, from fine to coarse.

HARDWARE STORE NUTCRACKER

A pair of curved-jaw locking pliers are the perfect tool for cracking hard-shelled nuts (especially walnuts). The adjustable rounded jaws can accommodate nuts of almost any shape or size, and the grip is strong enough to break through the hardest shell, leaving the tender flesh intact.

ONIONS IN THE MIST

When browning small amounts of onion, there's a tendency for drying and scorching, even if you use a high-quality pan. Keep small batches of onions moist with a plant mister, spritzing them lightly if they start to look dry. The water not only helps them caramelize evenly but also deglazes any flavorful browned bits (fond) stuck to the bottom of the pan.

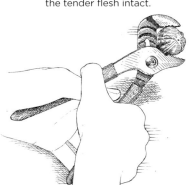 

PUTTING DOWN ROOTS

Keep root vegetables such as ginger, carrots, and beets usable for several months with this trick.

1. Fill a plastic container or clay pot with clean, dry sand. Bury the root vegetables in the sand, and store the container in a dark, cool cupboard or in the refrigerator.

2. When you're ready to use a vegetable, just brush off the sand and peel.

PERFECT CHERRIES—NAILED IT!

Here's a cheap, clever way to pit cherries without a specialized tool.

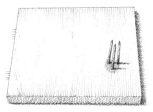

1. Drive three clean stainless-steel nails close together through a piece of clean, thin scrap wood in a triangle.

2. Gently push a cherry down onto the sharp tips of the nails to extract the pit. Entry and exit wounds are minimal.

HANDLING A HAM WITH A HACKSAW

A country ham's large size makes it unwieldy to cook, especially because the ham should be simmered in a stockpot before being roasted. To get around this problem, use a hacksaw to remove the hock end of the ham. The ham should then fit into a large stockpot or roasting pan. Save the hock for use in cooking beans or greens, or for making soup.

ALTERNATIVE TURKEY TOOL

If cutting the backbone out of a turkey or chicken to butterfly it is too much for your kitchen shears or knives, try a clean (or new) pair of garden clippers. After cutting the bird's skin with a knife, use the sturdy blades of the clippers to cut through the bones and wing tips.

5.1 GARAGE AND GARDEN SHED COOKING TRICKS

CLEVER CLEAVER SUBSTITUTE

If you don't have a meat cleaver or the heavy chef's knife or kitchen shears required for hacking up meat, you can make do with a new hatchet from the hardware store. Not only is this an excellent substitute, but it also costs under $10.

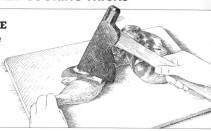

PASTRY TOOLBOX

Baking buffs know how quickly all the necessary tools of the trade can overtake limited space in their kitchen drawers. Avoid this problem by storing your baking gadgets (cookie cutters, icing spatulas, measuring cups, and the like) in an inexpensive plastic toolbox, purchased from a hardware store.

HARDWARE PIE

If you can't find your pie weights next time you're baking a pie (or if you just don't own any), improvise with a handful of nails, bolts, and screws. Placed on top of the aluminum foil on the dough, they work just as well as fancy weights. They will get very hot in the oven, however, so be careful when removing them.

MAKE ANY BOWL A NONSLIP BOWL

To keep bowls from slipping in the test kitchen, we usually set the bowl on top of a damp cloth. For a more permanent solution, apply rubber coating (the kind used to coat the handles of tools, available in hardware stores) to bowls that tend to run away. To create a nonskid surface on the bottom of a slippery bowl, dip its bottom in rubber coating. (Do not put the coated bowl in the dishwasher.)

INSTANT ICE WATER FOR PASTRY

A plant mister is a terrific device for distributing a minimal amount of water evenly over a mixture of fat and flour when making pie dough. Fill a mister bottle with about ¼ cup water and store it on its side in the freezer. When making pastry, just grab the bottle from the freezer and fill it with cold water, which quickly chills even further upon contact with the ice.

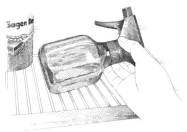

5.1 GARAGE AND GARDEN SHED COOKING TRICKS

OFFSET SPATULA SUBSTITUTE

If you're unwilling to pay premium kitchenware-store prices for a large offset icing spatula, try a large offset palette knife with a flexible blade from the hardware store, which is normally used for mixing small amounts of paint or Spackle. The knife works almost as well as an icing spatula, and it costs only a fraction as much. Palette knives can also be purchased at art supply stores.

CHOCOLATE CHISEL

Instead of using a knife to break apart chocolate or frozen liquids, consider keeping a cheap chisel from the local hardware store on hand. The chisel's sturdy edge does a better job—and keeps your knives' sharp, delicate edges out of harm's way. Place the chisel on chocolate or ice, angled away from you. Using short, quick strokes, chip into pieces of desired size.

TORCH YOUR DESSERT

Crème brûlée aficionados already know that you can use a toolshed butane torch instead of a little kitchen torch to get a faster and more crispy caramelized sugar layer on that classic dessert, but you can also get more from your torch by using it to brown already-baked meringue-topped pies, tartlets, and cakes.

WATERING YOUR PANS IN THE OVEN

Putting boiling water into a pan in the oven when baking bread helps achieve the desired crust. Unfortunately, this can lead to scalding or burning yourself if you are not careful. Try using a copper (not plastic) watering can with a long spout to solve this problem. This method also works perfectly when adding water to a bain-marie.

THE RULES OF REDUCING

While some cooks are comfortable eyeballing it when reducing liquid for a sauce, jam, or jelly, others like more precision. If you're in the latter group, a stainless-steel ruler can help. Simply dip the ruler into the pot to measure the initial level of the liquid, then check periodically to determine when it has reduced to the desired point. The ruler is cheap, heatproof, easy to clean, and reusable.

5.1 GARAGE AND GARDEN SHED COOKING TRICKS

FOLLOW THE RULER FOR PERFECT COOKIES

For the best-looking cookies, it's important to start with balls of dough that are all the same size. In order to get an accurate measurement, set a ruler on top of the mixing bowl. Rather than placing the ball of dough on top of the ruler (where it's hard to measure the equator), bring the ball up along the side of the ruler.

HANDLING HOT PANS

Pulling a hot baking sheet out of the oven while wearing oven mitts can be tricky, sometimes resulting in smushed cookies. Try putting curved-jaw locking pliers to work in your kitchen instead. Use the pliers to latch onto metal baking sheets (or other bakeware without handles) and then slide the sheets out of the oven.

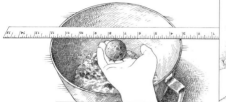

TAKING THE GUESSWORK OUT OF MEASURING

After a few cycles in the dishwasher, the size markings on plastic measuring cups can rub away, but your toolbox can help: With an electric drill fitted with a very thin bit (⅛ or ¹⁄₁₆ inch), drill holes in the cup handles to indicate volume—four holes for the quarter cup, three for the third, and two for the half. (The full cup is hard to misidentify.)

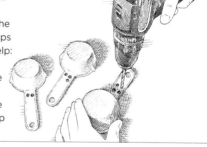

CORRALLING KITCHEN TWINE

Kitchen twine can be unwieldy to unravel, and the roll often gets dirty in the process. Keep yours clean by assembling one of these home-made dispensers.

A. Flowerpot

Stand a roll of twine upright on a saucer, then cover it with an overturned clay flowerpot.

1. Feed the twine through the hole in the bottom of the pot, pulling out as much as you need for each use.

2. Snip at the desired length.

B. Glass Jar

A simple glass jar can also keep kitchen twine from falling off the counter and unraveling in a mess. Using a hammer and nail or an ice pick, punch a hole through the center of the tin lid of a glass jar. Then place the ball of twine inside the container and thread the end through the hole in the lid.

STEEL WOOL COASTER

Store wet steel-wool scrub pads on an unpainted terra-cotta planter base to avoid getting rust all over the countertop. The clay material absorbs any water that drips off the used pad, and the pad stays rust-free.

A DIFFERENT KIND OF KITCHEN KNIFE

Removing stubborn caked-on food from stovetops or counters often requires scrubbing with steel wool or harsh cleaners, both of which can scratch delicate kitchen surfaces. Instead, grab a plastic putty knife. Its flexible edge gives you just enough leverage to pry off the stuck-on food without damaging the surface underneath.

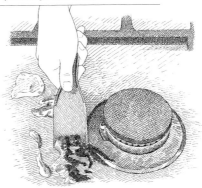

WELDER'S BRUSH GOES GRILLING

Thoroughly cleaning a grill grate while it's still hot is recommended to keep foods from sticking. A welder's brush, which can be purchased for a mere $2 at a hardware store, has a long wooden handle attached to a wire brush, just like those grill brushes that cost 10 times as much. Its long wires and narrow design allow for deep scrubbing between the bars on the cooking grate.

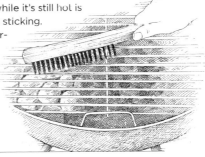

BRICKS ON THE GRILL

Butterflied chicken on the grill cooks faster and more evenly when weighed down, and a brick has the perfect size, shape, and inexpensive price tag for the job. Just set a rimmed baking sheet on top of the chicken and put two bricks in the pan, or place two aluminum foil–wrapped bricks directly on the bird.

5.1 GARAGE AND GARDEN SHED COOKING TRICKS

DRESSED TO GRILL

Grilling requires a lot of equipment. To keep everything at the ready and easy to find, and keep your hands free at the same time, try accessorizing with a carpenter's tool belt. Slip everything from grill brushes to your timer to a thermometer into its pockets and loops.

DRAINING WOOD CHIPS OUTDOORS

Soaking wood chips or chunks in water prevents them from burning too quickly on the hot coals. Rather than making a trip into the kitchen for a colander to drain soaked chips, use a clean, perforated flowerpot that you can store outside with your grilling tools. Dump the soaked chips into the flowerpot, allowing the water to drain out the bottom.

CHIMNEY STARTER PLATE

Many barbecue recipes require fresh, hot coals added midway through cooking to maintain the grill's temperature. However, that means finding a safe place for firing up coals in a chimney when the grill is already occupied. Here's an unusual solution: an unglazed terra-cotta flowerpot saucer. (Just make sure the saucer doesn't have a drainage hole.) The porous clay withstands the chimney's heat, and the saucer's lip catches ashes. (Always place the saucer on a concrete or stone surface away from flammable materials.)

LET THERE BE LIGHT!

Early- or late-season grillers (and diehards who grill through the winter months) often find themselves grilling the evening meal in the dark. In the absence of a well-placed outdoor light, try a camping headlamp (also known as a spelunker's or miner's light). This contraption not only allows you to point the light directly where you're looking but also keeps your hands free for cooking purposes.

5.2 SURPRISING KITCHEN-BATHROOM CROSSOVERS

BERRY DRYER

Instead of waiting around for strawberries or other fruits to dry before dipping them in melted chocolate, lay the just-washed berries on paper towels and blast them with a hair dryer turned to the "no heat" setting.

SALON TREATMENT FOR YOUR SALMON

Use a hair dryer to remove moisture from the skin of fish before frying it. That way, when you put the fish in the pan, the oil doesn't pop and splatter onto the stovetop, and you don't have to worry about getting burned.

STYLING CAKES

Professionally decorated cakes seem to have a molten, silky look. To get that same appearance at home, frost as usual and then use a hair dryer to "blow-dry" the frosted surface of the cake. The slight melting of the frosting gives it that smooth, lustrous appearance.

SHAVING CHOCOLATE

If chocolate is too hard, it can be difficult to pull off thick shavings to decorate a cake or pudding. Even if you do cut off nice shavings, warmth from your fingers can cause the pieces to melt as you try to place them on the dessert. Here's how to avoid both problems: Warm a block of bittersweet or semisweet chocolate by sweeping a hair dryer over it, taking care not to melt the chocolate. Holding a paring knife at a 45-degree angle against the chocolate, scrape toward you, anchoring the block with your other hand. Pick up the shavings with a toothpick and place them on the dessert.

BETTER BUTTER BLOW-OUT

To soften butter quickly for creaming, cut the butter into large cubes, place the cubes in the bowl of a stand mixer and, with the mixer running, use a hair dryer to direct hot air into and around the mixing bowl until the butter just begins to soften.

5.2 SURPRISING KITCHEN-BATHROOM CROSSOVERS

NO-STICK PROPOSITION

Weary of battling with stuck-on price tags and labels on dishware, glasses, and wine bottles? Here's a novel way to release them: Point a hair dryer set on high at the price tag or label until the glue softens, allowing it to be peeled off with ease.

RESTARTING A GRILL FIRE WITH STYLE

When a charcoal fire peters out, you can douse it with lighter fluid and toss on a match, which creates a thrilling ball of flame. Some grillers, however, prefer a tamer, safer, less chemical-infused approach. Assuming the grill is placed close enough to an outdoor power outlet, simply turn an electric hair dryer to high and aim it toward the base of the pile of coals. The airflow acts as a bellows to get the fire going again in just a few minutes—without a dangerous ball of flames. (If your grill isn't near an outlet, try a bike pump. Three or four blasts provide the intense burst of air that the fire needs for a bit more life.)

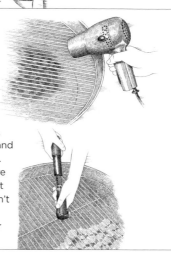

IMPROMPTU BOWL COVER

Plastic wrap is the usual choice for covering leftovers for storage or protecting rising dough, but a clean, unused shower cap (often found in complimentary toiletry packs in hotel rooms) also makes a perfect bowl cover. It is big enough to fit most large bowls and creates a more reliable seal than most plastic wraps.

HAIR BANDS COME IN HANDY

To keep open bags of frozen vegetables from getting freezer burn, we used to tie off the open end with a rubber band. The problem was that freezing made the rubber bands brittle; sometimes they broke and spilled the contents of the bag into the freezer. As a solution, we traded in the rubber bands for those bungee-like hair bands: They never get brittle and break in the freezer, and they're cheap (50 to a pack at the dollar store). They can also be used outside the freezer for anything from tying off bags of sandwich bread to holding together a pile of plastic utensils for a summertime picnic.

5.2 SURPRISING KITCHEN-BATHROOM CROSSOVERS

UNKINKING CORDS

To free up countertop space and keep long electrical cords on appliances from tangling with one another, fold each cord up tightly and then secure it with a plastic hair clip.

SECURING ELECTRIC CORDS

For an inexpensive way to neatly contain appliance cords on the kitchen counter, bundle the cord, then feed it into an empty cardboard toilet paper roll.

STRESS-FREE SPEEDY DOUGH RISING

To speed up bread making, try a clean microwavable neck wrap, the kind used to relieve stress. When heated for 1 to 2 minutes and then wrapped around a bowl of dough, it provides just enough heat to gently nudge the dough into rising in about half the time.

SWABBING SEPARATED EGGS

When separating eggs, a cotton swab is ideal for blotting up small specks of egg yolk that accidentally get in the whites.

MEASURE FOR MEASURE

If you don't use the plastic caps from cough syrup bottles, don't throw them away. Use them to measure liquids. The caps, which hold the equivalent of 2 tablespoons, stack neatly for easy stowing. They also work well for measuring out herbs, spices, and other ingredients in preparation for cooking, creating what's called *mise en place*.

PICKY SHRIMP PREP

Even when grilling shrimp with the shell on, many cooks like to remove the gritty vein running down the back. One easy way to accomplish this is to straighten the shrimp as much as possible, grab the exposed end of the vein with flat-edged tweezers, and pull it out gently.

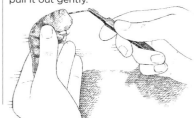

5.2 SURPRISING KITCHEN-BATHROOM CROSSOVERS

A DENTIST'S FAVORITE KITCHEN HELPERS

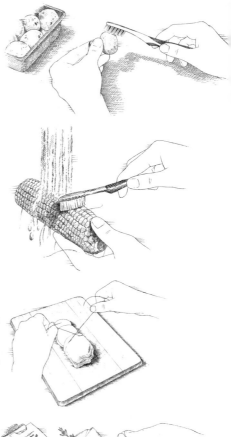

A. Mushroom Brushing

No need for those cute little specially brushes for cleaning all of those hard-to-reach spots on mushrooms—a clean, soft-bristled toothbrush provides a comfortable handle, and the small head slips easily under the gills to capture every stray bit of dirt. A run through the dishwasher cleans the soiled brush.

B. Corn Cleaning

For a no-fuss way to remove the long, clingy strands of silk from ears of corn, hold the corn under cool running water and use a clean, firm-bristled toothbrush to brush off the silk. The toothbrush can be cleaned in the dishwasher and used repeatedly.

C. Slick Slicing

Unflavored, unwaxed dental floss can be used for a variety of slicing tasks in the kitchen. Try using this solution for soft doughs, such as cinnamon rolls; soft cheeses, such as goat cheese; or fragile cakes, such as cheesecake. The floss won't pull, tear, or flatten as much as a knife.

D. Twine Replacing

Dental floss also makes a perfect stand-in for kitchen twine if you don't have any on hand. Use unflavored, unwaxed floss to tie up meat, poultry, and bouquets garnis.

E. Cake Leveling

Rather than use a long-bladed knife to level a cake, try this tip: After the cake has cooled, return the cake layer to the pan. Run the appropriate length of dental floss (or even clean, new fishing line) across the cake top, using the top edge of the pan as a guide. Pull the severed section from the top of the layer.

5.3 COOKING FROM THE LAUNDRY ROOM

DRY YOUR DINNER WITH YOUR DELICATES

If you make fresh spaghetti and fettuccine at home, finding a spot for drying the long strands can be a challenge. But you don't need a fancy pasta rack to solve this problem: Hang your fresh pasta over the bars of an adjustable wooden indoor clothes drying rack instead.

THERMOMETER HOLDER FOR THE GRILL

An ordinary wooden clothespin makes a convenient holder for the thermometer you use to monitor the temperature out on the grill. It has the benefit of staying cool to the touch while also protecting the head of the thermometer from the hot metal surface of the grill.

TOASTER OVEN TRICK

The small footprint of a toaster oven is great, but the compact size of this appliance leaves little room for a bulky oven mitt to reach in for your food. To avoid a burn, pull the rack out using a wooden clothespin instead.

PREPARING PICTURE-PERFECT PEAS

Stuffed snow peas make a pretty and fresh springtime appetizer, but neatly opening each pod, one by one, can be tiresome. A seam ripper borrowed from the sewing box can help make things faster and easier.

EXPLOITING THE LOOPHOLE

Many dish towels come with a loop sewn into the hem. Take advantage of this design by sewing a button into the waist of your apron so you can keep one of these towels at the ready at all times.

5.4 OFFICE SUPPLIES FOR KITCHEN BUSINESS

CHERRY CLIPPER

Half the battle of making a fresh cherry pie is pitting the cherries efficiently, with minimal bruising of their delicate flesh. One easy way is to use a paper clip.

1. Unfold one bend of a clean, large metal paper clip to create an elongated S-shape.

2. Holding the cherry in one hand, stick one end of the S into the stem end of the cherry, hook it around the pit, and flick the pit out.

SHARPEN YOUR OWN SKEWERS

Next time you run out of skewers while making large batches of kebabs, try a new use for the collection of wooden takeout chopsticks lingering in your kitchen drawer: You can transform them into sturdy skewers for meat or veggies by honing one end with a pencil sharpener.

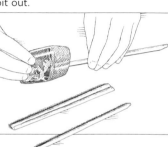

HOMEMADE KNIFE PROTECTOR

Storing knives in a drawer is not only dangerous but also potentially damaging to the knives. Here's a cheap way to protect your fingers and your knives.

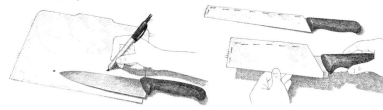

1. Set a knife on a manila folder, placing the blade of the knife parallel to the bottom edge of the folder. Use a pen to mark ½ inch beyond the tip and ½ inch above the spine.

2. Using these marks as guides, cut the folder into a rectangle. Staple the top edge and front of the rectangle at ½-inch intervals, leaving the back end open to slide in the knife.

ONE RULE FOR STICKY PIE DOUGH

Few things are more frustrating in the kitchen than having rolled-out dough stick to the counter. Rather than dirtying a bench scraper, slide a metal ruler under the dough (a tool which also comes in handy for making sure dough is rolled out to the right size). The ruler's thin edges pry the stubborn dough off just as well as a bench scraper does.

SECURING SLIPPERY CUTTING BOARDS

To keep a plastic cutting board from sliding around the counter as you chop, wrap a thick rubber band around each end, creating a stable nonskid surface for safe chopping. Want an even easier option? Just sprinkle a handful of rubber bands on the counter and place your cutting board on top, thereby preventing any slipping or sliding while you chop. If the bands get contaminated with juices from meat or poultry, just throw them out.

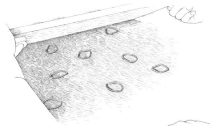

EXTRA GRIP FOR TONGS

We recommended the use of tongs to remove ramekins of custard from a water bath. Cooks who worry about the ramekins slipping in the tongs can try this tip: Slip rubber bands around each of the two pincers. The sticky rubber provides a surer grip.

JAR-OPENING ASSISTANT

Many cooks have a drawer full of rubber bands. Those rubber bands can provide much-needed extra grip when it's time to pry off a lid that is stuck to its jar. Simply slip the band around the jar lid and turn to open.

NO-SLIP PEPPER MILL

When your hands get wet during cooking, using a plastic or glass pepper mill becomes a slippery, frustrating task, but there's a simple remedy: Secure a thick rubber band at the top of the pepper mill. Grip the rubber band while grinding.

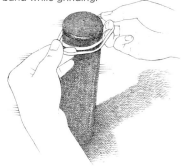

5.5 SECRET DOUBLE LIVES OF KITCHEN TOOLS

ICE WATER SHAKE-UP

When recipes like pie dough call for ice water, it can be a challenge to pour just the water, not the cubes as well. You can use a tool from your bar to ensure a controlled pour. Fill a cocktail shaker with the desired amount of water. Add ice and affix the lid. Shake vigorously, then pour the water through the strainer, leaving the ice in the base.

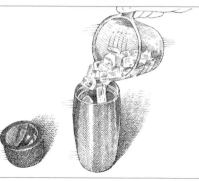

IMPROVISED EGG CUPS

If you're a fan of soft-cooked eggs but you don't want to invest in a whole set of tiny egg cups to steady them as you slice the tops off, try this solution from your liquor cabinet: a shot glass. Empty widemouthed shot glasses are the perfect size to keep the top of the egg propped above the rim of the glass.

SPICY TEA FOR SOUPS AND STEWS

Spices and herbs are a must in soups and stews, but some (like bay leaves, whole peppercorns, and cloves) have to be fished out before serving. To make removal easy, create individualized spice packets.

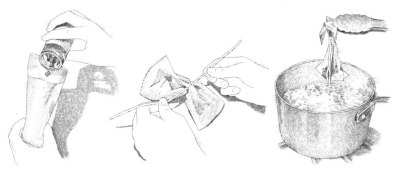

1. Fill a tea filter bag made for loose tea with spices.

2. Tightly tie the packet closed with kitchen twine and add it to the pot.

3. When your dish is ready, simply remove the packet.

TEA TWINE

When you need a short length of foodsafe string to tie a spice bag or secure a bunch of herbs and don't have any kitchen twine handy, try clipping the string off of a tea bag. The string is the perfect size for such small tasks. If a longer length is required, two lengths of string can be tied together.

DON'T LOSE YOUR TAMPER

Just because your espresso machine is seldom in use doesn't mean the tamper has to sit idle.

A. Try using it to pack brown sugar in your measuring cup.

B. An espresso tamper can also be used to smash peppercorns, garlic, and olives.

NO SUGAR SHAKER? NO PROBLEM.

To apply a light dusting of powdered sugar to brownies, cakes, or French toast without a special sugar shaker, you can substitute one of these multitasking tools from your kitchen.

A. Try a wide-plane rasp grater. A tablespoon of powdered sugar and a few quick taps create the same effect as a sifter or shaker, and the cleanup is a quick rinse under the faucet.

B. A tea strainer also works wonders as a stand-in shaker. Filled by a quick scoop into the sugar, it is much neater and easier to use than a sifter and won't create a dust storm.

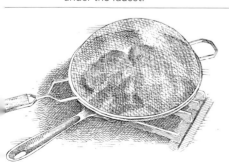

SCREENING WITH STRAINERS

When you don't have a splatter screen handy, try covering the pan with an overturned wire mesh strainer of an appropriate diameter.

5.5 SECRET DOUBLE LIVES OF KITCHEN TOOLS

EASIER SEED REMOVAL

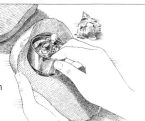

Removing the tangled mess of seeds and pulp from a pumpkin or winter squash can be a tricky, messy job. Instead of using a spoon, reach for a round metal cookie cutter. The sharp edges conform to the curves of the squash, making it easy to remove the seeds and stringy pulp.

QUICKER CUTTING

The next time you're serving French toast, pancakes, or waffles to a crowd of hungry kids, use a pizza cutter to cut the foods neatly and quickly into bite-size pieces.

HOT 'PICKS

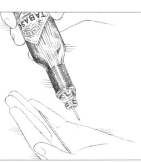

Here's a creative use for an empty hot sauce bottle: After washing it well, fill it with toothpicks and replace the plastic drip-dispenser top. The hole in the top is the perfect size to dispense just one toothpick at a time when the bottle is shaken upside down.

RECYCLING RUBBER GLOVES

No-skid rubber mats are useful for stabilizing cutting boards and preventing them from slipping around on the counter. Instead of buying one of these handy accessories, you can make one from your recycled rubber kitchen gloves.

1. Cut off the hand portion of a glove at the wrist; discard the hand. Slit the wrist section open into a flat piece, then cut in half lengthwise.

2. Place the rubber pieces on the counter and then place the cutting board on top.

OM IN THE KITCHEN

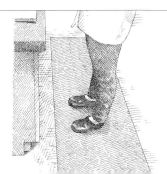

Specially designed chefs' floor mats offer cooks comfort when standing in the kitchen—but at a steep price. For a creative solution, try using a yoga mat instead. Its surface prevents slips and offers a surprising amount of cushioning; plus, it easily rolls up for storage when not in use.

CINNAMON STIR STICK

To add honey to your cup of tea—and a hint of cinnamon at the same time—try this trick: Twirl a cinnamon stick in a jar of honey to pick up the desired amount, then transfer to the cup of tea. Use the stick to stir and dissolve the honey. To get more than one use out of each cinnamon stick, rinse, dry well, and store in an airtight container.

NO MATCH FOR SPAGHETTI

Flambéing alcohol in a skillet can be dangerous if you don't have a long, chimney-style match. Luckily, there's an easy, inexpensive solution that you probably already have on hand: a single strand of dry spaghetti.

1. Light the spaghetti on the flame of a gas burner.

2. Use the spaghetti to safely ignite the alcohol.

USING YOUR NOODLE

If you don't have the special scalloped-edge square cookie cutter called for in a recipe, try using the wavy edge of a dry lasagna noodle to cut your rolled-out cookie dough. In some ways, this trick is actu-ally better than a cookie cutter because the long noodle can cut more dough at once, and without the wasted in-between scraps left by a stamp-style cutter.

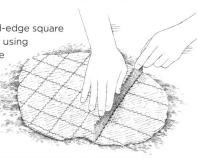

IMPROMPTU BASTING BRUSHES

Not many households stock extra pastry brushes to use just for basting, especially for foods on the grill. If you find yourself short a brush to apply marinades and sauces, you can get the job done with a large lettuce leaf. Or try a juiced lemon half: Spear a fork into the pointed end of the spent half-lemon, and use the cut side to apply the sauce to the food. Of course, this is best when you have a lemony sauce.

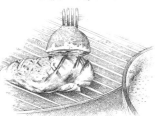

ALTERNATIVE BISCUIT CUTTER

If you're unable to find a biscuit cutter while in the midst of baking one day, reach for a canning jar ring. While its edge is slightly duller than that of the traditional tool, it easily stamps through dough and creates a perfect circle every time.

SHAPING PATTIES

Crab cakes must be uniformly shaped if they are to cook evenly. Here's a way to shape them, as well as hamburgers and other patties, with a simple item you probably already have on hand.

1. Line a small two-piece Mason jar lid with plastic wrap.

2. Press enough of your mixture into the lid to fill it completely and evenly.

3. Remove the patty by gently pushing the lid up from the bottom.

BETTER BROILED GRAPEFRUIT

Broiled grapefruit is quick and easy: Halve the grapefruit, top the cut halves with honey or brown sugar, and place them under the broiler element. The problem? The citrus's curved base makes the fruit likely to tip, spilling the topping and the juice. Set each half in a canning jar lid band to keep them stable and upright.

STABILIZING ARTICHOKES FOR STEAMING

Without a steaming apparatus, it can be tricky to keep artichokes upright in the pan as they steam. If you simply sit an artichoke on its stem end, the air will not circulate for even cooking, and the bottom of the artichoke can easily overbrown by the time the leaves are tender. For the perfect solution, set each artichoke in the band of a canning jar lid, which will keep the artichoke stable and protect the stem end from the bottom of the pan.

5.7 **THE MANY MAGICAL USES OF CANNING GEAR**

HOMEMADE COOLING RACK

When you need extra cooling racks to place your pans on, try placing canning jar lid bands on your counter. The elevation of the bands allows for just enough air circulation.

RING AROUND THE BAKING MAT

Rather than securing your rolled-up nonstick silicone baking mat with a rubber band for storage, use a canning jar lid band to keep it from unrolling. Using the mat is as easy as sliding off the band, and the metal is sturdier than a rubber band, which can tear and break.

GETTING A GRIP ON RAMEKINS

Using tongs to remove slippery ramekins of custard from a water bath can be tricky. In the test kitchen, we wrap rubber bands around each tong pincer to provide a sure grip. However, if you have them, you can also use canning tongs to remove individual ramekins. With their rounded grip designed to curve around jars, canning tongs won't slip.

BAR BACK(UP)

When entertaining, it's nice to be able to make cocktails to order without the hassle of stopping to wash the cocktail shaker between drinks. Instead of buying multiple shakers, you can fashion an extra with a widemouthed 1-quart Mason jar and two corresponding lids.

1. Drill several holes in one lid. File down any raised metal.

2. Screw on the band over the unpunctured lid and shake. To pour, replace the lid with the one with holes in it.

MASON JAR MILK STEAMER

1. To steam milk for cappuccino in the microwave, fill a Mason jar no more than halfway, put on the lid, and shake the jar vigorously for 30 seconds.

2. Remove the lid and microwave the milk for 30 seconds at high power to both warm and stabilize the foam.

RINSING GRAINS

To rinse rice and other small grains without losing them down the drain, follow this suggestion.

1. Pour the rice or other grain into a widemouthed 1-quart Mason jar, preferably with cup measures marked on the side, replace the lid with a piece of screen, and secure it with the jar lid's band.

2. Run water through the screen into the jar; swish, shake, and drain. Repeat as many times as necessary.

SHAKER MAKER

When your shaker jars and strainers are otherwise occupied and you need a very fine dusting of flour, confectioners' sugar, cornmeal, or the like, make a homemade version of a shaker using this method.

1. Place the ingredient in a Mason jar and cover the mouth with a piece of waxed paper. Screw on the jar band. Poke several small holes in the waxed paper. (A single layer of cheesecloth will also work in place of the waxed paper.)

2. Now go ahead and shake out the contents. This is especially useful when a very lightly floured surface is necessary.

3. You can screw on the lid cover with the waxed paper or cheesecloth still in place to keep the jar airtight for storage.

POUR SOME SUGAR

If you're tired of spilling dry ingredients like baking soda and sugar when measuring small amounts from the box or jar, try transferring them to canning jars—and adding a spout.

1. Using a sharp knife or razor, cut the top off an empty salt container with a built-in spout.

2. Fill an empty widemouthed canning jar with the desired ingredient, place the salt-carton top on the rim, and screw on the jar band to secure it.

MESS-FREE MUFFIN MAKING

Instead of portioning batter into a muffin tin using a spoon or a measuring cup—which tend to dribble batter on the counter— try an unusual tool: a canning funnel. The gadget neatly fits into each cup and allows you to deposit batter without any drips.

TAKE YOUR CAKE FOR A SPIN

Frosting a cake without a rotating cake stand can be a pain because you either end up awkwardly hovering around it or you have to be on pins and needles the whole time you're adjusting it on the counter. A fancy stand will solve the problem, but if you don't make cakes all that often, improvising a cake stand will save you from buying yet another kitchen gadget. All you need is the insert from a tube pan and a Mason jar. Turn the insert upside down and fit the tube into the Mason jar. Put the cake, on a platter lined around the edge with parchment paper, on top of the insert; now you can rotate the whole cake while you frost it. The tube pan stays stable in the jar. When you're done all you have to do is remove the parchment paper.

CHAPTER 6

FOOD STORAGE HACKS

How to Keep Food Fresh and Stop Wasting Money

FRIDGE TRIAGE BOX

To cut down on food waste and keep yourself from throwing away expired food that gets pushed to the back of the refrigerator and forgotten, try putting anything in danger of going bad into a box or basket on the top shelf. Now every time you open the door, you'll be reminded of what should be consumed first.

EATING ALL YOUR VEGETABLES

Rather than allow vegetable scraps to wither (or get lost) in the crisper drawer, toss any leftovers into a reserved clamshell container. This way, you can easily find them if you need a small amount of chopped vegetables, such as for an omelet or a salad.

NEXT-LEVEL SANDWICHES

Many cooks complain that fresh herbs such as parsley or basil are sold in bunches much larger than they need to make just one or two recipes. Often, the leftover herbs just rot in the refrigerator and have to be thrown out.

To keep fresh herbs from going to waste, try adding them to sandwiches in place of lettuce or other greens for a delicious flavor boost.

DIY DRIED HERBS IN A FLASH

Stuck with a plethora of herbs growing in your garden? Try this quick, easy way to dry and store them.

1. After washing and drying the herbs, place them on a clean paper towel and microwave them on high power for 30 to 40 seconds.

2. Crumble the dried herbs and store in an airtight container (use within three months for best flavor).

STORING GINGER

Fresh ginger can be stored in the freezer or in a pot of dry sand to extend its shelf life, or you can try this method.

1. Peel and cut the ginger into 1-inch pieces and place in a canning jar or other glass jar.

2. Fill the jar with sherry, cover with an airtight lid, and store in the refrigerator for up to six months. This technique not only preserves the ginger but also gives you ginger-flavored sherry to use in Asian recipes.

RECYCLING LEFTOVER PICKLE JUICE

Instead of tossing out a jar of pickle juice after finishing the last pickle, use the tangy liquid to make a new condiment. Add thinly sliced onions to the juice and let them marinate in the refrigerator for a few days. The drained onions can be used as a topping for hot dogs or hamburgers or in salads. This method also works well with the spicy packing juice from vinegar peppers.

DRESSING UP LEFTOVER CONDIMENTS

Next time you end up with the dregs of a delicious jam, jelly, or mustard in your fridge, make the most of every last morsel by mixing up some salad dressing. Add olive oil, vinegar, salt, pepper, garlic, and herbs or spices when the jar is nearly empty, screw on the lid, and shake away. In seconds you have a perfect dressing and nothing is wasted!

CROUTONS IN A CRUNCH

Homemade croutons are a great way to recycle stale bread. Here's a quick method for making them that doesn't even require an oven.

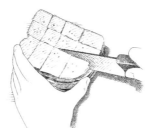

1. Brush four slices of bread with oil or melted butter on both sides and sprinkle with 1 teaspoon kosher salt and 1 teaspoon chopped fresh herbs.

2. Cut the bread into 1-inch pieces and place it in a single layer on a large microwave-safe plate.

3. Microwave on high power for 4 to 5 minutes until the cubes begin to brown. Remove the cubes from the microwave; they will crisp as they cool.

Chocolate Clusters

✓ WHY THIS RECIPE WORKS: Somehow, no matter what the recipe says, you almost always end up with leftover melted chocolate after decorating cookies or dipping fruit. Instead of throwing away the extra, use it to make a treat. Chocolate clusters are easy to make and can incorporate a variety of different flavor combinations, depending on what you like and have on hand. You can also think of this recipe as a way to use up other ingredients—the end of a bag of shredded coconut, or various nuts and dried fruits, or candies. See below for some of our favorite combinations.

Toasted nuts, dried fruit, chopped candies
Melted chocolate

1. Add nuts or other mix-ins to melted chocolate and toss so they are evenly coated.

2. Spoon coated ingredients onto parchment paper and wait for them to harden. Once cooled, confections can be stored in airtight bag or container.

Recommended Combinations
- Toasted almonds and shredded coconut
- Toasted walnuts and mini marshmallows
- Dry-roasted peanuts and chopped plain M&M's
- Plain rolled oats and raisins

HOMEMADE PITA CHIPS

The next time you have stale pita bread sitting around, turn it into a delicious snack rather than throwing it away.

1. Cut two 8-inch pita breads into wedges and arrange them on a baking sheet. Brush the wedges with 2 tablespoons olive oil and then sprinkle with ½ teaspoon table salt and ¼ teaspoon dried herbs.

2. Place the baking sheet on the lower-middle rack of a 350-degree oven and bake until crisp, about 8 minutes. Flip the chips and continue to bake until fully toasted, about 8 minutes longer.

TWO NEAT TRICKS FOR STRAINING BACON GREASE

A. Tea Infuser

Straining cooled bacon grease before saving it for future use helps avoid spoilage, but the potentially messy task often requires an extra set of hands. Here's a clever way to work alone: Set a tea infuser over a Mason jar. Designed to rest in a mug, the infuser also sits securely on the jar's rim so that you can focus on careful pouring.

B. Foil Lining

Handling hot bacon drippings is a messy proposition. Try this great tip for neatly storing the drippings for later use.

1. Line a small heatproof bowl with two small sheets of heavy-duty aluminum foil and carefully pour the hot bacon fat into the foil-lined bowl.

2. After the fat cools and solidifies, lift out the foil and fold it over the fat. The fat can then be refrigerated or frozen.

KEEPING WINE GOOD TO THE LAST DROP

A good bottle of wine is a terrible thing to waste, but sometimes leftovers are unavoidable. Use these tips to keep your vino fresh and drinkable for days after opening the bottle.

A. Recorking a wine bottle to preserve leftovers can be a challenge if the cork no longer fits into the neck of the bottle. Use a rasp grater to shave off a portion of the cork so that it can be easily reinserted into the bottle.

B. Allowing red wine to "breathe," or briefly exposing it to air, can enhance its flavor. But prolonged exposure causes it to over-oxidize and take on an unpleasant, vinegar-like taste. Gadgets like vacuum pumps minimize air exposure to preserve the flavor of leftovers, but you can get the job done with this homemade solution: Completely fill an airtight container, like a small, lidded Mason jar or an empty water bottle, with the leftover wine (the wine must reach the very top of the container to eliminate all air). Screw on the top and refrigerate for up to one week

C. If you're following the tip above and storing leftover wine in an airtight container, but you have only a small amount of wine left over, you can add clean marbles to the jar until the wine reaches the brim. No air; problem solved.

A.

C.

CHOPSTICKS TO THE RESCUE

Most cooks like to keep a pump soap dispenser near the kitchen sink for hand washing. This is much more convenient than a slippery bar of soap on the kitchen counter, but there's one problem: It's wasteful to discard the last drops of soap that always collect in the bottom of the bottle. We found a fast, neat way to get the soap from the old bottle to a new one: Insert a long chopstick into the neck of the new bottle and invert the old bottle on top. The soap will cling to the chopstick and trickle down more readily.

6.2 PROTECTING PANTRY GOODS AND PERISHABLES

KEEPING DRY GOODS DRY

Here's a way to beat the humidity that can turn opened dry goods in your pantry stale: Fill empty paper tea bags (or small pouches of cheesecloth) with rice and place them inside the storage containers before reclosing. The rice absorbs any extra moisture and can easily be replaced as necessary.

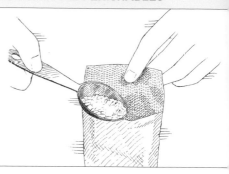

SUMMER FLOUR STORAGE

Bakers who live in humid climates probably know firsthand that flour absorbs moisture from the air, which in turns adds weight when you weigh it out for a recipe. Here are two ways to limit the rate of moisture absorption.

A. Store your flour in the freezer. This method also eliminates the possibility of bug infestations in the flour.

B. Those who may not have enough freezer space can try this tip: Store flour in a microwave oven. When you need to use the microwave, just remove the flour, replacing it when you're finished.

CAKE FLOUR ARRANGEMENTS

Bakers who make cakes infrequently may not have a covered storage container especially for cake flour. However, rather than simply storing cake flour as it came in the box, try transferring it to a zipper-lock bag and storing the bag in the original box. Then you just lift the bag out of the box, open it up wide, and dip the measuring cup right in. No more spills from pouring flour out of the box.

TERRA-COTTA FOR SAVING BROWN SUGAR

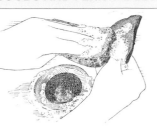

Here's a novel use for the pieces of broken terra-cotta pots that accumulate around the garden potting bench: Store one with your brown sugar to keep it from drying out and clumping.

1. Find a shard of terra-cotta about the size of a small saucer, with no sharp edges. Scrub it free of dirt and soak it in water for 15 minutes.

2. Blot the piece with a towel before placing it at the bottom of your brown sugar container. It will slowly release moisture, keeping the sugar soft.

BROWN SUGAR IN THE BAG

Pouring brown sugar out of its narrow box into a measuring cup can be a messy, frustrating chore. Streamline the task by transferring the brown sugar to a large, heavy-duty zipper-lock bag for storage. Not only does the sugar remain moister during storage, but a cup measure fits inside the bag easily and can be loaded up by pressing the sugar into it through the plastic. No pouring, spilling, or sticky hands.

STORING VANILLA BEANS

Vanilla beans, expensive as they are, warrant proper storage when fresh to preserve their suppleness. To keep vanilla beans from drying out, store them in a tall bottle (such as a clean caper bottle) filled with vanilla extract. The beans stay moist, full of flavor, and ready to use.

DOUBLE-DECKER EGG STORAGE

It's not uncommon to purchase a new carton of eggs before you've used up the old one. To save fridge space and make sure the older eggs get used first, place the newer carton upside down on a shelf and set the older eggs in the now-inverted cups on the bottom of the carton.

NO-TEARS ONION STORAGE

Onions are a staple of many different types of cooking, but they can be tricky to store—they need a cool, dry place or they quickly spoil. Here are a few tips for protecting your onion stash.

A. **B.**

C. **D.**

A. It's always best to use up foods that have been sitting in the pantry for a while before breaking into a fresh supply. Here's a trick for doing this with onions: Using a permanent marker, lightly mark a small X on the skin of each onion in your storage bin. Leave any new onions you add to the bin unmarked. Use the marked onions first. When all of the marked onions have been used, mark the remaining onions.

C. Instead of discarding empty clementine orange containers, keep the stackable crates in your pantry for storing onions, potatoes, and other items that benefit from exposure to air.

B. The high sugar content of Vidalia onions, which is what endears them to cooks, also makes them spoil more quickly if they are stored touching each other. Turn to an unusual place— the hosiery drawer—to avoid this issue. Place a Vidalia onion in the leg of an old but clean pair of pantyhose. Tie a knot in the hose, just above the onion. Repeat this process up the entire leg of the pantyhose.

D. Looking for a convenient way to store onions, shallots, and garlic in a dark, cool place with plenty of air circulation? Try dusting off your bamboo steamer. The baskets stack easily and allow just enough air circulation to prevent mold.

6.2 PROTECTING PANTRY GOODS AND PERISHABLES

HELLO, MY NAME IS... LEFTOVER CHEESE

If leftover cheese hunks aren't returned to their original packaging, it can be hard to remember what type of cheese you're storing. To keep track, snip the label from the original packaging and store it with the leftovers.

GOAT CHEESE BUNKER

Rather than rewrapping a log of fresh goat cheese every time you use a portion, store it in a covered butter dish. That way, the cheese is neatly protected and easy to use.

KEEPING FISH EXTRA-FRESH

Fresh fish and shellfish are best purchased and served on the same day. If fish must be stored, even briefly, it is best kept on ice. Instead of keeping seafood in a messy container of melting ice, place a layer of sealed frozen ice bricks (the kind used in picnic coolers) along the bottom of the meat drawer in the refrigerator. Place the wrapped fish on top of the ice bricks. For firm-fleshed fish and shellfish, place additional ice bricks on top. Replace melted ice bricks with fully frozen bricks as necessary.

COOL TUNA

Tuna fish salad sandwiches are quick and easy. But it can be annoying to wait for the freshly made tuna salad to chill after opening a new can and making the salad. Solve this problem by storing cans of tuna fish in the fridge for fast-tracked lunch anytime. (This tip is recommended only for water-packed tuna.)

COVERING UP LEEKS

Long vegetables such as leeks and celery often don't fit in produce bags. To remedy this, save empty sandwich bread bags that are long enough to completely contain the stalks.

6.2 PROTECTING PANTRY GOODS AND PERISHABLES

ARMOR FOR DELICATE PRODUCE

Fragile produce such as lettuce can easily get damaged and crushed when kept in flimsy supermarket produce bags. Save plastic "clam-shell" containers, the kind that tender greens are sold in, and use them as a sturdy alternative for storing your washed lettuce and other delicate produce.

1. Poke holes in the container for airflow.

2. Gently layer washed greens with paper towels.

3. Snap the lid shut and store in the fridge.

CARBONATING YOUR SALAD GREENS

Blowing into a bag of salad greens (thereby increasing the carbon dioxide level) keeps the contents fresh longer, but it's not very sanitary. For a cleaner carbon dioxide source, try a few puffs from a countertop seltzer maker before sealing the bag.

KEEPING THE FRESHNESS IN FRESH CHILES

Fresh chiles like jalapeños and serranos have a relatively brief shelf life in the refrigerator. To help them keep their crisp texture and fresh flavor, slice them in half and submerge them in a brine solution (1 tablespoon salt per cup of water). Chiles stored like this will retain their crispness, color, and bright heat for several weeks. After a quick rinse to remove excess brine, they are indistinguishable from fresh chiles. After a month they will begin to soften, but they are still perfectly usable in cooked applications for several more weeks.

KEEPING AVOCADO GREEN

Avocado flesh turns brown very quickly once it is exposed to air. Try this solution for preserving the color of extra avocado halves.

1. Rub 1 tablespoon of olive oil over the exposed avocado flesh.

2. Allow the excess oil to drip into a shallow bowl, then place the avocado half cut side down in the center of the oil puddle, creating a "seal." Store the avocado in the refrigerator.

6.2 PROTECTING PANTRY GOODS AND PERISHABLES

CARING FOR BERRIES

To extend the life of blueberries and strawberries, wash them in a mild distilled white vinegar solution: 1 part vinegar to 3 parts water. Then dry them and store them in a paper towel–lined airtight container. The vinegar kills bacteria without imparting flavor, and the berries stay fresher for longer.

BETTER BREAD KEEPING, TWO WAYS

Exposure to air can make bread quickly go from fresh to stale. Try these techniques to keep your loaves as fresh as possible.

A. Bottle-Top Bread Bag

1. Cut off the neck of an empty plastic bottle; reserve the neck and lid.

2. Pull the top edge of the plastic bread bag through the bottle's neck.

3. Press the air out of the bag, fold the top down, and screw on the bottle's lid to seal.

B. No Twist Tie, No Problem

The twist ties that seal bread bags have an uncanny ability to disappear. If this happens to you, try securing the bag by twisting it shut and folding the excess back on itself, over the remaining bread. This works best after a few slices have been eaten.

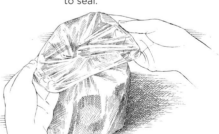

CLEAN CONDIMENTS

You can store your condiments upside down in the fridge to get the most out of them. Unfortunately, if caps aren't shut tight or there's residue on the tops, they can make a mess. Using a cut-up egg carton to hold the inverted bottles helps keep the fridge clean; plus, the edges of the egg holders help the upside-down bottles stay upright.

LABEL CONSCIOUS

You can use the free address labels you receive in the mail for more than just outgoing envelopes and packages. The easy-peel strips are perfect for sealing opened chip and cereal bags and they retain their sticking powers.

PROTECTING OUR VITAL COOKIE RESOURCES

A. If you have trouble eating all your cookies before they go stale, here's a new technique for keeping them moist and fresh: Layer parchment paper, a tortilla, parchment, and then a layer of cooled cookies in your cookie tin. Repeat until the tin is full, ending with a layer of cookies. The tortillas fit tidily into the tin, where their moisture keeps cookies soft for days.

B. Decorative cookie jars may be convenient and attractive, but they are not airtight. However, there is a way to store cookies in an attractive jar and preserve their freshness at the same time. Simply line the inside of the jar with a large zipper-lock bag, place the cookies in the bag, and seal tightly.

C. Putting a small piece of bread in the cookie jar with cookies that have gone stale is a classic trick. Take this one step further by adding a small piece of bread to zipper-lock bags of cookies that have been packaged ahead of time for a potluck or bake sale to make sure that the cookies will be soft and fresh when you dig into them.

D. Because sugar absorbs moisture from the air, storing crispy cookies with a few cubes of sugar keeps them from getting soft and chewy. In tests, cookies stored this way retained a just-baked crispness for two days.

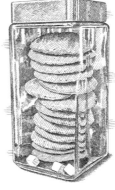

SAVING CAKE

A. To keep leftover cake moist as long as possible, store the remaining portion under a cake dome along with a whole peeled apple. The moisture from the apple helps to keep the air under the dome humid and thus discourages the cake and frosting from drying out.

B. Use this method to prevent leftover layer cake from staling: Arrange a folded piece of parchment paper to fit over the exposed edges. Pressing the parchment onto the cake lessens air exposure and keeps the next slices as good as the first.

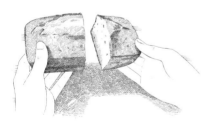

C. The best way to keep a pound cake moist is to cut slices from the middle of the cake, not the end. The cake can then be sandwiched back together and wrapped in plastic wrap. With the cut sides insulated this way, the cake stays moist longer. This tip will also work for other items baked in a loaf pan, including quick breads.

KEEPING LEFTOVER PIE INTACT

Storing uneaten pie can be tricky. Toppings such as fresh fruit, meringue, and whipped cream can get crushed against a container. However, when turned upside down, the lid of a large round storage container acts as the perfect plate for the leftover pie, while the container's bowl acts as a dome that preserves the topping's integrity.

LOST POWER INDICATOR

Try one of these solutions for gauging whether your refrigerator lost power while you were on vacation.

A. Place three ice cubes in a zipper-lock bag on a freezer shelf before leaving. If the cubes have melted together upon your return, you know the fridge shut off while you were away.

B. Take an empty plastic soda bottle, fill it halfway with water, seal it, and place it on its side in the freezer. Once the water has frozen, stand the bottle upright in the freezer so that the ice is now oriented vertically against one side of the bottle. When you return from vacation, if the ice has re-formed at the bottom of the bottle, it's time to clean out the fridge and freezer.

ENERGY-EFFICIENT FREEZING

Throw a few 2-liter soda bottles partially filled with water into your freezer. The extra mass helps keep the freezer cold during defrost cycles.

THE EFFICIENCY OF THE MUFFIN TIN

Many cooks like to freeze small portions of homemade stocks and soups in individual containers such as recycled yogurt cups. But if your freezer is more than a few steps away from the stovetop—say in the garage or basement—it may be hard to get the containers to the freezer without spilling a cup or two. To avoid any potential mess or lost food, try placing a container in each cup of a muffin tin and you'll be able to carry the whole lot with ease.

SINGLE-SERVING SMOOTHIES

If you like to drink smoothies for breakfast, you know that prepping several different kinds of fruit every morning can be a hassle. You can prep a whole week's worth of smoothie ingredients by peeling and cutting up all the fruit and then portioning enough for one smoothie into each of five zipper-lock freezer bags. Freeze the portioned fruit and then simply pull out a bag and blend its contents with yogurt or juice as needed in the morning. As an added bonus, with the fruit frozen solid, there's no need for ice, which can water down a smoothie anyway.

FREEZER FILING

Long-term freezer storage comes with a downside: Even if food is clearly labeled, it often gets buried—and then risks being forgotten. To keep track of inventory, freeze food flat in labeled zipper-lock bags and then arrange the bags in a desktop file organizer. This system keeps the freezer tidy and takes up much less space.

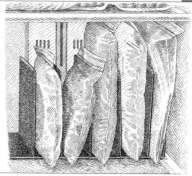

RUBBER BAND LABELS

Broccoli and some other vegetables come neatly contained by thick rubber bands. Recycle the bands by using them to label items destined for the freezer. Stretch a band around the top and bottom of a container (which also helps keep a loose lid in place) and write the container's contents on the band with a permanent marker. You can even flip the band over to get more uses out of it.

THRIFTY COOK'S VACUUM SEALER

Here's an approach to vacuum sealing without the bulky, pricey machine or special bags. Sealed according to this method, chicken breasts stored in the freezer for a month exhibited almost no ice crystals (they are a sure sign of freezer burn).

1. Pack the food snugly into the corner of a large zipper-lock bag. Starting from the side closest to the food, close the zipper almost all the way, leaving a small opening at the end opposite the food. Insert a straw ½ inch into the opening.

2. Place the bag in a pot of water. Slowly pull down on the bag with one hand while massaging out the air through the straw with your other hand. When all of the air is removed from the bag and the water level almost reaches the top, remove the straw and seal the bag.

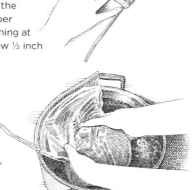

6.4 FRESH TIPS FOR THE FREEZER

WASTE-FREE FROZEN STORAGE

Savvy cooks often keep bags of frozen fruit and vegetables on hand in case they need something in a pinch. The question is, what's the best way to store the leftovers from a large bag? Try this efficient trick.

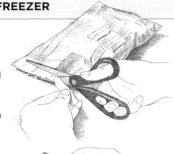

1. Using scissors, cut a thin strip from the top of the bag to open it.

2. After removing the desired amount of fruit or vegetables, twist the bag shut to remove excess air and secure by tying the cut strip of plastic at the base of the twist.

NO MORE MYSTERY MEAT

After wrapping meat in plastic wrap and placing it in a zipper-lock freezer bag, cut off the grocery label and put it inside, facing out. At a glance you know the exact cut, weight, and—most important—date of purchase, allowing you to gauge how long the meat has been lingering in the freezer.

USING UP LEFTOVER MEAT

Instead of tossing out scraps of cured meat such as dry sausage or prosciutto, place leftovers in a zipper-lock bag and store them in the freezer. When making tomato sauce, soups, or stews, add the meat to the simmering pot for extra flavor.

ADDING BACON FLAVOR TO ANYTHING

If you like the flavor that a small amount of bacon fat adds to food but don't want to fry a slice of bacon every time you need it, try this creative way to portion leftover bacon drippings for future use: Pour leftover drippings into a bowl and refrigerate. Once solid, the drippings can be scooped into teaspoon portions and frozen. The frozen portions of bacon drippings can be stored in a zipper-lock bag and substituted for butter or oil in any dish where a meaty flavor is desired.

ALL WRAPPED UP IN BACON

Freezing is a great way to preserve bacon, but if it's frozen into a solid slab, it's impossible to remove just a few slices when needed. One option is to roll the slices into cylinders before freezing them, but if you prefer to keep them flat, try this wrapping method.

1. Place a single slice of bacon on one end of a 16 by 12-inch piece of waxed paper. Fold the paper over the bacon, then top with another slice.

2. Continue folding and stacking in an accordion fashion.

3. Place wrapped slices in a zipper-lock bag and freeze until ready to use.

EASIER MEAT DEFROSTING

Frozen ground meat is problematic when you only need to use a small quantity. You can solve this problem by transferring the ground meat to a large zipper-lock bag before freezing. Using your fingers, press through the bag to divide the mass into four equal portions, and then place the bag flat in the freezer. When it's time to cook, simply break off the amount of meat that you need.

PORTION CONTROL

Put coffee filters (or flattened cupcake liners) to unusual but effective use by placing them between pancakes, pork chops, meat patties, and other items while stacking them for storage in the freezer. You can then easily remove individual portions without having to defrost the entire supply.

Perfect Steak Straight from the Freezer

✓ **WHY THIS RECIPE WORKS:** Conventional wisdom holds that frozen steaks should be thawed before cooking, but is that step really necessary? We cooked steaks straight from the freezer and the frozen steaks actually browned just as well and as fast as thawed steaks. Furthermore, they had thinner bands of gray, overcooked meat directly under the crust, and they lost less moisture during cooking. While we still prefer to start with steak that's never been frozen for the best texture, if you do have frozen steaks on hand, we highly recommend cooking them straight from the freezer. To ensure that the steaks brown evenly, add oil to the skillet until it measures ⅛ inch deep. Frozen steaks will splatter more during searing, so use a large skillet. This recipe makes 2 servings.

> 2 **boneless strip steaks, 1 inch thick, trimmed and frozen**
> **Kosher salt and ground black pepper**
> **Vegetable oil**

1. Adjust oven rack to middle position and heat oven to 275 degrees. Season entire surface of steaks liberally with salt and pepper. Add oil to skillet until ⅛ inch deep. Heat over high heat until smoking. Sear steaks until browned, 90 seconds per side.

2. Transfer steaks to wire rack set in rimmed baking sheet; transfer baking sheet to oven. Cook until meat registers 125 degrees (for medium-rare), 18 to 20 minutes. Transfer steaks to clean wire rack and let rest, loosely tented with aluminum foil, for 10 minutes. Serve.

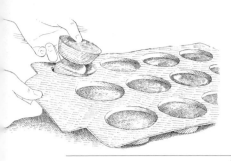

A MORE FLEXIBLE WAY TO FREEZE LEFTOVERS

In the test kitchen, we routinely freeze extra homemade stock and pesto in metal muffin tins or plastic ice cube trays. For an even easier freezing process, use silicone molds instead. The flexible material releases frozen blocks with ease, eliminating the hassle of banging, twisting, or warming traditional tins and trays.

FROZEN ASSETS

Casseroles often produce too much food, but rather than scale down the recipes, you can make the full yield and freeze the leftovers in individual portions for quick single-serving meals.

1. Let the casserole cool and then slice it into individual servings. Arrange the servings on a baking sheet and place the sheet in the freezer.

2. Move the frozen servings to a zipper-lock freezer bag. Reheat as needed.

SINGLE-SERVING SOUP STORAGE

Homemade soup is a winter treat that's easy to freeze. But most people freeze it in large multiserving portions that make for a lot of unnecessary defrosting when the need for just one or two servings arises. Try this easy system for freezing convenient single servings.

1. Set out a number of 10- or 12-ounce paper cups for hot beverages and fill each with a portion of cooled soup (but not all the way to the top). Label, wrap, and freeze each cup.

2. Whenever you want a quick cup of soup, remove as many servings as necessary from the freezer and microwave them until they're hot and ready to serve.

MASHED POTATOES IN A MOMENT

Here's a great tip for using up leftover mashed potatoes: Freeze the cooled potatoes in individual portions so that they are quickly available for a meal.

1. Once your leftovers have cooled, use a large ice cream scoop or measuring cup to place 1-cup portions of mashed potatoes on a baking sheet lined with parchment paper. Transfer the baking sheet to the freezer and allow to freeze solid.

2. Once frozen, transfer to a large zipper-lock bag and return to the freezer. To reheat, place a portion in a microwave-safe bowl, cover with microwave-safe plastic wrap, and microwave at 50 percent power for about 5 minutes, stirring occasionally, until heated through.

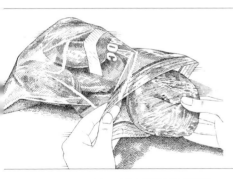

SPLIT AND FREEZE

When freezing English muffins or bagels they often fuse together, becoming difficult to separate when you are ready to toast them. To expedite breakfast preparation, split each English muffin or bagel in half and then place the halves back together. Wrap with plastic wrap and freeze.

FLAVOR SECRET IN THE FREEZER

Save your Parmesan rinds and do as the Italians do: Toss one into a soup or stew. It's an age-old trick for adding savory depth. Stored in a zipper-lock bag in the freezer, the rinds will keep indefinitely (no need to thaw them before using).

MAKE-AHEAD PIE DOUGH

Many bakers prefer to make pie dough in large batches and freeze it. To minimize the time it takes to thaw and roll the dough, you can use a 9-inch cake pan to create even rounds for freezing.

 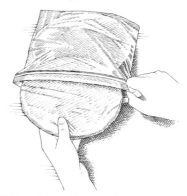

1. Line a 9-inch cake pan with plastic wrap. Gently press pie dough into the pan in an even layer. Wrap the dough in plastic and freeze until firm.

2. Once frozen, the dough rounds can be removed from the cake pan and stored in a large zipper-lock bag until needed.

USING UP LEFTOVER BROWNIES

If you find yourself with the strange problem of having an unusable excess of brownies or cookies, don't let them go to waste. Try freezing them for later use as toppings for sundaes and other desserts.

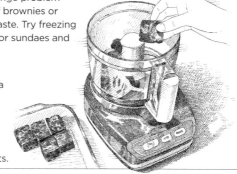

1. Pulse slightly stale brownies or cookies in the workbowl of a food processor until they form coarse crumbs. Store in a zipper-lock bag in the freezer.

2. Sprinkle the frozen crumbs onto ice cream or other desserts.

LEFTOVERS ARE A PIECE OF CAKE

After eating only one or two slices from a cake, you may want to freeze the rest. But you probably won't want to defrost the whole cake later when you want just another piece or two. To avoid this problem, first slice up the whole cake. Then wrap a piece of waxed paper around the point and against the sides of each slice. Reassemble the cake and freeze. Now you can remove as many slices as you like without defrosting the whole thing.

PREVENTING ICE CREAM TRAGEDIES

When exposed to air, ice cream quickly develops unappealing ice crystals and freezer burn.

A. To help avoid freezer burn, cover the ice cream remaining in the carton with heavy-duty plastic wrap before replacing the container in the freezer, pressing the wrap right down onto the surface of the ice cream.

B. For an even better way to cut down on air exposure and keep ice cream as fresh as possible, try the following method (which also frees up freezer space): As the ice cream is eaten, cut off the empty part of the container with scissors or a knife. Then replace the lid and return the container to the freezer.

QUICK AND EASY SINGLE SCOOPS OF ICE CREAM

Some home refrigerators freeze ice cream so hard that it has to sit on the counter for several minutes to soften before it can be scooped. When you've got an ice cream craving, that can feel like a very, *very* long wait. To avoid this unfortunate delay, try this method to portion out ice cream in advance.

1. Scoop ice cream or frozen yogurt into a muffin tin lined with muffin papers, and then freeze.

2. Once frozen, the paper-lined portions can be stored in a zipper-lock bag in the freezer for easy, ready-when-you-are servings. Just peel off the paper and place the ice cream in a bowl. This is also a great method for quickly firming up homemade ice cream, which is notoriously soft when it comes out of the machine.

6.5 FROZEN RESERVES: INGREDIENTS AT THE READY

BREAD CRUMBS

After a barbecue, you almost always end up with leftover buns. Rather than discarding the extra hamburger or hot dog rolls, tear them into pieces and freeze the pieces in a zipper-lock bag until you need fresh bread crumbs. Then just 10 to 20 pulses in the food processor turns the leftovers into ready-to-use crumbs, no thawing necessary. This is also a great way to use up the unwanted heels from loaves of sandwich bread or artisanal bread that you can't finish before they get stale. (If you don't have a food processor, you can grate the bread on the large holes of a box grater.)

BUTTERMILK

While many recipes call for buttermilk, few of them will require a whole container of the real stuff, and it can be a challenge to use it up before it goes bad. Try this tip to keep unused buttermilk leftovers from spoiling.

1. Place some small paper cups on a tray and fill each with ½ cup of buttermilk.

2. Place the tray in the freezer.

3. Once the buttermilk has frozen, wrap each cup with plastic wrap and store them in a large zipper-lock bag. Defrost the amount you need in the refrigerator before you bake.

CARAMELIZED ONIONS

Caramelized onions lend a complex, earthy sweetness to many dishes, such as burgers, focaccia, pizza, omelets, and mashed potatoes. However, a batch of this flavorful ingredient can take upwards of an hour to make. We came up with a way to ensure that there's always a stash on hand: Make a large batch and then portion the cooked onions into zipper-lock freezer bags, rolling them from the bottom up to expel as much air as possible. Seal the bags and store them in the freezer, where they will keep for up to three months. When you need a small amount to sweeten a dish, just take out a bag and thaw.

CITRUS ZEST

If you find that you often use only a teaspoon or so of the zest from a lemon or orange, try freezing the rest to avoid waste. Remove the zest from the rest of the fruit and deposit it in ½-teaspoon increments on a plate. Transfer the plate to the freezer. Once the piles are frozen, place them in a zipper-lock bag. Frozen zest keeps for up to three weeks.

FRESH GINGER

Fresh ginger is often sold in large pieces that may not be used up in one recipe. To keep it from going to waste and save it for long-term storage, use this easy tip: Cut leftover unpeeled ginger into 1-inch pieces and place them in a zipper-lock bag. Store the bag in the freezer for one month or longer. Whenever fresh ginger is needed, simply pull a piece from the freezer, allow it to thaw, peel it, and then grate or chop as required for your recipe.

FRESH HERBS

Often, home cooks buy a bunch of parsley only to end up using just a small fraction, leaving the rest to go bad. Luckily, there's a good way to keep leftover parsley usable indefinitely. This method also works with sage, rosemary, and thyme.

1. Chop leftover fresh herbs by hand or in the food processor, transfer by the spoonful into ice cube trays, and top with water to cover. For a standard ice cube tray, place 2 tablespoons chopped herbs and approximately 1 tablespoon water in each cube.

2. Once the cubes are frozen, transfer them to a zipper-lock bag and seal. Store until you want to add them to sauces, soups, or stews.

RICE

The next time you make rice, prepare a double batch and freeze the leftovers. They can be reheated in the microwave, used to make fried rice, or added to soups and stews. To freeze, spread the hot rice out on a baking sheet to cool. Break up any large clumps. Place the cooled rice in a zipper-lock bag and freeze until needed.

TOASTED NUTS

Toasted nuts are often used in recipes such as pesto or cookies, but it can be annoying to have to toast small amounts for each dish. Here's a solution: Toast several cups of nuts on a baking sheet in a 350-degree oven for 3 to 5 minutes. When the nuts are cool, transfer them to a zipper-lock bag and freeze them. Do not use pretoasted frozen nuts for recipes in which a crisp texture is desired, such as salads.

TOMATO PASTE

Recipes often call for only a tablespoon or two of tomato paste. Unfortunately, the rest of the can usually ends up turning brown in the refrigerator and then being discarded. Eliminate this waste by using the following tip.

1. Open both ends of the tomato paste can. Remove the lid from one end and use the lid at the other end to push the paste out onto a sheet of plastic wrap. (This method also works as a neat way of getting other solid ingredients, such as frozen juice and almond paste, out of cans.)

2. Wrap the tomato paste in plastic wrap and place it in the freezer.

3. When the paste has frozen, you can cut off just as much as you need for a particular recipe and then return the frozen log to the freezer.

WINE

Instead of tossing out that last bit of wine from an unfinished bottle, freeze it. Then when you need a little wine to finish a sauce, there is no need to open a fresh bottle. Measure 1 tablespoon of wine into each well of an ice cube tray and freeze. Use a paring knife to remove each wine cube, and store them in a zipper-lock bag. Add the frozen cubes to sauces as desired.

Citrus-Infused Vodka

WHY THIS RECIPE WORKS: If you don't want to freeze leftover citrus peels or zest, why not booze it up a bit? Infused spirits are a great, simple way to make a flavorful cocktail. You can keep your infusions economical by using citrus peels left over from juicing (any fruit will work). Mix and match with simple syrup, sparkling water, juices, and garnishes for easier-than-they-seem party cocktails. For best results, use organic citrus fruits and wash them thoroughly. Initially, infused vodka will be cloudy but it will turn clear with age. Take care to avoid the bitter white pith when peeling the citrus. This recipe makes one 750-milliliter bottle of infused liquor and takes four days to fully infuse.

13 (3-inch) strips lemon, orange, or grapefruit zest (1¼ ounces; 3 lemons, 2 oranges, or 1½ grapefruits)

1 (750-ml) bottle vodka

1. Bring 1 quart water to boil in small saucepan. Add zest to boiling water and cook until beginning to soften and dull in color, about 30 seconds. Strain zest well and transfer to blender. Add vodka (saving bottle for storage of finished infusion) and process until zest is finely minced, about 30 seconds. Pour into 1-quart jar, cover, and store in cool, dark place until fully infused, about 4 days.

2. Set funnel over empty vodka bottle and line with coffee filter. Strain infused vodka through filter, discarding zest. Infused vodka can be stored in cool, dark place indefinitely.

CHAPTER 7
REHEATING + REVIVING FOOD HACKS

AKA Culinary Magic

7.1 DON'T THROW THAT OUT; IT'S STILL GOOD!

RECONSTITUTING HARDENED ALMOND PASTE

Almond paste is expensive and seldom used, which means that leftovers often sit around and harden before they can be used up. When faced with rock-hard almond paste, try the old trick for softening brown sugar: Place the paste in a zipper-lock bag along with a slice of bread. In a couple of days, the almond paste will be restored to its normal, pliable self.

REPAIRING ROCK-HARD BROWN SUGAR

If you discover in the middle of a recipe that your brown sugar has dried out and formed rock-hard clumps, you can use a coffee grinder to quickly break up what you need (up to ¼ cup at a time) so that you can proceed with your recipe. A grater is also a useful tool for this problem; running the block of sugar along the tool's sharp holes quickly breaks it down into a measurable, usable state.

RESTORING CLUMP-FREE SUGAR

When white sugar cakes up and forms a solid brick, you can use a potato masher to break it into granules again.

RENEWING CRYSTALLIZED HONEY

All honey hardens and crystallizes over time, but you don't need to throw it out when this happens. To bring honey back to its translucent, liquid state, use a pot of simmering water or a microwave. Put the opened jar of honey in a saucepan filled with about an inch of water and place over very low heat, stirring the honey often, until the crystals melt. Alternatively, heat the opened jar in the microwave on high power in 10-second increments, stirring intermittently, until it has liquefied. Once cooled, use the honey or screw the lid back on for storage. The honey will eventually recrystallize, but it should flow freely for several weeks.

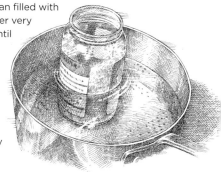

RESCUING OVERSOFTENED BUTTER

The fat in butter is partially crystalline and highly sensitive to temperature changes. When butter is properly softened to 65 or 70 degrees, the tiny crystals can effectively surround and stabilize the air bubbles that are generated during creaming. When heated to the melting point, however, these crystals are destroyed. They can be reestablished, but only if the butter is rapidly chilled. (Returning it to the refrigerator will cool it too slowly.) To quickly cool down partially melted butter, mix in a few ice cubes. After less than a minute of stirring, the butter will cool to a softened stage—right below 70 degrees. Simply remove the ice and the butter is ready to use.

REFRESHING DRY VANILLA BEANS

A. As Easy as Sliced Bread

Return moisture to hardened vanilla beans by placing them in an airtight container overnight (or better yet, for two nights) with a slice of bread. The moisture from the bread should soften the beans enough to let you split them and scrape out the seeds.

B. Restorative Cream Bath

Splitting dry, shriveled vanilla beans and removing their seeds is nearly impossible. To avoid wasting this expensive ingredient, use this trick to revive over-the-hill vanilla beans.

1. Cut the vanilla beans in half crosswise and place them in a microwave-safe bowl or measuring cup. Add enough cream or half-and-half to cover the beans.

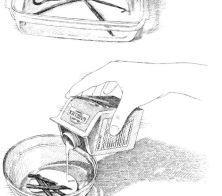

2. Microwave the mixture on medium power for 1 to 2 minutes until the beans are soft and supple (the cream should not boil). Remove the beans from the cream, split them lengthwise, and scrape out the seeds. Don't discard the vanilla-flavored cream: It can be cooled and used in coffee.

Vanilla Extract

✓ **WHY THIS RECIPE WORKS:** Even dried-out vanilla beans can be used to create a pretty impressive bottle of homemade vanilla extract. It's well worth the two-month wait. Pop off the lid of your homemade vanilla and you'll find the scent is pure and unadulterated. The taste? A full-bodied, well-rounded flavor that makes the best store-bought pure vanilla extract taste cheap. If you can find them, Grade B beans, labeled "extract beans," contain less water and are ideal for homemade extract. This recipe makes 1 cup.

8   vanilla beans (1 ounce), preferably Grade B
1   cup vodka

1. Cut vanilla beans in half lengthwise. Using tip of paring knife or spoon, scrape out seeds and transfer to small saucepan. Cut pods into 1-inch pieces and add to pan.

2. Add vodka, cover, and cook over medium-low heat until mixture is steaming, about 2 minutes. (Do not open lid while pot is over flame or alcohol will ignite.)

3. Pour mixture into jar with tight-fitting lid and let cool to room temperature. Cover with lid and store in dark place for at least 6 weeks or up to 10 weeks, shaking jar gently once a week.

4. Line fine-mesh strainer with 2 coffee filters and set over liquid measuring cup. Strain vanilla through filters, then transfer from measuring cup to clean jar with tight-fitting lid. Vanilla extract will keep indefinitely.

REJUVENATING DRIED-OUT MARSHMALLOWS

Marshmallows have a tendency to become hard and stale over time. Try this tip to restore their freshness: Place the stale marshmallows and one slice of white sandwich bread in an airtight container. After 24 hours, the marshmallows will be soft and ready for snacking or floating on hot chocolate. Discard the bread.

RESUSCITATING STALE COOKIES

To restore the warm and chewy "Just out of the oven" texture to stale, hardened cookies, place them on a microwave-safe plate and heat them in the microwave on high power for 10 seconds. Be careful if the cookies are hot, but be sure to eat them before they cool completely and lose their softness again.

REPLENISHING FRESHNESS IN BREAD

Toasting slices is one way to revive stale bread. But what if you want to reverse the staling of an entire loaf? Here's our method: If the bread is crusty, briefly pass it under a running faucet of cold water (for softer loaves, skip this step). Wrap the loaf tightly with aluminum foil, place it on the middle rack of a cold oven, and set the temperature to 300 degrees. After about 30 minutes (15 to 20 minutes for small or narrow loaves like baguettes), remove the foil and return the loaf to the oven for about 5 more minutes to crisp the crust. The effect lasts for only a few hours or so, so make sure to serve or use your revived bread immediately.

RECRISPING CHIPS

Microwaving stale potato or tortilla chips restores crispness beautifully. Spread 2 cups of chips on a Pyrex pie plate and microwave on high for 1 minute. Place the hot chips on a double layer of paper towels and allow them to come to room temperature before serving.

RECOVERING PLIABLE TORTILLAS

Some tortillas have an annoying tendency to crack and break when you fold them into wraps or burritos, especially if they're a few days old. To make them more pliable, briefly warm them in the microwave.

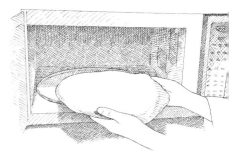

1. Place a stack of tortillas on a large microwave-safe plate and cover it with a damp dish towel.

2. Microwave on high power for 15 to 30 seconds. Carefully remove the towel and use the tortillas immediately.

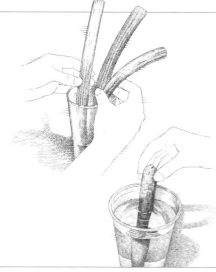

RECHARGING CELERY AND CARROTS

Over time, even the crispest celery and carrots become limp, but there's a simple technique for refreshing lifeless veggies.

1. Trim and discard the bottom end of each celery stalk and peel the carrots.

2. Place the carrots or celery in a tall, narrow container with at least 2 inches of water (more for carrots). Refrigerate overnight, until they are crisp and sprightly. The vegetables absorb the water, which crisps them back up.

RECYCLING NUTMEG NUBBINS

When you have grated a whole nutmeg seed to the point where you are risking your fingertips, don't throw the little nub away. Eliminate waste by grinding the leftover nutmeg with a mortar and pestle. It is actually quite soft and pulverizes quite easily.

7.2 TIPS FOR LEFTOVERS WORTH EATING

REWARMING LEFTOVERS

Judging the interior temperature of reheated leftovers such as lasagna or a casserole can be difficult. To avoid serving leftovers that are tepid at the center, try this trick.

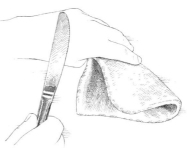

1. Before taking the casserole out of the oven, poke the center with the blade of a butter knife or dull dinner knife, and leave it in place for 15 to 30 seconds.

2. Remove the knife and then touch the side of the blade very gently to the back of your hand. If the metal is hot, so, too, is the center of the casserole.

REVIEWING YOUR ASSUMPTIONS ABOUT THAWING

We did a lot of testing to determine the best way to heat a frozen casserole, and we found that the simplest method was actually the best—we put our frozen casseroles straight into a cold oven without defrosting. This method allowed the casserole to defrost gently as the oven came to temperature. Defrosting the casserole before baking took longer without giving us better results, and putting a frozen casserole in a hot oven resulted in casseroles with bubbling tops over icy centers.

REVITALIZING LEFTOVER FRENCH TOAST

After a big weekend breakfast, there are inevitably a few uneaten pancakes or slices of French toast. Instead of discarding the leftovers, try this method for saving them and reheating them later.

1. Layer parchment paper between the cooked French toast slices or pancakes, wrap in plastic wrap and then in aluminum foil, and store in the freezer.

2. To reheat, unwrap and heat the French toast or pancakes for 10 to 12 minutes on a baking sheet in a 350-degree oven and serve with hot maple syrup. The breakfast treats can also be reheated in a toaster oven.

REVISITING COLD SOFT-COOKED EGGS

Making a large batch of soft-cooked eggs for the week is super convenient, but reheating them once they've been refrigerated can be a little tricky. One quick method is to place the cold egg(s) in a bowl—or, if taking your breakfast on the go, a food storage or deli container—and fill the vessel with hot water. Let sit for 3 minutes, drain, and serve.

RECLAIMING LEFTOVER RICE

For leftover rice that tastes just as fluffy and moist as a fresh-made pot, try this method.

1. Fill a saucepan with ½ inch of water. Place a steamer basket lined with a damp coffee filter in the pan.

2. Add leftover rice; cover and cook until heated through, about 5 minutes. Fluff with a fork and serve.

REDEEMING LEFTOVER POLENTA

Freshly cooked polenta has a terrific creamy texture, but leftovers cooled in the refrigerator turn thick and stiff. To restore your leftover polenta to its original creamy state, try the following technique: Using quick pulses, process the cold polenta in a food processor, adding a few tablespoons of warm water for every cup of cooked polenta, until the mixture is creamy. Transfer the processed polenta to a microwave-safe bowl, cover with microwave-safe plastic wrap, and heat on high power until warm.

REANIMATING LEFTOVER PASTA

Day-old pasta often becomes dry and unappetizing, but you can save yourself from mediocre leftovers by planning ahead. Simply save some of the original pasta cooking water (or make a substitute with water and cornstarch—see page 280) and stir it into the leftovers when you're reheating them. You'll end up with leftovers that are almost as moist and tender as the original dish.

REVIVING LEFTOVER PIZZA

Leftover pizza is a treat that can easily be ruined by a spin in the microwave (it gets soggy). Our favorite reheating method for pizza uses the oven. Place the cold slices on a rimmed baking sheet, cover the sheet tightly with aluminum foil, and place it on the lower rack of a cold oven. Then set the oven temperature at 275 degrees and let the pizza warm for 25 to 30 minutes. This approach leaves the interior of the crust soft, the cheese melty, and the bottom hot and crisp but not dehydrated. If you'd rather not heat up the oven for a single slice of pizza, just turn to the stovetop burner. Place the pizza in a cold nonstick skillet, cover it, and turn the burner to low. About 8 minutes in the pan gives the cheese time to melt while the bottom crisps perfectly—no more soggy slices.

RETHINKING LEFTOVER FISH

Fish is notoriously susceptible to overcooking, so reheating previously cooked fillets is something that makes nearly all cooks balk. But almost everyone has leftover fish from time to time, and the best technique for dealing with it depends on what kind of fish you've got. To reheat thicker fish fillets, use a gentle approach: Place the fillets on a wire rack set in a rimmed baking sheet, cover them with aluminum foil (to prevent the exterior of the fish from drying out), and heat them in a 275-degree oven until they register 125 to 130 degrees, about 15 minutes for 1-inch-thick fillets (timing varies according to fillet size). For thin fish, it's very difficult to reheat without drying out and overcooking. Your best bet is to try serving leftover cooked thin fish in cold applications like salads.

RECONDITIONING LEFTOVER FONDUE

Fondue is a fun and delicious special-occasion food but one of the downsides is that it always eventually cools down and firms up. Keep the cheese flowing with this method for serving and reheating: Fill a microwaveable bowl one-third full of boiling water, then nest a slightly smaller microwaveable bowl inside it. Pour the fondue into the smaller bowl and serve. To reheat, microwave the double-bowl setup for 2 to 3 minutes, stirring halfway through microwaving.

REINVIGORATING LEFTOVER TURKEY

Microwaving leftover turkey often dries it out. Try one of these ingenious methods to warm your leftovers while keeping the meat moist.

A. Place slices of leftover turkey in a steamer basket set in a pot of simmering water, then cover the pot with a lid and check it every few minutes. The turkey heats up quickly and stays juicy.

B. Wrap leftover portions in aluminum foil, stacking any sliced pieces, and place them on a wire rack set in a rimmed baking sheet. Transfer to a 275-degree oven and heat until the meat registers 130 degrees. Timing will vary based on the shape and size of the leftover turkey pieces.

C. Place any large skin-on pieces skin side down in a lightly oiled skillet over medium-high heat, heating until the skin recrisps.

RECONSTITUTING FROZEN GRAVY

Defrosting and reheating leftover gravy is a tricky task—the sauce tends to weep and separate when rewarmed. This is because when gravy is thickened with flour or cornstarch (the two most common thickeners), the starch granules release long, straight chains of glucose called amylose. The stringy amylose molecules tangle and form a net-like structure that gives the gravy its thick consistency. When gravy cools, the amylose crystallizes and the net-like structure breaks down, causing it to weep or break. But this unattractive trait is fixable. Simply bring your defrosted gravy to a full boil and then whisk it vigorously to return it to its normal thick, emulsified consistency.

REHEATING LEFTOVER STEAK (SO IT DOESN'T SUCK)

Our best method for cooking steaks—slowly warming them in the oven and then searing them in a hot skillet—turns out to be the best method for rewarming leftover steak, as well. The reheated steaks come out only slightly less juicy than freshly cooked ones, and their crusts are actually more crisp. Place leftover steaks on a wire rack set in a rimmed baking sheet and warm them on the middle rack of a 250-degree oven until the steaks register 110 degrees (roughly 30 minutes for 1½-inch-thick steaks, but timing will vary according to thickness and size). Pat the steaks dry with a paper towel and heat 1 tablespoon of vegetable oil in a 12-inch skillet over high heat until just smoking. Sear the steaks on both sides until crisp, 60 to 90 seconds per side. Let the steaks rest for 5 minutes before serving. After resting, the centers should be at medium-rare temperature (125 to 130 degrees).

CHAPTER 8

COMPANY'S COMING HACKS

Clever Ways to Impress Your Friends

TWO WAYS TO MAKE TEA FOR TWELVE

A. To brew a large batch of tea without the mess of fishing out hot tea bags, tie the tea bag strings together, then slide a skewer or chopstick through the knot before tightening it. Position the skewer across the top of the pot, with the tea bags dangling in the water. When the tea has finished brewing, remove the skewer and all the tea bags simultaneously.

B. Try this trick to keep the tea bags from getting lost in the water, whether you're making hot or iced tea. Crimp the tabs of the bags to fit through the holes of a slotted spoon and prop the spoon across the opening of the pot or pitcher while the tea steeps. The strings aren't pulled in, and removing the bags is as simple as lifting the spoon.

PRESERVING PIPING-HOT PANCAKES

A warm oven can be used to keep pancakes hot, but this method sometimes results in a dried-out breakfast. Try the following trick for keeping pancakes as hot and moist as when they first come out of the skillet.

1. Bring 2 cups water to a simmer in a large saucepan. Place a large heatproof plate on top of the saucepan.

2. As the pancakes are cooked, place them on the warm plate until serving time.

HEATED BREAKFAST DISHES ARE CLASSY

A. When you pour hot coffee into a cold mug, the mug absorbs heat, making the coffee cool down faster. To keep coffee hot longer, preheat the mugs by filling them with hot tap water and letting them sit while the coffee brews. When the coffee is ready, pour out the hot water.

B. Prevent room-temperature plates from cooling down a perfect hot breakfast. While your bread is toasting, place the plates on top of the toaster oven. The radiating heat warms them right up and delivers eggs, pancakes, and other breakfast items to the table still hot.

TOAST FOR A TABLEFUL

Most electric toasters only accommodate two to four slices of bread—a problem if you're hosting a large group for breakfast or brunch. Here's an easy way to toast enough bread for a crowd: Place an oven rack in the middle position and a second rack in the lower-middle position. Then place a baking sheet on the lower rack. Heat the oven to 450 degrees, then arrange bread slices between every other bar of the upper rack, resting on the baking sheet. Toast the bread until the top sides are lightly browned, about 6 minutes. Using tongs, flip the slices and continue toasting the second side, about 6 minutes longer.

KEEPING MAPLE SYRUP WARM

There's nothing like pouring warm maple syrup over hot French toast or pancakes. To keep the syrup from getting cold during breakfast, pour the freshly warmed syrup into an insulated coffee carafe or thermos before bringing it to the table.

SUMMER SALAD CHILL-DOWN

Serving cold dishes at a hot summer picnic can be a recipe for mediocre food. Here are two tips for keeping your salads and cold dishes cool and fresh on the buffet table.

A. Dutch Oven Cooler

Fill an enameled cast-iron Dutch oven with ice water and let it stand until the pot is thoroughly chilled, about 5 minutes. Dump out the water and dry the pot and then transfer chilled food, such as potato or macaroni salad, into the pot for serving. The pot will retain the cold temperature much longer than would a glass or plastic serving bowl.

B. Lettuce on Ice

Fill one or two large zipper-lock bags with ice cubes and a few table-spoons of salt. (The salt helps to keep the ice cold longer.) Place the sealed bags in the bottom of a large serving bowl and cover them with lettuce leaves. Spoon your salad onto the lettuce leaves. It will stay cold for at least 1 hour.

POTLUCK PERFECTION

All too often, hot potluck dishes cool off quickly. Keep your soups and stews (and even mashed potatoes) warm on the buffet table for more than an hour by serving them in an attractive, insulated ice bucket.

DISH ID

Bringing food to a potluck or other get-together can be a bit of a risk—many a good dish has been lost in the shuffle over the years. Give your platters and trays a fighting chance at making it home by writing your name and phone number or address on the bottom in dry-erase marker. It makes for easy identification post-meal and easily washes off later.

TAGGING WITH TOOTHPICKS

When grilling for a crowd, you need a way to tell well-done burgers and steaks from medium-rare at a glance. Try assigning each level of doneness a number of toothpicks (e.g., one for medium-rare, two for medium, three for well-done) and pegging the proper marker into the meat as it comes off the fire.

BBQ TRICK FOR BAKERS

When serving condiments at backyard barbecues, use a jumbo muffin tin to contain extras like ketchup, mustard, relish, and chopped onion. The toppings stay together and you have only one container to clean at the end of the party. (A popover pan also works.)

A SIMPLE TRICK FOR SWEETER ICED TEA

No one enjoys undissolved granules of sugar in an iced tea. Solve the problem by keeping a jar of sugar syrup, known as simple syrup, in the refrigerator. To make the syrup, combine 1 cup water and 1 cup granulated sugar in a small saucepan. Set the pan over medium heat and whisk frequently, until the sugar dissolves completely. Simmer for 4 minutes, remove from the heat, and let cool. For more flavor, simmer one of the following ingredients with the water and sugar (strain the flavoring ingredients out of the syrup once it cools):

- ½ scraped fresh vanilla bean and seeds for Vanilla Simple Syrup
- 3 tablespoons packed mint leaves for Mint Simple Syrup
- 3 ounces fresh berries (raspberries, blackberries, or blueberries) for Berry Simple Syrup
- 2-inch piece of ginger cut into four coins for Ginger Simple Syrup
- 2 teaspoons grated citrus zest (lemon, lime, or orange) for Citrus Simple Syrup

CONCENTRATED FLAVOR FOR SUMMER DRINKS

Create inventive summer drinks by stirring scoops of frozen juice concentrate into pitchers of unsweetened iced tea to taste. Lemonade, limeade, and orange juice are all great choices.

WATERMELON ICE CUBES

Everyone loves lemonade on hot days. To make it extra fun, freeze diced watermelon to put in the glasses instead of ice cubes. The watermelon's water content helps it freeze easily, and the lemonade-spiked watermelon makes a delicious treat after the drink is gone.

UNDILUTED FRUIT PUNCH

Chilling fruit punch or sangria with ice cubes can water it down. Here's a clever and delicious alternative.

1. Freeze assorted chunks of fruit, such as apple, orange, pineapple, pear, peach, and grapes, on a baking sheet for 1 to 2 hours (depending on the size of the fruit).

2. Add the frozen fruit to the drink. Not only does the fruit help keep the drink cold, it can also be eaten at the end.

DIY INSTANT WINE BUCKET

For a way to quickly chill a bottle of white wine at a picnic, try cutting the top off an empty plastic 2-liter soda bottle, filling it about one-third of the way with ice and water, and placing the wine bottle inside. The wine will be crisp and cool in minutes.

EMERGENCY BBQ BOTTLE OPENER

During backyard barbecues, it's all too easy to misplace one of the most important tools: the bottle opener. To quench your thirst during grillside endeavors, you can use grill tongs as a substitute church key. They have an opening inside the handles just large enough to catch the edge of a bottle cap. Sandwich the top of the bottle inside the handle and you can gently pop the cap off.

NO-DRIP ICE CREAM CONES

When you eat ice cream in a cone, the melting ice cream often drips through the bottom of the cone and onto your hands or clothing. Here are two tasty solutions to this tragic problem.

A. Dip the bottom of the cone (at least ½ inch) into the melted chocolate of your choice (dark, milk, or white). Place the cone upside down on a cooling rack until the chocolate sets, fill it with ice cream, and serve. (Grasp the cone above the chocolate so it won't melt.)

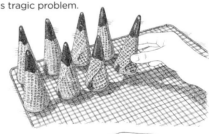

B. Place a mini marshmallow or upside-down Hershey's Kiss in the cone before loading it up with ice cream, creating a barrier between the melting ice cream and the cone tip.

EASY, FANCY ICE CREAM SANDWICHES

Though homemade ice cream sandwiches are a wonderful treat even with no embellishment at all, it is fun and easy to dress them up a little. Spread sprinkles, toasted shredded coconut, toasted chopped nuts, or mini chocolate chips on a plate and dip the edges of the ice cream sandwiches into them. Press down firmly yet gently to make sure the decorations adhere to the ice cream.

FROSTBITE-FREE ICE CREAM SCOOPING

Instead of freezing your fingers off while clutching tubs of ice cream to serve up at the next picnic or birthday party, use this tip: Wrap a dish towel around the middle of the ice cream carton and twist the ends together. To scoop, grasp the twisted section of the towel firmly; this will give you a good grip—without the frostbite.

Instant Aged Bourbon

✓ **WHY THIS RECIPE WORKS:** A fine aged bourbon is a beautiful thing, but it doesn't come cheap. And you might not always want to bring out the top-shelf stuff at a big rowdy party. So when we heard that inexpensive bourbon could be doctored to make it taste more like the good stuff, we had to give it a try. We bought several bottles of bourbon costing around $15 for 750 milliliters and experimented with spiking each with small amounts of different flavorings. We used a bottle of 12-year-old W.L. Weller bourbon (about $50) as a benchmark. In the end, three pantry staples proved most effective at mimicking the effects of barrel aging: vanilla extract provided vanillin (a flavor compound found in oak), liquid smoke added earthy depth, and dry sherry (which undergoes at least three years of oxidative aging) contributed many of the aromas and flavors associated with well-aged bourbon. You and your party guests might not find the spirits to be as good as real oak-aged bourbon, but you'll be pleasantly surprised by the enhanced complexity of the altered booze. Our tasters unanimously preferred it to the unadulterated low-end samples. This recipe makes one 750-milliliter bottle of doctored bourbon.

1 **tablespoon dry sherry**
¾ **teaspoon vanilla extract**
⅛ **teaspoon liquid smoke**
1 **750-ml bottle inexpensive bourbon**

Pour sherry, vanilla, and liquid smoke into bottle with bourbon, replace cap, and shake.

8.3 COOL COCKTAIL PARTIES

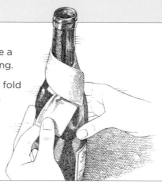

WINE BOTTLE BIB

To keep drips from staining your tablecloth, tie a paper collar around wine bottles before pouring.

1. Fold a paper towel in half lengthwise, then fold it in thirds lengthwise (like a business letter). Wrap the strip around the neck of the wine bottle, overlapping the ends.

2. Tuck one end of the strip under the other and pull the free end to tighten the strip snugly around the neck of the bottle.

AERATE WINE IN A FLASH

Red wines—especially young, undeveloped ones—benefit from a breathing period after opening to break down tannins and sulfur compounds by exposing as much of the wine as possible to oxygen. Typically, this is done by pouring the wine into a wide, shallow vessel and letting it rest for several hours, but decanting can also be accomplished by simply pouring the wine between two pitchers 15 times. Wines that are decanted this way taste bright and balanced, with more complex aromas coming to the fore.

MAKESHIFT MARTINI SHAKER

Cocktails like martinis and Manhattans should be shaken, not stirred, and not just because James Bond says so. Shaking the cocktail with the ice chills the mixture more thoroughly than simply stirring it. A spillproof coffee mug with a screw-on lid makes a fine substitute for a proper martini shaker. Just be sure to place your finger over the sipping hole when you shake.

HOME-FILTERED VODKA

When it comes to cooking and baking with vodka, we usually recommend that you spend the money on a premium bottle, but there is a cheaper option. Vodka is charcoal filtered to remove impurities. Generally speaking, the better-quality vodka is more highly filtered. So if your cheap vodka hasn't been filtered much before it hits the shelves, just do it yourself. Pour it through an at-home water filter four times. This works great for improving vodka that you're going to use in a recipe or in a mixed drink. If you want the liquor for straight-up drinking, seasoned palates will notice a difference.

GUARANTEED CHILL FOR GIBSONS

Use frozen onions in your Gibson (a martini garnished with onions instead of olives) instead of the traditional pickled onions. They will help keep the cocktail chilled while also imparting the ideal essence of onion.

CHILLING IN THE LAUNDRY ROOM

Especially around the holidays, refrigerator space available for chilling beverages for a party is often at a premium. For an unusual solution, turn your top-loading washing machine into something of an icebox. Fill the washer's basket with ice cubes, then nestle in the drinks. When the party is over and the ice has melted, simply run the washer's spin cycle to drain the water.

KEEPING COOL WITH YOUR BUNDT PAN

When you aren't baking cakes with your Bundt pan, you can use it to bring a whole new cool factor to your parties with these two tricks.

A. In the Punch Bowl

1. Arrange a layer of thinly sliced citrus rings over the bottom of the pan. Pour enough cold water over the fruit to barely cover. Freeze until firm, then add enough water to cover the fruit by 1½ inches. Freeze until firm.

2. When you're ready to use the ice ring, run the bottom of the mold under warm water until the ice ring releases. Place the ring in your punch bowl.

B. On the Snack Table

1. Fill a Bundt pan halfway with water; freeze until firm. Just prior to serving, run the bottom of the mold under warm water to loosen the ice ring.

2. Place the ring in a large serving bowl and set a container of cocktail sauce or other dip in the center. Top the ice with shrimp, crudités, or fruit.

Crispy Spiced Chickpeas

✔ **WHY THIS RECIPE WORKS:** Party snacks can be predictable and boring—dumping a bag of potato chips into a bowl is hardly going to impress your guests. Instead, try this surprisingly quick and easy (and totally addictive) recipe for ultracrisp fried chickpeas, seasoned with smoked paprika (an alluring spice that packs a smoky punch). Make sure to dry the chickpeas thoroughly with paper towels before placing them in the oil to prevent splattering. To ensure crisp chickpeas, keep the heat high enough that the oil continues simmering the whole time after you add the chickpeas. Check for doneness after about 12 minutes; let cool slightly before tasting a few. If they are not quite crisp yet, continue to cook for 2 to 3 minutes longer, checking occasionally for doneness. Fried chickpeas can be stored in an airtight container for up to 1 day. This recipe makes 6 servings.

- 2 **(15-ounce) cans chickpeas**
- 1 **teaspoon smoked paprika**
- 1 **teaspoon sugar**
  Salt and pepper
- 1 **cup olive oil**

1. Rinse chickpeas and pat thoroughly dry with paper towels. Combine paprika, sugar, ½ teaspoon salt, and ¼ teaspoon pepper in large bowl. Heat oil in large Dutch oven over high heat until just smoking.

2. Add chickpeas and cook, stirring occasionally, until deep golden brown and crisp, 12 to 15 minutes. Using slotted spoon, transfer chickpeas to paper towel–lined baking sheet to drain briefly, then toss with spices. Serve.

8.3 COOL COCKTAIL PARTIES

ENGINEERING CRUDITÉS

Height is an important visual element in an appealing crudité presentation. Even with an assortment as simple as cherry tomatoes and carrot and celery sticks, you can use the following tricks to create a little extra height.

A. Give celery and carrot sticks extra lift (and freshness) by standing them up in glasses or cups with a few ice cubes in the bottom.

B. To elevate a bowl full of bite-size items such as cherry tomatoes or trimmed broccoli florets, overturn a small glass or ceramic bowl to use as a stand for the bowl holding the veggies. (If your bowls are slippery, put a small piece of folded plastic wrap between the two to keep the top bowl in place.)

FAST TRACK TO SOFT CHEESE

Soft, creamy cheeses like Brie and Camembert firm up in the refrigerator and should be brought to room temperature before serving, but that can take as long as two hours. For a faster route, place the wedge of chilled cheese in an airless zipper-lock bag in 4 quarts of 80-degree water. Submerging the wedge in the water bath gently warms the cheese to 72 degrees in less than an hour.

EDIBLE TOOTHPICKS FOR HORS D'OEUVRES

Any number of hors d'oeuvres—including small meatballs, crab cakes, marinated mushrooms, bits of semisoft cheese, and squares of Spanish omelet—are served with toothpick skewers. Add a little salty crunch to the equation and avoid the problem of used toothpick disposal by spearing hors d'oeuvres with slender pretzel sticks, which can be eaten right along with the tasty tidbit they have skewered.

GIVING SAUCES THE SQUEEZE

Dispensing condiments like sour cream at a party can get messy—globs end up on the tabletop and serving spoons inevitably travel from one bowl to another. Instead, try using clear plastic squeeze bottles, which simplifies serving and cleanup.

GO BANANAS WITH YOUR SILVER

Did you know that you can use a banana peel to polish tarnished silverware? After you enjoy a banana, rub the inside of the peel along the silver and you'll see the magic happen. Just wipe it off with a clean cloth afterward to have sparkling silverware again. This trick doesn't work with really dark spots, but it's great for lightly tarnished utensils.

WARMING THINGS UP AT THE DINNER TABLE

A. Warmed dinner plates make any meal feel special. If your oven is already in use (or if any of your dishes aren't ovensafe), you can warm all the dishes you need by running them through the dishwasher on the dry cycle.

B. It is also always nice to serve food from a warm dish, but it's particularly nice with mashed potatoes and pasta, which otherwise cool off quickly. Warm your serving bowls for these foods by draining the water in which they've been cooking into the bowl and letting it warm up. Just make sure the bowl is heatproof.

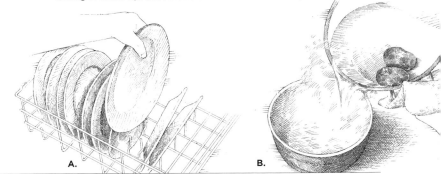

A.   B.

DESIGNATED SERVING PLATTERS

It's always nice to have help transferring food to serving bowls and platters for a large dinner party or holiday meal. But sometimes the host is busy cooking and unavailable to match the food with the serving piece of choice. To get around this situation graciously and efficiently, try labeling the serving dishes and corresponding containers of food ahead of time with small Post-it Notes to make it clear which foods and dishes go together.

PRESENTING PERFECT FISH FILLETS

A large fish fillet or whole fish makes an impressive presentation, but it can be a challenge to remove the delicate item from a baking sheet without it falling apart. For an easier transfer, reach for a flexible cutting board. Slide the cutting board under the fish and use it to gently transfer the fish onto a serving platter, using a spatula if necessary.

PROTECTING ROAST'S BROWN CRUST

For many of us, the crispy brown skin is the most sought-after morsel of a roasted chicken or turkey. The same can be said of the crust that forms on the outside of a roast. But when the roast rests before it is carved and served, the bottom crust is often soft-ened by the juices that accumulate in the platter. Get around this problem by letting the roast rest on a wire rack, thereby elevating the meat over the puddle of juices.

SPOONING A WHOLE ROAST CHICKEN

One of the most difficult parts of roasting a whole chicken is trans-ferring the hot bird from the roasting pan to the carving board. Get a better grip with this method.

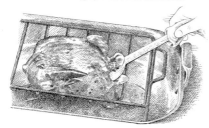

1. Insert the bowl of a long wooden spoon into the chicken's cavity.

2. Grasp the handle of the spoon with a towel, tilt the chicken slightly toward the handle, and lift it out of the pan.

TURKEY TURNING

Although we usually recommend holding large wads of paper towels to turn a hot turkey during cooking, some cooks feel more secure using oven mitts. To keep the mitts from getting dirty and greasy, slip clean plastic produce bags over the mitts to protect them.

STUFFING MUFFINS

One of the greatest holiday essentials is the crisp topping of baked stuffing. To please everyone at the table, bake individual portions of stuffing in muffin tins so that there is plenty of crispy goodness to go around: The sides and top of each "muffin" become browned and crunchy. (A bonus: the baking time for the stuffing is also reduced.)

HOLDING MASHED POTATOES

Finishing the mashed potatoes at the same time as the roast, the gravy, and the green beans can become quite a juggling act. Free up some of those precious few last minutes (and some valuable stovetop space) by making your mashed potatoes a couple of hours ahead of time and keeping them warm in a slow cooker on the low setting. All they need is a quick stir before serving.

KEEPING FOOD WARM

Tired of burning butter that's being melted and scorching mashed potatoes while trying to keep them warm over low heat? Try this easy way to tame the flame: Place a cast-iron skillet over a low flame, then place your saucepan right in the skillet.

GRAVY CARAFE

To keep gravy warm at the table, as well as easy to pour, try using an insulated coffee carafe. It cuts down on spills and keeps gravy hot throughout the meal.

A PRETTIER PIECE OF PIE

Prying out the first piece of pie often results in a broken mess. Try these tricks for a perfect first slice.

A. Foil Helper

1. Fold a 12 by 12-inch sheet of aluminum foil in half, then in half again to make a 6-inch square. Fold this square diagonally to form a triangle. Before fitting your pie dough into the plate, press one point of the triangle into the center of the pie plate and let the other two points hang over the edge.

2. Bake, cool, and then slice the pie following the triangle's lines. Pull up on the overhang and use a spatula to lift out the slice.

B. Making the (Extra) Cut

Forgot the foil? Try this: After making the two cuts to form the first slice, make a third cut as if to form the second slice. This makes it easier to slide out the first piece tidy and intact.

ANYONE CAN FROST LIKE A PRO

A cake makes an impressive ending to any meal. Here are a few simple tricks that can take your decorating skills to the next level.

A. DIY Cake Comb

A cake "comb" is an easy way to make patterns in the icing on a cake. Make your own at home with nothing but a pair of decorative scissors (like pinking shears) and a plastic lid or discarded credit card. After frosting, use the serrated edge to create a ridged design.

B. Makeshift Cake Stands

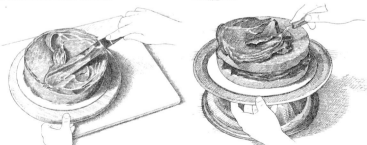

Frosting a cake is made much easier when it's elevated on a cake stand. For infrequent bakers, a lazy Susan makes an admirable stand-in. Alternatively, try placing the cake on a cardboard round, then on an overturned 12-inch pizza pan or similarly sized baking sheet. Set the pan on an upside-down flat-bottomed bowl. The bowl provides height, and the pan can be rotated as needed.

THE SECRET OF THE SWIRLS

Cupcakes topped with swirled frosting may look like the work of a professional baker, but there's a way to bring this fancy technique home.

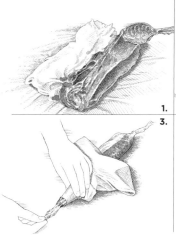

1. 2.
3. 4.

1. Spoon a line of colored frosting down the center of a large piece of plastic wrap and then spoon a second color alongside it. Fold the plastic in half lengthwise.

2. Roll the frosting into a log, twisting and knotting one end of the plastic.

3. Insert the open end of the log into a pastry bag and pull the plastic tightly through the piping tip. Snip off the excess plastic.

4. Pipe the frosting onto cupcakes as usual.

SERVING ROCK-HARD ICE CREAM

Taken straight from the freezer, small pint-size containers of premium ice cream often are frozen too hard to scoop easily. Here's an unusual solution to this problem: Place the container on its side on a cutting board and cut off slices, right through the cardboard, with a serrated blade or an electric knife. Peel the cardboard off the sides and serve. The lid will sit flush up against any ice cream left in the container for easy storage. This method lends itself to artful presentations, such as sandwiching each disk between two cookies for easy ice cream sandwiches, or cutting the disks into interesting shapes using cookie cutters.

CUSTARD'S LAST STAND

Individually portioned desserts such as custard are a great make-ahead solution when entertaining, but only if you have enough refrigerator space to accommodate multiple ramekins. Maximize space by placing a tiered cooling rack in the fridge. With multiple shelves, you can chill several servings at once.

Homemade Chocolate Magic Shell Ice Cream Topping

✔ **WHY THIS RECIPE WORKS:** Chocolate sauce that instantly hardens when poured over ice cream is a treat with a party-worthy presentation. When we sampled Smucker's Magic Shell over ice cream, we were impressed by the way it hardened upon contact but less fond of its cloyingly sweet, boringly mild chocolate taste. A quick review of the ingredients revealed that the "magic" was the third ingredient listed: coconut oil. Coconut oil is extremely high in saturated fat, which makes it solid at room temperature and brittle at cooler temperatures. Combining melted coconut oil in a 2:3 ratio with melted chocolate produced a satiny mixture that solidified into a perfect, shatteringly thin shell with a rich chocolate flavor. This recipe makes ¾ cup.

- ¼ **teaspoon vanilla extract**
- ⅛ **teaspoon instant espresso powder**
- **Pinch salt**
- 4 **ounces semisweet chocolate, chopped**
- ⅓ **cup coconut oil**
- 1 **teaspoon unsweetened cocoa powder**

Stir vanilla, espresso powder, and salt together until espresso dissolves. Microwave chocolate and coconut oil at 50 percent power, stirring occasionally, until melted, 2 to 4 minutes. Whisk in vanilla mixture and cocoa until combined. Let cool to room temperature, about 30 minutes, before using. Chocolate shell can be stored at room temperature in airtight container for 2 months; microwave, stirring occasionally, until melted and smooth, 1 to 2 minutes, before using.

CHAPTER 9

11TH-HOUR HACKS

You Made a Mistake, Now Let's Fix It

LAST-MINUTE SIDE DISH

For a quick way to make a bowl of steamed broccoli or cauliflower for the dinner table, just put the vegetables in a microwavable zipper-lock bag or microwave-safe dish with a cover with two or three ice cubes. Microwave for a minute or so for a super-fast side dish.

EMERGENCY MEATBALLS

Need quick meatballs for that impromptu spaghetti dinner? Try this shortcut, which uses sausages.

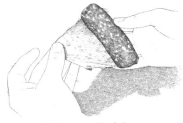

1. Remove all of the sausage filling from its casing.

2. Roll small sections of the filling into balls and fry them in a skillet. Make sure to cook thoroughly.

MADE-AHEAD DISH SHORTHAND

Streamline dinner and minimize last-minute work on food from the freezer by leaving a note to yourself. Next time you freeze a make-ahead dish, wrap it up and then place a sticky-note on top of the wrapped food that lists the finishing instructions. Wrap the whole thing in an extra layer of plastic wrap. Now in the rush before dinner you'll have all the information you need to finish the dish without having to dig up the recipe again.

PASTA WATER REPLACEMENT

If you forgot to save pasta water for thinning sauce and instead poured it all down the drain, there's an easy fix: Mix ¼ teaspoon of cornstarch with 1 cup of water and microwave it for 1 to 2 minutes until hot. A splash or two of the slightly thickened liquid creates a sauce with just the right consistency.

BOILING WATER ON THE DOUBLE

Boiling four or five quarts of water for pasta can be slow and frustrating, especially if you're running out of time before dinner. Speed up the process by boiling the water in two pots. When both pots are boiling, carefully pour the water from the second pot into the stockpot, and you're ready to go.

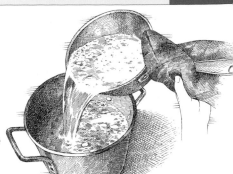

INFUSED OIL FAST

Oils infused with garlic, herbs, or other flavors can make the perfect final touch for a pasta recipe, salad, or side dish. However, large bottles of flavored oil don't always keep well and they may not have the strong, fresh taste that you're looking for. If you don't like keeping these expensive products around or you find that you've run out in the middle of cooking, try this solution for a lighting-fast, convenient way to make small amounts of fresh infused oil for a particular dish: Put a few tablespoons of olive oil in a microwave-safe bowl with chopped garlic, red pepper flakes, or herbs, and microwave for about a minute (until the oil is warm but not hot). The oil will be infused with whatever flavor you want in no time at all.

QUICK CHILL FOR THE WHIPPED CREAM BOWL

It's always a good idea to chill the bowl and beaters or whisk you plan to use when whipping cream, but full refrigerators and freezers may not accommodate bulky bowls. If you find yourself in this situation, try the following method: Fill a zipper-lock bag with ice cubes and place it in the bowl. A bag filled with 20 ice cubes will chill a 12-inch stainless-steel bowl in about 5 minutes. Another way to chill a stainless-steel bowl is to toss in a couple of frozen freezer packs. They will turn the bowl icy cold in about 10 minutes.

PANCAKE SYRUP BACKUP PLAN

Homemade pancakes and waffles just aren't the same without syrup. If you run out of pancake syrup with breakfast already on the table, you can make a super quick and delicious substitute from a basic pantry staple: Just melt brown sugar by microwaving it. Add water to get a consistency that you like. You can also add butter or mix in flavoring from ingredients such as almond or vanilla extracts, depending on your taste.

Quick Lemon-Parsley Compound Butter

✓ WHY THIS RECIPE WORKS: Compound butters are usually prepared by softening butter, mixing in flavorings, shaping the mixture into a log, and then rechilling the butter so that it can be sliced and spread on meat, fish, breads, or muffins. Our hacked version of this fancy condiment uses a whole stick of salted butter straight from the refrigerator, no mixing or rechilling necessary. A quick slice and roll ensures flavor in every portion, perfect for last-minute dinner plans. Wrap any leftovers and freeze for future use. See below for other flavor combinations to replace the parsley and lemon. This recipe makes 8 tablespoons.

- 8   **tablespoons salted butter, chilled**
- ¼   **cup minced fresh parsley**
- 4   **teaspoons grated lemon zest**

Unwrap butter and halve lengthwise. Combine parsley and zest in wide, shallow dish. Roll butter in seasonings. Slice and serve.

Garlic-Herb Butter: 2 tablespoons minced fresh sage (or 1½ teaspoons dried); 1 tablespoon minced fresh parsley; 1 tablespoon minced fresh thyme (or ¾ teaspoon dried); 2 garlic cloves, minced

Rosemary-Parmesan Butter: 6 tablespoons grated Parmesan cheese; 4 teaspoons minced fresh rosemary (or 1 teaspoon dried); 2 garlic cloves, minced; ¼ teaspoon red pepper flakes

Sweet Orange Butter: 2 tablespoons vanilla sugar; 1 teaspoon grated orange zest

FOILING A FAST SIMMER

If it's hard to get your stovetop burners to maintain a very low flame (necessary when trying to cook soups or stews at a bare simmer so they don't burn), improvise a flame tamer out of a thick ring of aluminum foil. Set the foil ring on the burner, then place the pot on top of the foil.

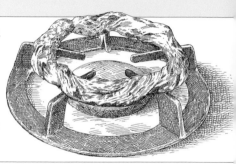

WHEN A PAN GETS OVERLY FOND

Searing meat in a pan produces a crusty brown fond, which is key to great flavor in many soups, stews, and sauces. But when those dark brown bits begin to turn black, it's a good thing gone bad. When searing cutlets over high heat, for example, the areas of the pan between the pieces of meat are often the first to blacken. To guard against this, shift the food to cover the darker spots. The juices released from the meat will help to deglaze the pan. When searing a large quantity of meat in batches, it may be necessary to deglaze the empty pan with water, wine, or stock between batches.

BROWNED BUTTER'S OILY BUDDY

Blackened butter will impart a bitter flavor to a finished dish and should be thrown away. However, slightly browned butter has a pleasantly nutty flavor and is often specifically called for in recipes. To keep butter from browning further after you get it to just the right stage, add a small amount of vegetable oil to the pan. With its higher smoke point, vegetable oil helps keep the butter from burning.

A LEAFY FIX FOR UNDERCOOKED MEAT

If you have already taken meat off the heat, rested it, and sliced it, only to discover it's underdone, you might be tempted to simply put it back in the oven or the pan, but that will only make it dry out and turn gray. Instead, place the sliced meat on a wire rack set in a baking sheet and cover each slice with a lettuce leaf. Then put the pan under the broiler for a few minutes. The meat will gently steam under the lettuce, without drying out.

SOLVING A STICKY SITUATION

Food that initially sticks to the pan usually releases on its own after a few minutes, when a crust begins to form from the heat. As long as the food is not burning, you should wait a minute or two before worrying about any stickiness. If it's still sticking on stubbornly, dip a thin, flexible spatula in cold water and slide the inverted blade underneath the food to loosen it.

MOISTENING DRY CAKE

If you find yourself with a dry, overbaked cake, brushing the cake with a flavored simple syrup can restore moistness. The technique works with yellow, white, and chocolate cakes.

1. Bring ½ cup each of water and sugar to a simmer in a small saucepan. Cook, stirring occasionally, until the sugar dissolves. Remove from the heat and add 2 tablespoons of liqueur, such as Framboise, Frangelico, Chambord, or Kahlúa.

2. After turning the cake out onto a wire rack, poke the top with a skewer and brush each layer with a few tablespoons of the flavored syrup. Let the cake cool as directed before frosting.

SPREADING STIFF FROSTING

Trying to ice a cake with stiff frosting can yield unappealing flecks of torn-off cake. To keep things spreadable, heat up a spatula or spoon in hot water before slathering on the frosting.

1. Dip the metal spatula (or spoon) into hot water for 5 seconds.

2. Remove and dry completely.

3. Spread the frosting on the cake, repeating the process as necessary.

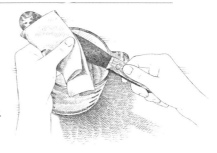

9.2 RECIPE RESCUE

GOLDILOCKS IN THE KITCHEN

Soups, stews, and sauces often need some last-minute adjustments, even if the recipe was followed to the letter. Why? The moisture and fat content of foods can vary a great deal. Here are some tips for how to tweak your dish.

TOO THICK

If your recipe turns out too thick, gradually add more water, broth, canned tomatoes, or whatever liquid is appropriate. Remember to correct the seasoning before serving.

TOO THIN

Simmering the liquid until the desired consistency is reached is the simplest option but not necessarily the best one. Time will not always permit a lengthy simmer, which may also overcook any meat or vegetables in the dish. Instead, you can try one of these options:

A. Butter

Cold butter whisked into a sauce just before serving adds richness and body.

B. Cornstarch

Soups and stews can be thickened with cornstarch, provided it is first dissolved in a small amount of water to prevent lumps.

C. Bread

Another option for a soup is to soak several pieces of crusty bread in some of the broth and then puree the bread in a blender or food processor until smooth. Add the mixture to the soup and stir to combine.

D. Instant Mashed Potato Flakes

A sprinkle of dehydrated instant mashed potato flakes can also help bring a gravy or stew to the desired consistency in seconds without changing how the dish tastes.

WHEN SEASONINGS GO AWRY

If you've added too much salt, sugar, or spice to a dish, the damage is usually done. In mild cases, however, the overpowering ingredient can sometimes be masked by the addition of another from the opposite end of the flavor spectrum. Consult this list for ideas. And remember to account for the reduction of liquids when seasoning a dish—a perfectly seasoned stew will likely taste too salty after several hours of simmering. Your best bet is to season with a light hand during the cooking process and then adjust the seasoning just before serving.

IF YOUR FOOD IS...

A. Too Salty

Add an acid or a sweetener, such as vinegar, citrus juice, canned unsalted tomatoes, sugar, honey, or maple syrup.

B. Too Sweet

Add an acid or seasonings, such as vinegar or citrus juice, chopped fresh herbs, or a dash of cayenne, or, for sweet dishes, a bit of liqueur or espresso powder.

C. Too Spicy or Acidic

Add a fat or sweetener, such as butter, cream, sour cream, cheese, olive oil, sugar, honey, or maple syrup.

RESCUING A BROKEN SAUCE

Sometimes a finicky sauce, such as beurre blanc, can separate and break if it gets too hot. But all is not lost. Simply remove the pan from the heat and whisk an ice cube into the sauce until it comes back together.

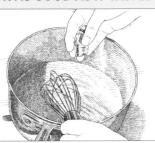

SMOOTHING OUT LUMPY GRAVY

Trying to thicken gravy by sprinkling in flour often results in unsightly lumps and a consistency that is still too thin because the starch is not dispersed. Solve the problem by using the following steps. (This technique does not work with mushroom or giblet gravy.)

1. Fill a blender no more than half full with the lumpy gravy and process until the gravy is smooth, about 30 seconds.

2. To thicken the gravy, pour it back into a saucepan and bring it to a simmer. Any remaining small lumps can be strained out with a fine-mesh strainer.

SAVING A FALLEN SOUFFLÉ

Myth: You can't make a fallen soufflé rise again. Reality: Yes, your soufflé will fall after it's been out of the oven for about 5 minutes. But returning it to a 350-degree oven will convert the water back into steam and reinflate it (although it will lose about ½ inch of height).

HELP! THIS COOKIE IS BURNT!

When baking lots of cookies, it's inevitable that some of them will end up overbrowned or even burnt in some spots. But all is not lost! Save those sweet efforts by gently grating the burnt layer with a rasp-style grater. Note that there are limits; this tip works well with lightly singed cookies but can't rescue thoroughly burnt ones.

Roux in the Microwave

✓ **WHY THIS RECIPE WORKS:** Roux, a cooked mixture of flour and fat, is often used to thicken sauces and stews. Roux can be cooked to a lighter or darker shade depending on the needs of your dish—longer-cooked, darker roux will have more pronounced flavor but less thickening power. (Cook the béchamel for a soufflé too long and it won't have the same thickening power or structural integrity, and if you shortchange the cooking time for the roux in a stew recipe, you could end up with a gloppy, overly thickened dish.) No matter the type, a roux is usually prepared at the start of a recipe, before liquids and other ingredients are added to the pot, and can take a while to cook. What happens if you get to the end of your recipe and find that your stew or sauce is too thin—and dinner is only minutes away? Here's a way to make a quick last-minute roux in the microwave that can be added to your cooked dish. Make sure to use a microwave-safe measuring cup or bowl for this recipe. We recommend placing it on a dry dish towel when you remove it from the microwave since it's best to avoid placing very hot tempered glass directly on a cold surface. This recipe makes ¼ cup.

2 **tablespoons all-purpose flour**
2 **tablespoons oil**

1. Mix flour and oil together. Microwave for 1½ minutes. Stir, then microwave for 45 seconds. Stir, microwave for 45 seconds, and stir again.

2. For darker roux, continue microwaving and stirring in 15-second intervals.

3. Stir roux, 1 tablespoon at a time, into stew or gravy until desired consistency is reached.

9.3 MAKE IT LOOK AS GOOD AS IT TASTES

FIXING A SPLIT CAKE

If you've ever found yourself with broken cake halves after removing a finicky cake from a pan, you'll appreciate this trick. Repair the fracture by allowing the cakes to cool, then spreading a thin layer of soft buttercream frosting over the broken surfaces and reattaching the pieces. Then set the cake in the refrigerator for about an hour to allow the frosting to harden before continuing to assemble and frost it.

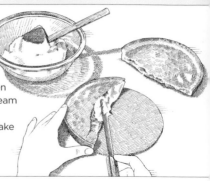

BROKEN-CUPCAKE PARFAIT

Instead of panicking when your cupcakes stick to the muffin tin, improvise with the crumbly (but still tasty) pieces by alternating cake and frosting to fill small, individual plastic cups. Simply rename the dessert "Fancy Cake Parfait Cups" and no one will be the wiser!

UNCRACKING CRACKED CHEESECAKE

Even when every precaution is taken, the occasional cheesecake will develop unsightly cracks. Here's a simple method for repairing them.

1. Remove the sidewall from the springform pan while the cheesecake is warm. Wrap a cloth ribbon snugly around the cake, preferably one that covers the sides completely (about 3 inches wide for most pans).

2. Secure the ribbon with a binder clip, and leave in place until the cake has cooled completely.

WHIPPING PUDDING INTO SHAPE

If a pudding or pastry cream has become lumpy during cooking, use this restaurant trick to smooth things out: Using an immersion blender, quickly blend the pudding until smooth. Then pass the pudding through a fine-mesh strainer to remove any remaining solid bits.

FIXES FOR WHIPPED CREAM WOES

A. Unwhipping Overwhipped Cream

If you accidentally go too far and overwhip the cream, try this trick to ensure all is not lost.

1. Add unwhipped cream to the overwhipped mixture 1 tablespoon at a time.

2. Gently fold in, adding more unwhipped cream until the desired consistency is reached.

B. Stabilizing Weepy Whipped Cream

Cream begins to break down soon after whipping. To prepare whipped cream in advance, try adding marshmallow crème to keep it stable. Whip in 6 tablespoons of crème for every cup of heavy cream, along with ½ teaspoon of rum extract or vanilla extract. Cover and refrigerate. The crème keeps the cream from deflating for up to a day and also adds a pleasantly sweet marshmallow flavor.

WHEN WINE GETS CORKED UP

Fix the frustration of fishing out bits of cork that have fallen into a bottle of wine with one of these remedies.

A. Add a Strainer

1. Cut cheesecloth into a 2-inch square, fit it over the bottle, and secure it with a rubber band.

2. Pour through the cheesecloth, leaving any bits of cork behind.

B. Use a Straw

To remove the pieces altogether, insert a straw into the neck of the bottle and over the cork crumb, then place a finger over the end of the straw and lift it out. A vacuum is created that traps the cork crumb for removal.

CHAPTER 10

FOOD
TRANSPORT
HACKS

Getting Your Dish from A to B, Safely

10.1 FLAWLESS FOOD ON THE GO

TRANSPORTING FROZEN GROCERIES

To eliminate the need to rush straight home after a trip to the supermarket, store a Styrofoam cooler in the trunk of your car for holding perishable groceries. The cooler keeps ice cream and other frozen foods from melting and prevents fragile items like eggs and fruit from rolling around and getting damaged.

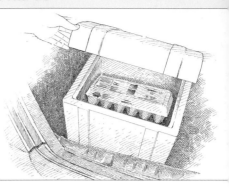

CARPROOFING PLATTERS OF PREPARED FOOD

Driving around a curve a little too fast or braking suddenly can mean disaster for a platter of food that you are transporting in your car.

To thwart potential messes, simply line the trunk of your car with a large, damp beach towel before placing the platter in the trunk. The towel prevents the dish from slipping. If you have multiple dishes, try bunching the towel between them to provide extra cushioning and stability.

TIPS FOR TENTING PLASTIC WRAP

Covering potluck-bound dishes with plastic wrap protects the food, but it can also pull away the top layer when removed. To preserve the presentation, use several pastry tips to prop up the plastic when transporting the dish and remove them prior to serving. If you don't have pastry tips, you can also create props by folding twist ties in half. Just before serving, touch up the top of your dish.

KEEP A LID ON IT

Transporting a casserole to a potluck can be a messy task. To lock the glass lid of a casserole dish in place and prevent spills, try this technique: Secure a rubber band on the handle of the lid and stretch it to attach it to one of the handles of the dish. Then secure a second rubber band on the handle of the lid and stretch it to attach it to the other handle of the dish.

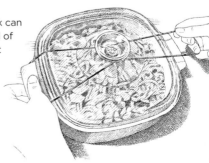

NO FOOD CARRIER? NO WORRIES!

If you don't have an insulated food carrier, don't fret—you can improvise. Wrap a casserole straight out of the oven in aluminum foil, then in a large beach towel, and then in plastic wrap. While the casserole wrapped this way will not stay at a safe temperature for the same length of time as in an insulated carrier (only about an hour, versus nearly 3 hours in a good carrier), it does give you long enough to travel moderate distances and still keep the food hot.

NO MORE DISH SLIPPAGE

Have you ever thought to yourself, "Gee, I wonder what I could do with my leftover nonskid shelf liner?" If you happen to have a large casserole or cake to tote from point A to point B, here's what to do: Line the bottom of a cake carrier, box, or other container with a small piece of surplus nonskid shelf liner to keep the contents from sliding into the walls of the carrier while in transit.

CRISPER CASSEROLE CRUSTS

To keep a casserole topping crisp while traveling to a potluck dinner, place a paper towel or clean dish towel over the top of the dish before wrapping it in aluminum foil. Steam from the hot casserole is absorbed by the towel instead of condensing on the foil and dripping back onto the casserole.

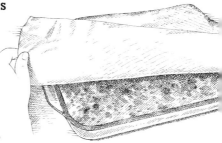

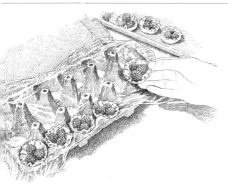

TRANSPORTING FRAGILE PASTRIES AND HORS D'OEUVRES

If you've ever tried to transport small, delicate tartlets, deviled eggs, or other bite-size treats for family parties or neighborhood potlucks, you know how difficult it can be to get them to their final destination safely. Here's one idea for making the trip a little safer: Pack the items in a cardboard egg carton lined with plastic wrap.

STUFFED MUSHROOM CADDY

For easier transport of stuffed mushroom caps, use mini muffin tins. Each mushroom perches neatly in a muffin cup, and not a single bread crumb is lost on the way to the party.

DEVILED EGGS ON THE GO

Deviled eggs are all about presentation—bright yellow filling piped into the hollow of a cooked egg white—so safely packing them for a picnic or a party can be daunting. Here are two tricks to help.

A. Prevent overturned eggs by placing each one in a paper cupcake liner and then arranging them in a single layer in a plastic storage container.

B. To completely sidestep the problem of stabilizing already-filled deviled eggs, pack the prepared filling in a zipper-lock bag, then simply place the egg white halves and the bag of filling in a cooler for transport. Just before serving the eggs, snip the corner of the bag and pipe the filling into the whites.

TRAVEL-READY FROZEN DINNER

Skip the canned beans and franks on a stick and upgrade to skirt or flank steak on your next camping trip (works for tailgating, too).

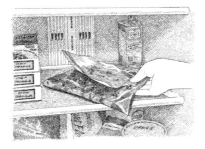

1. At least one day in advance, combine the meat with a low-acid marinade (that won't turn the exterior of the meat mushy) in a zipper-lock bag and place the bag in the freezer. You want about ¼ cup of marinade for every pound of beef.

2. About 3 hours before you're ready to grill, remove the steak from the freezer and place in a cooler. It should stay cold but defrost in time for cooking.

SALAD IN A BAG

Instead of carting a container with you when you bring salad to a party (and then inevitably leaving it behind), pack your salad with all of its extras in an extra-large zipper-lock bag. Just before serving, add the dressing, give the bag a quick shake, and empty the salad into one of your host's serving bowls.

HAVE CUPCAKES, WILL TRAVEL

Beautifully frosted cupcakes make a great single-serving dessert for parties and picnics, but transporting them neatly can be a challenge. Here are a few tips to help your treats survive their trip.

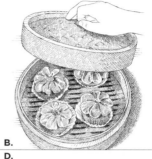

A. | **B.**
C. | **D.**

A. To easily transport cupcakes without having to buy a cupcake carrier, use a large shirt box (found at drugstores and other outlets). Cut evenly spaced Xs in the top of the box and then nest the cupcakes inside them.

B. Rather than buying a carrier dedicated to transporting baked goods, try toting yours in a bamboo steamer basket. Cupcakes (and pie) fit snugly inside, the lid protects the contents, and a ribbon tied from bottom to top secures it en route.

C. Sometimes you may want to transport just one cupcake. To safely transport a cupcake or any other delicate pastry, lay the lid of a clean pint-size deli container upside down and place your cupcake on it. Invert the container, slip it over the cupcake and down onto the lid, and seal it shut, thus creating a safe shell around the cupcake.

D. If the aesthetics of the cupcake are less important to you, another way to preserve the frosting is to cut the cake of the cupcake in half horizontally and flip the top half upside down so that the icing is in the middle, making a cupcake sandwich. Wrap the cupcake in plastic wrap or a plastic bag, and you're good to go.

TRAUMA-FREE PIE TRANSPORT

Your freshly baked pie deserves better than to be squished in transit to a party. Turn to another type of pie for a clever container—pizza pie. Hit up your local pizzeria and request a clean pizza box (a small 10-inch-square one is just the right size) for keeping flat-topped pies, such as pecan and pumpkin, safe. (This tip won't work with domed pies, like lemon meringue, but see below for one that will.)

PASTA-TOPPED CREAM PIE?!

The last ingredient you'd expect to pair with your beautiful cream pie is pasta, but hear us out. Instead of risking a mussed-up topping with a close-fitting cover during transport, stand a few strands of uncooked spaghetti in the pie and suspend a sheet of plastic wrap over the pasta. Don't try this with toothpicks, which are likely to sink down into the pie.

WHIPPED CREAM ON THE GO

When bringing a pie for dessert, you might want to serve it with fresh whipped cream. Since this accompaniment doesn't travel well, try this efficient way to transport cream and "whip" it all in one container.

1. For about 1 cup of whipped cream, place ½ cup of heavy cream and 1½ teaspoons of sugar in a pint jar and secure the lid. Keep cool until ready to use.

2. To make whipped cream, shake the jar until the contents double in volume, about 4 minutes. Serve immediately. (The volume will be a bit less than cream that's been whipped in a stand mixer but still thick.)

TRANSPORTING ICE CREAM

For a clever way to transport homemade ice cream without it turning into soup, use your ice cream maker's chilled freezer bowl as a mini cooler. It holds up to a quart of ice cream, sherbet, or sorbet, and when flexible ice packs are placed snugly against the sides and top of the container, the frozen treat stays solid for hours.

MEMORY KEY

It's always frustrating to put the effort into making a brown-bag lunch to take to work or school only to forget it at home in the fridge. For a no-fail solution, try placing your keys in the fridge next to your lunch: That way, you can't leave the house without it.

SALAD ON THE GO

Lunchtime thoughts often turn to salad, even for those who pack their own lunch to eat at work. But salads present a problem when prepared early and eaten later in the day. Many cut items dry out, and dressing causes the greens to turn limp. Here are some simple ways to solve these problems.

A. To transport a small amount of dressing, use one of the jars in which dry spices are packed. Their small size and tight seal are perfect for the job.

B. To completely avoid the need to bring a separate container of dressing, try a multilayered approach to fitting everything in one container: Add the dressing to the bottom of the container; cover it with chopped vegetables, fruit, beans, and cheese; and place the greens on top. To dress the salad, simply shake the container.

C. If the salad is to include juicy items, such as tomatoes, or items that might dry out if pre-cut, such as cheese, bring them intact and pack a paring knife, nestled safely inside of a plastic travel toothbrush holder.

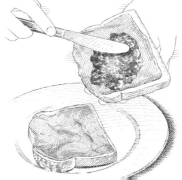

PERFECT PB&J

Anyone who's packed a peanut butter and jelly sandwich knows the disappointment of discovering that the bread in contact with the jelly has gotten soggy. To avoid the unpleasant texture this creates, spread peanut butter on both bread slices and then top the peanut butter on each side with jelly.

10.2 BRING A BETTER BROWN-BAG LUNCH

STABILIZING SANDWICHES

Be they grinders, hoagies, subs, or po' boys, overstuffed sandwiches in bulky rolls are an American favorite. But they can be pretty sloppy to pack and to eat, with fillings spilling out every which way. Neaten up these sandwiches by pulling out some of the interior crumb in the top and bottom halves of the bread. This creates a trough in the bottom half for fillings and a cap on the top for toppings for mess-free eating.

A CUT ABOVE

Slicing a particularly hearty—or crusty—sandwich in half can force the fillings out the sides of the bread, making an unmanageable mess of your lunch. Here's one solution.

1. Using a bread knife, cut the top slice of bread in half before placing it on the assembled sandwich.

2. Gently hold the pieces together and use the existing cut to guide the knife through the filling and the bottom slice of bread.

CHEESIER SANDWICHES

Large round slices of cheese such as provolone can be too big to fit onto a piece of sandwich bread. For a neater fit, use this clever trick, which is especially useful for making grilled cheese, when you don't want any of the cheese to leak out.

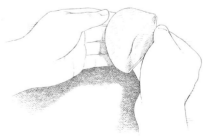

1. Fold the cheese slice into quarters, breaking it into four pieces.

2. Arrange the cheese on the bread with the squared edges facing out and the rounded edges facing in.

SANDWICHES FOR PICNICS

Next time you head to the beach or the park for a picnic, instead of wrapping sandwiches individually, try stacking the prepared, unwrapped sandwiches in the bread bag you've emptied to make the sandwiches. You can even recycle the original tab to seal the bag shut.

BAGEL BUNKER

If you often bring bagel sandwiches to work, you may have noticed that it's not so easy to fit them into sandwich-size zipper-lock bags. (And in larger bags, they shift around, spilling their contents everywhere.) Here's a fix: use an clean, empty CD spindle. The sandwich fits perfectly into the crush-proof case, and its filling stays in place.

APPLE ARMOR, PEACH PROTECTOR

A piece of fruit is a great snack to bring to work, but if it's bruised and mushy by the time you're ready to eat it, it loses its appeal. Fix this problem by using a foam drink cozy to shield apples, peaches, and other round, easily damaged fruit from bumps and jostles in your bag during your commute.

THE COOLEST LUNCH AROUND

To keep foods destined for lunch boxes chilled as long as possible, try this easy solution.

1. Fold a paper towel in thirds, saturate it with water, and then fit it inside the bottom of a storage container. Put the container in the freezer.

2. When you're packing lunch in the morning, place the food in a zipper-lock bag, set the bag in the frozen plastic container, and put on the lid. The food will stay cool until lunchtime.

Homemade Instant Oatmeal

✓ **WHY THIS RECIPE WORKS:** A quick bowl of hot oatmeal can start the day on a warm note or make a perfect comfort snack in the middle of the afternoon. Single-serving packets of instant oatmeal are available at almost every supermarket and they promise convenience and ease—but their gluey texture and unappealing flavors mean it usually just isn't worth it. Here's a way to have the best of both worlds: homemade instant oatmeal. This DIY version is simple, portable, inexpensive, and customizable with your favorite flavors and toppings. You can keep a few in your backpack or desk drawer for an easy and delicious bowl of oatmeal whenever you want one. This recipe makes 1 serving.

½ **cup quick-cooking or 1-minute oats**
¼ **teaspoon cinnamon**
1 **tablespoon packed brown sugar**
   Pinch salt
1 **tablespoon dried fruit, chopped nuts, chocolate chips, spices, or other add-ins**

1. Combine all ingredients in sandwich-size zipper-lock bag or small jar.

2. To cook, empty bag into a bowl or mug and add ⅔ cup boiling water (if oatmeal is in jar, simply add water directly to jar). Stir, cover with plastic wrap, and let sit for 5 minutes. Uncover, stir again, and serve.

10.3 YOUR KITCHEN ON VACATION

ORGANIZED ROAD TRIPS

When packing munchies for a long car trip, instead of piling up an impenetrable mass of snacks in a bag, use an empty box from a case of wine. The cardboard insert (used to separate the bottles) creates compartments for holding soda cans, napkins, utensils, fruit, and the like. It's so easy to find the food that kids (and preoccupied adults) can help themselves.

PORTABLE KITCHEN

If you often find yourself missing must-have ingredients or favorite kitchen tools when cooking while away from home, try packing a few sharp knives and other indispensable items like a garlic press, a pepper grinder, your favorite type of salt, and a bottle of extra-virgin olive oil into a plastic container to take along. Multiple containers can easily be stacked on top of each other and lowered into a paper grocery bag.

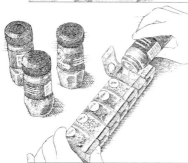

TRAVELING SPICES

If you want to cook while vacationing in rental properties but are afraid of finding old, flavorless dried spices gathering dust in the kitchens and don't want to buy all new ingredients, try using a jumbo pill organizer to transport small amounts of your favorite spices—one in each of the compartments.

PACK THE SALT AND PEPPER

Most vacation homes supply plenty of table salt but rarely have the kosher salt you may want for grilling—plus, the pepper on hand is usually a flavorless preground kind of unknown vintage. Rather than pack a big box of salt and a pepper mill, just make a mix of kosher salt and fresh-ground pepper to bring along in a zipper-lock bag.

SAFE KNIFE TRANSPORT

There are a number of ways to safely travel with a kitchen knife. One option is to insert the blade into a paper towel roll. Most rolls easily accommodate the blade of an 8- or 10-inch chef's knife. Another option is to cut a slit in a thick piece of corrugated cardboard and slip the knife into the opening. Or try wrapping knives in cone-shaped paper coffee filters for safe transport to picnics and cookouts.

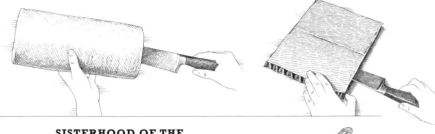

SISTERHOOD OF THE TRAVELING PANINI

Here are two tricks for mimicking these popular griddle sandwiches in a rental kitchen without having to pack a panini press.

A. Cast-Iron Double-Team

1. Set a large, seasoned, oiled cast-iron skillet over medium-high heat; place the assembled sandwich inside.

2. Place a smaller cast-iron skillet (or other heavy pot) on top of the sandwich to press. Cook until the bottom of the sandwich is golden brown, then flip and repeat the process on the other side.

B. Tea (Kettle) Sandwiches

Fill a tea kettle with water and use it to weigh down the sandwiches as they cook. If you prefer, fill a saucepan with water and use it in the same manner. Remember to wipe the kettle or pan bottom before its next use.

RECIPE REMINDER SOUVENIR

If you're the kind of person who always finds new regional recipes on the road, here's a tip to help you remember your new discoveries and the special trips where you first heard about them: Buy a few postcards of the area you're visiting and write the recipes on the back of the postcards. A normal postcard will fit right into a recipe box so you'll always have a visual memento of the places where you found your new favorite recipes.

CHAPTER 11

KITCHEN HACKS

ON THE BOOKS

Working Off the Page and On the Screen

11.1 TECH TIPS FOR FOODIES

ORGANIC TABLET STYLUS

If you're using your tablet computer to refer to recipes while cooking, you'll probably find that you don't want to touch the screen mid-prep with hands covered in oil, flour, or raw chicken juices. Instead of having to repeatedly wash your hands, try picking up a baby carrot to use as a stylus for scrolling. When you're done cooking, simply throw the carrot away.

MAKING A STAND IN THE DIGITAL AGE

Following recipes on an e-reader is super convenient, but it's sometimes difficult to read the screen when it's flat on the countertop. Here are two handy fixes that make it a little easier to bring your tech into the kitchen.

A. Knife Stand Podium DIY

1. Use Velcro to attach a piece of wood that's a few inches longer than the e-reader horizontally on the slanted part of a knife block.

2. Rest the e-reader on top of the wood for a stand that's built right in to something you already have sitting on the counter.

B. Plate Stand Recycling
Try putting an old-fashioned plate stand to use. The easel-like tool secures the tablet and keeps it upright for easy reading. (The stand also works for traditional cookbooks.)

SMART (PHONE) GROCERY LIST

Use this smart trick to keep track of what you need to pick up at the store: Simply snap a picture on your phone of items as soon as they're empty or right before you use the last one and then add the photos to an album titled "Groceries." You can scroll through the photos at the store and delete the pics as you make your purchases.

DIGITAL SHOPPING LIST

Instead of writing down the ingredients you need for a particular magazine or cookbook recipe, try this high-tech solution: Snap a picture of the ingredient list with your smartphone. You can easily reference it at the market to be sure to grab exactly what you need.

DIGITAL RECIPE FILE

Keep a photo album on your smartphone with pictures of the ingredient lists from your favorite go-to recipes. That way, the next time you're out shopping and you haven't made a list ahead of time, you can swipe through your collection right at the store.

MOBILE TASTING RESULTS

Keep track of new products you've tried and how they turned out by keeping a taste-test photo album on your smartphone: Use the camera to snap a picture of anything you try with either a thumbs-up or a thumbs-down alongside it. Next time you're at the store you'll have a built-in shopping guide you can scroll right through to know exactly what to buy.

KEEPING ACCURATE INVENTORY

Create a checklist that catalogs the contents of your pantry. Your computer makes it easy to alphabetize and update the list. Keep a printed copy of the list taped to the inside of your cabinet to help you track your staple ingredients. Then you can just take a quick picture of the up-to-date checklist with your phone before you go to the supermarket for a reminder of which pantry items you have in stock and which ones you need to pick up.

COOKBOOK PAGE PROTECTORS

To protect cookbooks from splatter you can shield open pages with heavy-duty clear protector sheets, which are available at any office store. Two taped-together sheets fit neatly over an open cookbook. This cover can be wiped clean with a damp cloth and reused.

KEEPING A COOKBOOK FLAT

To keep the open pages of a cookbook or magazine flat, readable, and clean while cooking, put a clear glass (Pyrex) baking dish over them.

PRESERVING YOUR COOKBOOKS

When the pages of a cookbook get soiled or moist from wayward recipe ingredients, use this trick to keep them from sticking together.

1. Blot the pages dry with paper towels.

2. Slip a piece of waxed paper between the pages before closing.

PICTURE-PERFECT RECIPES

To keep recipes splatter-free, try printing them out on water-resistant photo paper. The paper is sturdy enough to prop up during cooking and can easily be wiped clean with a damp towel. Its heavy weight also makes it more durable than a regular recipe card, and the 4 by 6-inch size fits perfectly in a recipe box.

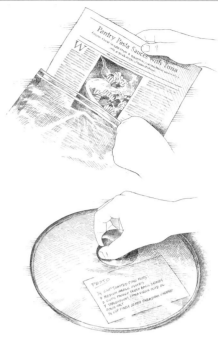

PROTECTING CHERISHED RECIPES

To protect recipes from the splotches and splatters of usual kitchen duty, many cooks use plastic page protectors, available at office supply stores. If you find yourself without page protectors, try one of these solutions.

A. Zipper-lock bags serve the purpose admirably. Lay the zipper-lock bag flat on the counter, slide the sheet of paper right into it, and zip shut. 1-gallon bags work nicely for 8½ by 11-inch sheets, while sandwich-size bags are perfect for recipes on index cards.

B. Clean, dry glass pot lids also do the job. Place the lid over the sheet of paper, or even over an open cookbook or magazine. The weight of the lid will keep it open.

READ LIKE A TEST COOK

We have no qualms about minor splatters on our cookbook pages. The real problem occurs when messy hands scramble to hold the pages open. In the test kitchen, we work from photocopies tacked to a standing clipboard (found in most office supply stores). Without all the advertising that bulks up most magazines, *Cook's Illustrated* is actually light enough to be held on one of these clipboards. Just clip a plastic sheet protector (available at stores that sell school supplies) over the page for added protection.

INGENIOUS RECIPE HOLDERS

A. Slip one or more recipe cards into a 5 by 7-inch freestanding Lucite picture frame, which slants backward slightly for easier reading and also keeps the cards free from splatters during cooking.

B. Thread the recipe card on fork tines and then set the fork in a water glass.

C. To keep a whole magazine spread in plain view (and out of harm's way) while cooking, place the open magazine in an empty napkin holder.

C.

STAND-IN COOKBOOK STAND

Put your large salad bowl to an unconventional use as a cookbook stand. Simply prop the open book against the side of the overturned bowl. Unlike a flat countertop, the bowl elevates the book at an angle for easy reference during cooking.

RECIPE ROUNDUP

Try this solution for keeping recipes at eye level while cooking: Use a magnet to secure recipe cards to the metal hood above your stove. Not only are they near the stove but you can arrange several cards in a row for easy reference when you're preparing a complete meal. If you don't have a metal hood, try propping a baking sheet or cookie sheet against the wall and hanging the recipe on it with binder clips. (If your baking sheet is magnetic, you can use magnets to attach the recipes.) The baking sheet takes up almost no room when leaning against the wall which frees up space, and your recipe is safer from drips than it would be on the counter.

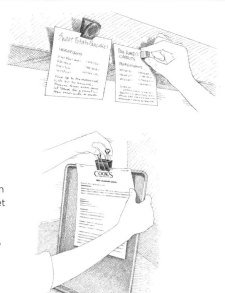

BOOK LOCK

Cooking from cookbooks in a small kitchen can be an issue—with limited counter space, books are often in the way and can get dirty, or worse, ruined by oil, molasses, honey, ketchup, etc. In addition, pages in a stiff book often flip on their own so it's all too easy to lose your place in the middle of a recipe. To solve these problems, set the opened cookbook in a rimmed baking sheet and stretch two rubber bands across the pages on either side, along the edges of the book (this also works great with magazines). Then you can lean the book against a wall for easy, out-of-the-way, protected reading, and the pages won't flip on you.

TRAINING TOMORROW'S COOKS

Accurately reading a recipe is key to success in the kitchen, and this is a great lesson to teach young aspiring chefs and bakers. To help children as they learn, print out the recipe you're working on together and place it inside a clear sheet protector. As you use each ingredient and complete each step, they can cross it off with a dry-erase marker. This is also good for cooks who might have more experience in the kitchen but still want to double-check that they haven't skipped anything in a complex recipe.

SHOWING YOUR WORK

Rather than converting ingredient proportions every time you halve or double a favorite recipe, try this tip: Calculate the new measurements just once and list them in the same order as the ingredients in the recipe on a narrow slip of paper or a Post-it note. Clip or stick the paper with the new measurements next to the original measurement column in the recipe; no more strained memory or guesswork.

TEMPERATURE CHEAT SHEET

If you can never remember the target doneness temperatures for various cuts of meat and poultry, desserts, and bread, try attaching a laminated index card featuring the desired internal temperatures for the foods you make most to your thermometer's protective case. That way you can avoid second-guessing yourself or scrambling for a reference book when you're in the middle of cooking.

HANDY INSTRUCTIONS IN BULK

Many thrifty cooks save money by purchasing staple ingredients in bulk. Here's a tip for making it easier to prepare these foods: When you transfer the bulk-purchased foods, such as rice, polenta, or pancake mix, into storage containers, write instructions for preparing that food on a mailing label and stick it to the container. Then when you go to make rice for dinner, the instructions are right there.

HANDY WEIGHT CHART

Sometimes even a conscientious baker will forget to tare the digital scale (i.e., zeroing out the weight of the empty container before adding ingredients) while making a recipe. To avoid the annoyance of having to remove the ingredients from the container and reweigh, plan ahead for these moments by making a weight chart for your favorite bowls and measuring cups and taping it to the inside of a cabinet door. Determining the ingredient weight is as easy as subtracting the container weight from the total.

CHAPTER 12

SUBSTITUTION
HACKS

You Know Better But You Still Do It, So Do It Right

A NONALCOHOLIC SUBSTITUTE FOR WINE IN COOKING

Amount: ½ cup wine

Substitutes:
• ½ cup broth + 1 teaspoon wine vinegar (red or white, per recipe)
• ½ cup broth + 1 teaspoon lemon juice

Notes: Add the vinegar or lemon juice just before serving.

A SUBSTITUTE FOR WINE IN COOKING

Ratio: 1:1

Substitutes:
• Equal amount dry vermouth for white wine
• Equal amount sweet vermouth for red wine

Notes: When refrigerated, an open bottle of vermouth will last for at least three months, much longer than wine. Tone down sweet vermouth with a few drops of red wine vinegar or lemon juice.

A SUBSTITUTE FOR FORTIFIED WINE

Ratio: 1:1

Substitutes:
• Equal amount white wine for sherry
• Equal amount red wine for port

Notes: Add light brown sugar in ¼-teaspoon increments to mask the sharper alcohol flavor of the wine.

A SUBSTITUTE FOR CREAM SHERRY

Amount: ½ cup cream sherry

Substitute:
½ cup dry sherry + 2 teaspoons dark brown sugar

Notes: This substitute is suitable for recipes but not for drinking.

A SUBSTITUTE FOR RUBY PORT

Ratio: 1:1

Substitute:
Equal amount tawny port

Notes: Any flavor differences are mostly erased by cooking.

A SUBSTITUTE FOR MIRIN

Amount: 2 tablespoons mirin

Substitute:
2 tablespoons white wine (or sake) + 1 teaspoon sugar

Notes: Sweet sherry will also work as a mirin substitute.

A SUBSTITUTE FOR UNSWEETENED CHOCOLATE

Amount: 1 ounce unsweetened chocolate

Substitutes:
- 3 tablespoons unsweetened cocoa powder + 1 tablespoon vegetable oil
- 1½ ounces bittersweet or semisweet chocolate (remove 1 tablespoon sugar from recipe)

Notes: For intensely chocolaty recipes, do not replace all of the chocolate with cocoa powder; it has a drastic effect on texture.

A SUBSTITUTE FOR BITTERSWEET OR SEMISWEET CHOCOLATE

Amount: 1 ounce bittersweet or semisweet chocolate

Substitutes:
- ⅔ ounce unsweetened chocolate + 2 teaspoons sugar
- 1 ounce chocolate chips

Notes: These substitutes are both better for sturdier recipes like brownies rather than delicate custard, airy cake, or silky pudding.

A SUBSTITUTE FOR TAHINI

Ratio: 1:2

Substitute:
3 parts peanut butter + 1 part sesame oil (blend, then use half the quantity of tahini called for)

Notes: You can also make your own tahini by grinding sesame seeds in a blender with just enough toasted sesame oil to make a smooth mixture.

A SUBSTITUTE FOR REGULAR PEANUT BUTTER

Amount: 1 cup sweetened peanut butter

Substitute:
1 cup natural peanut butter + 1 tablespoon white sugar

Notes: Stir the natural peanut butter thoroughly before using it to bake in order to incorporate the oil that floats on the top of the jar.

A PEANUT-FREE SUBSTITUTE FOR PEANUT BUTTER

Ratio: 1:1

Substitute:
Equal amount sunflower seed butter

Notes: This substitute works in any application and even comes in both smooth and crunchy varieties.

12.3 MILKY WAYS

A SUBSTITUTE FOR WHOLE MILK

Amount: 1 cup whole milk

Substitutes:
- ⅝ cup skim milk + ⅜ cup half-and-half
- ⅔ cup 1 percent low-fat milk + ⅓ cup half-and-half
- ¾ cup skim milk + ¼ cup half-and-half
- ⅞ cup skim milk + ⅛ cup heavy cream

A DAIRY-FREE SUBSTITUTE FOR MILK

Ratio: 1:1

Substitute:
Equal amount soy milk

Notes: Sweetened soy milk is acceptable in baking but unsweetened is better for savory applications. Add soy milk off the heat to avoid curdling.

A SHELF-STABLE SUBSTITUTE FOR MILK

Ratio: 1:1

Substitutes:
- Equal amount reconstituted instant milk
- 1 part evaporated milk + 1 part water

Notes: These substitutes work in almost all applications, with small compromises in flavor and texture.

A SUBSTITUTE FOR HALF-AND-HALF

Amount: 1 cup half-and-half

Substitutes:
- ¾ cup whole milk + ¼ cup heavy cream
- ⅔ cup skim (or low-fat) milk + ⅓ cup heavy cream

A SUBSTITUTE FOR HEAVY CREAM

Ratio: 1:1

Substitute:
Equal amount evaporated milk

Notes: This substitution works in soups and sauces, but not in whipping applications or baking recipes.

A SUBSTITUTE FOR BUTTERMILK

Amount: 1 cup buttermilk

Substitutes:
- 1 cup whole milk + 1 tablespoon lemon juice
- 1 cup whole milk + 1 tablespoon distilled white vinegar
- 1 cup whole milk + 1 teaspoon cream of tartar

Notes: Lemon juice is our first choice; some tasters detected off-flavors from vinegar and cream of tartar. These substitutes do not work in raw applications, such as buttermilk dressing.

ANOTHER SUBSTITUTE FOR BUTTERMILK IN BAKING

Ratio: 1:1

Substitute:
Equal amount low-fat plain yogurt

Notes: When you need a runnier batter, use half yogurt and half low-fat milk (or water) to thin the consistency.

A SUBSTITUTE FOR SOUR CREAM

Ratio: 1:1

Substitute:
Equal amount plain whole-milk yogurt (or flavored yogurt in recipes where the flavors won't clash)

Notes: Whole-milk yogurt and sour cream can be swapped for each other in most baking recipes.

A SUBSTITUTE FOR YOGURT

Amount: 1 cup yogurt

Substitute:
⅔ cup Greek yogurt + ⅓ cup water

Notes: The water is added to compensate for the whey that is drained from Greek-style yogurt.

A SUBSTITUTE FOR CRÈME FRAÎCHE

Amount: 1 cup crème fraîche

Substitute:
1 cup heavy cream + 1 tablespoon cultured buttermilk (let sit at room temperature until thickened)

Notes: For a substitute you can use immediately, use 1 cup sour cream + 2 tablespoons heavy cream, but be aware that it will separate if boiled.

Dairy-Free Whipped Cream

✓ **WHY THIS RECIPE WORKS:** When we heard that it was possible to make dairy-free whipped "cream" using the thick layer of coconut fat from the top of a can of regular (not low-fat) coconut milk, our curiosity was piqued. Our test batches, although not as lofty as true whipped cream, had a pleasant mild coconut flavor and enough velvety billows to make us think that this unlikely ingredient could provide an acceptable dairy-free alternative. With a little more experimentation, we came up with two tips for success. First, the creamy part of coconut milk isn't always separated from the watery part; we found that refrigerating the can for a few hours helps form two distinct layers. Second, it's important to skim off only the very thick, fatty portion of the milk, or the cream won't whip properly. This recipe makes 1 cup.

> 1 **(10-ounce) can coconut milk, chilled**
> 1½ **teaspoons sugar**
> ½ **teaspoon vanilla extract**
> **Pinch salt**

1. Chill mixing bowl and whisk attachment in freezer for at least 20 minutes.

2. Using spoon, skim top layer of cream from coconut milk (about ¾ cup of cream) and place it in chilled bowl with sugar, vanilla, and salt.

3. Using stand mixer fitted with whisk, whip cream on low speed until small bubbles form, about 30 seconds. Increase speed to high and continue whisking until cream thickens and light peaks form, about 2 minutes. Serve immediately or cover and refrigerate for up to 4 hours.

12.5 A FEW GOOD EGGS AND ONE COOL BEAN

A SUBSTITUTE FOR EGGS IN BAKING

Amount: 1 egg

Substitutes:
- ¼ cups silken tofu
- 2 ounces plain whole-milk (or low-fat) yogurt mixed with ½ teaspoon vegetable oil

Notes: These work best in baking recipes that call for only one or two eggs.

A SUBSTITUTE FOR EGGS IN BREADING

Ratio: 1:1

Substitutes:
- Equal volume of mustard
- Equal volume heavy cream

Notes: Simply dip the food to be breaded in the cream or mustard instead of egg before coating in bread crumbs.

A SUBSTITUTION CHART FOR EGGS OF ALL SIZES

Large		Jumbo	Extra-Large	Medium
1	=	1	1	1
2	=	1½	2	2
3	=	2½	2½	3½
4	=	3	3½	4½
5	=	4	4	6
6	=	5	5	7

Notes: For half an egg, whisk the yolk and white together and use half of the liquid.

A SUBSTITUTE FOR DRIED BEANS

Amount: 1 cup dried beans

Substitute:
3 cups canned beans

Notes: This substitution is recommended for dishes where the dried beans would be cooked, drained, and then added (such as a salad or a quick pasta dish). In a recipe that requires dried beans to cook slowly along with the other ingredients, canned beans are not a good substitute. Cooking canned beans for the same amount of time as dried beans will cause them to disintegrate.

A SUBSTITUTE FOR UNSALTED BUTTER

Ratio: 1:1

Substitute:
Equal amount of salted butter (remove ½ teaspoon salt from recipe for every stick used)

Notes: The amount of salt can vary from brand to brand, so we still generally recommend using unsalted butter, especially in baking.

A SUBSTITUTE FOR BUTTER IN BAKING

Ratio: 1:1

Substitute:
1 mashed avocado for every stick of butter (replace up to half the butter in a recipe)

Notes: Recommended only in recipes with strong chocolate flavors.

A HEALTHY SUBSTITUTE FOR SHORTENING

Ratio: 1:1

Substitute:
Equal amount of refined coconut oil

Notes: This substitution works great in combination with butter in pie dough and biscuit recipes.

SUBSTITUTES FOR DIFFERENT OILS IN BAKING

Ratio: 1:1

Substitute:
Equal amounts of vegetable, corn, or canola oil

Notes: These three oils can be used interchangeably in small amounts. Do not use olive oil unless called for.

A SUBSTITUTE FOR REGULAR OLIVE OIL

Amount: ½ cup regular olive oil

Substitute:
⅛ cup extra-virgin olive oil + ⅜ cup canola oil

Notes: This combination mimics the milder taste of regular, or "pure," olive oil.

A SUBSTITUTE FOR BUTTER IN ROUX

Ratio: 1:1

Substitute:
Equal amount of oil

Notes: This works best in dishes that involve multiple flavors; if the roux is for a simple sauce, stick to butter.

Eggless Mayo

✓ **WHY THIS RECIPE WORKS:** Eggless mayonnaise sounds like an oxymoron, and every mayo alternative we've ever tried has been a far cry from the velvety richness of the real deal. But when we stumbled across an unusual "milk mayonnaise," made with just milk, lemon juice, garlic, pepper, and oil, we were intrigued. It turns out that the casein proteins in milk perform a stabilizing function similar to the lecithin in egg yolks: Casein proteins allow droplets of oil to remain suspended in the milk, creating a creamy texture. We tweaked the recipe to make it even more foolproof, adding mustard (another good emulsifier) for extra stability and upping the amount of lemon juice, as citric acid denatures the milk's casein proteins, increasing their emulsifying properties. Our egg-free emulsion is just as billowy and creamy as regular mayo but with a lighter, cleaner taste. This recipe makes 1 cup.

- ⅓ **cup milk**
- 1 **teaspoon mustard**
- 1 **teaspoon lemon juice**
- 1 **garlic clove, minced**
- ¼ **teaspoon salt**
- ⅛ **teaspoon sugar**
- ¾ **cup vegetable oil**

Whisk all ingredients except oil together in tall-sided clear container just wide enough to fit immersion blender. Pour in oil and place immersion blender at bottom of container. Blend on low speed until thick emulsion forms in lower half of container. With blender still running, slowly pull it up to incorporate rest of oil. Serve immediately or refrigerate for up to 1 week in airtight container.

A SUBSTITUTE FOR CAKE FLOUR

Amount: 1 cup cake flour

Substitute:
⅞ cup all-purpose flour + 2 tablespoons cornstarch

Notes: With just 6 to 8 percent protein, cake flour imparts a more tender, delicate, fine-crumbed texture to baked goods.

A SUBSTITUTE FOR BREAD FLOUR

Amount: 1 cup bread flour

Substitute:
1 cup all-purpose flour

Notes: Breads and pizza crusts made with this substitution may bake up with slightly less chew, but the results will be acceptable.

A WHOLE-WHEAT SUBSTITUTE FOR WHITE FLOUR

Amount: 1 cup white flour

Substitute:
¼ cup whole-wheat flour + ¾ cup white flour + 2 tablespoons liquid

Notes: This ratio is designed for best results; don't replace more than 25 percent of the white flour in a recipe with whole-wheat.

A SUBSTITUTE FOR INSTANT YEAST

Ratio: 1:1

Substitute:
Equal amount of active dry yeast

Notes: Apart from the differences in their methods of incorporation, these two types of yeast are interchangeable.

A SUBSTITUTE FOR BAKING POWDER

Amount: 1 teaspoon baking powder

Substitutes:
• ¼ teaspoon baking soda + ½ teaspoon cream of tartar (use right away)
• ¼ teaspoon baking soda + ½ cup of yogurt, buttermilk, or sour cream

Notes: ¼ teaspoon of baking soda is the leavening equivalent of 1 teaspoon of baking powder.

A SUBSTITUTE FOR CORNSTARCH AS A THICKENER

Amount: 1 tablespoon cornstarch

Substitute:
2 teaspoons potato starch

Notes: Using potato starch in a sauce may cause it to be slightly more gooey or velvety than a cornstarch sauce.

A SUBSTITUTE FOR TABLE SALT

Amount: 1 tablespoon table salt

Substitutes:
• 1½ tablespoons Morton Kosher salt or fleur de sel
• 2 tablespoons Diamond Crystal Kosher salt or Maldon sea salt

Notes: Kosher salt and coarse sea salt do not dissolve as readily as table salt, so avoid them in baking recipes.

A SUBSTITUTE FOR FRESH HERBS

Amount: 1 tablespoon minced fresh herbs

Substitute:
1 teaspoon dried herbs

Notes: Dried herbs are best used in longer-cooking recipes like soups and stews. Avoid dried basil, chives, dill, parsley, and tarragon; these are tasteless.

A SUBSTITUTE FOR FRESH GARLIC

Amount: 1 garlic clove

Substitute:
¼ teaspoon garlic powder

Notes: This should only be used when garlic is a background flavor in a recipe, not the predominant flavor.

A SUBSTITUTE FOR PREPACKAGED PUMPKIN PIE SPICE

Amount: 1 teaspoon pumpkin pie spice

Substitute:
½ teaspoon cinnamon + ¼ teaspoon ginger + ⅛ teaspoon nutmeg + ⅛ teaspoon allspice

Notes: We think this homemade mix actually tastes better than the store-bought version.

A SUBSTITUTE FOR SOY SAUCE

Ratio: 1:1

Substitute:
Equal amount of tamari

Notes: The two sauces can be used interchangeably in recipes.

A SUBSTITUTE FOR FISH SAUCE

Ratio: 1:1

Substitute:
3 cups water + ¼ ounce dried sliced shiitake mushrooms + 3 table-spoons salt + 2 tablespoons soy sauce (simmer until reduced by half, strain, cool, and store in the fridge for up to 3 weeks)

Notes: For a quick non-vegetarian substitute you can also combine 1 tablespoon of soy sauce and 1 finely minced anchovy fillet.

A SUBSTITUTE FOR BROWN SUGAR

Amount: 1 cup brown sugar

Substitutes:
• 1 cup granulated sugar + 1 tablespoon molasses
  (for light brown sugar)
• 1 cup granulated sugar + 2 tablespoons molasses
  (for dark brown sugar)

Notes: Pulse the molasses in a food processor along with the sugar, if desired, or simply add it along with the other wet ingredients.

A SUBSTITUTE FOR SUPERFINE SUGAR

Amount: 1 cup superfine sugar

Substitute:
1 cup granulated sugar ground in food processor for 15 seconds

Notes: This is handy for cold drinks, as it dissolves more readily than granulated sugar.

A SUBSTITUTE FOR CONFECTIONERS' SUGAR

Amount: 1 cup confectioners' sugar

Substitute:
1 cup granulated sugar + 1 teaspoon cornstarch ground together in blender (not food processor)

Notes: This substitute works very well for dusting over desserts, but less so in icings and glazes.

LIQUID SUBSTITUTES FOR SUGAR

Ratio: 1:1

Substitute:
Equal amount of honey, molasses, or maple syrup (reduce the liquid in the recipe by ¼ cup for each cup of liquid sweetener added)

Notes: Use this formula to replace up to half of the white or brown sugar in a recipe with liquid sweetener.

A SUBSTITUTE FOR HONEY

Ratio: 1:1

Substitute:
Equal amount of light agave nectar

Notes: This substitution works in most baking applications.

A SUBSTITUTE FOR CORN SYRUP

Ratio: 1:1

Substitute:
Equal amount of brown rice syrup

Notes: The two syrups can be used interchangeably in recipes.

A SUBSTITUTE FOR COCONUT MILK

Ratio: 1:1

Substitute:
1 part whole milk + 1 part shredded coconut (bring to a simmer, cover and let steep for 15 minutes; grind in a blender or food processor, steep another 15 minutes, and strain)

Notes: This makes an acceptable substitute for curries and stir-fries, but it's less reliable in baked goods. Do not use canned cream of coconut as a coconut milk substitute.

A SUBSTITUTE FOR TAMARIND

Amount: 2 tablespoons tamarind paste

Substitute:
⅓ cup lime juice + ⅓ cup water

Notes: Tamarind paste is a key ingredient in pad thai.

A SUBSTITUTE FOR APPLE CIDER

Amount: 1 cup apple cider

Substitute:
¾ cup apple juice + ¼ cup unsweetened applesauce

Notes: The applesauce mimics the residual solids in apple cider.

A SUBSTITUTE FOR GRAHAM CRACKER PIE CRUST

Ratio: 1:1

Substitute:
Equal volume of animal crackers

Notes: This substitute works in graham cracker crust recipes because animal crackers have a similar amount of fat and sugar.

A SUBSTITUTE FOR PANCETTA

Ratio: 1:1

Substitute:
Equal amount blanched bacon (plus a small amount of oil)

Notes: Using bacon as a substitute will add some subtle smokiness, so make sure this works with the other flavors in your dish.

A SUBSTITUTE FOR ANCHOVIES

Amount: 1 teaspoon minced anchovy

Substitute:
1 tablespoon of finely chopped water-packed tuna

Notes: This substitute is nearly indistinguishable in both sauces and dressings if finely minced.

Note: Page references in *italics* indicate recipe photographs.